Publications of the
CENTRE FOR REFORMATION AND RENAISSANCE STUDIES

D1563524

Renaissance and Reformation Texts in Translation, 10

GUEST VOLUME EDITOR   Nicholas Terpstra

Victoria University
in the
University of Toronto

'Profile portrait of Girolamo Savonarola'
Copper engraving from G. Savonarola, *Prediche so-pra Iob*. Venice: per Niccolo Bascarini, 1545,
frontispiece.

Girolamo Savonarola

A Guide to
Righteous Living
and Other Works

Translated and Introduced by
Konrad Eisenbichler

Toronto
Centre for Reformation and Renaissance Studies
2003

CRRS Publications
Centre for Reformation and Renaissance Studies
Victoria University in the University of Toronto
Toronto, Ontario M5S 1K7
Canada

National Library of Canada Cataloguing in Publication

Savonarola, Girolamo, 1452-1498.
    A guide to righteous living and other works / by Girolamo Savonarola ;
translated and introduced by Konrad Eisenbichler.

(Renaissance and Reformation texts in translation ; 10)
Translated from Italian.
Includes bibliographical references and index.
ISBN 0-7727-2020-7

    1. Savonarola, Girolamo, 1452-1498. 2. Florence (Italy)--History--
1421-1737. I. Eisenbichler, Konrad II. Victoria University (Toronto, Ont.).
Centre for Reformation and Renaissance Studies III. Title. IV. Series.

DG737.97.A25 2003   945'.51   C2003-905996-0

Typesetting and printing: Becker Associates

Contents

Poems

Sermons

Pastoral Works

Index of Names

List of illustrations

Cover illustration: 'Savonarola in his study.' Woodcut from G. Savonarola, *Libro ... de la semplicita de la vita christiana*. Florence: Lorenzo Morgiani ad istanza di Piero Pacini, 1496, title page.

Frontispiece: 'Profile portrait of Girolamo Savonarola.' Copper engraving from G. Savonarola, *Prediche sopra Iob*. Venice: per Niccolo Bascarini, 1545, frontispiece.

1. 'Sic transit gloria mundi' The execution of Savonarola and his two companions. Woodcut from *Processo di Savonarola*, n.p., n.d. [Venice, 1498], frontispiece.

2. 'View of Florence in the 1490s' Woodcut from Bernardino, *Le bellezze e i casati di Firenze*. Firenze, n.d.

3. 'Savonarola preaching from the pulpit.' Woodcut from G. Savonarola, *Compendio di Revelatione*. Florence: ad istanza di Piero Pacini da Pescia, 23 aprile 1496, title page; also in *Predica dell'arte del ben morire*, Berlin, 1926, p. [1]

4. 'Savonarola blessing a group of women in their convent courtyard.' Woodcut from G. Savonarola, *Operetta molto divota sopra e dieci comandamenti di Dio*. Florence, 1490s, f. 28r.

5. 'Savonarola giving one of his treatises to the abbess of the Dominican convent of the Murate in their chapel.' Woodcut from G. Savonarola, *Operetta molto divota sopra e dieci comandamenti di Dio*, Florence, Lorenzo Morgiani e Giovanni di Magona, ca. 1495, title page; also in *Predica dell'arte del ben morire*, Berlin, 1926, p. [8].

6. 'Savonarola leading a group of saintly women into heaven.' Woodcut from G. Savonarola, *Compendio di Revelatione*. Florence: ad istanza di Piero Pacini da Pescia, 1496, f. 28v.

Acknowledgements

In the course of this work I have incurred many debts on both sides of the Atlantic and even across the Pacific.

I must, first of all, thank my Florentine friends and colleagues who first urged me to look at Savonarola and then invited me to present my thoughts at the various international conferences they organized both before and during the 500th anniversary of the friar's death. In particular I wish to thank Gian Carlo Garfagnini, Claudio Leonardi, Cesare Vasoli, and Armando F. Verde for their initiative in organizing these events and for inviting me to take part in them. Grazie!

The numerous participants at these conferences provided me with many insights and much intellectual stimulation. I eagerly acknowledge the contributions of scholars such as Francesco Bausi, Anna Benvenuti, Rossella Bessi, Julia Bennavent, Giorgio Chittolini, Giovanni Ciappelli, Romeo De Maio, Christopher Fulton, Cristina Acidini Luchinat, Patrick Macey, Mario Martelli, Ottavia Niccoli, Lorenzo Polizzotto, Olga Zorzi Pugliese, Roberto Rusconi, Ludovica Sebregondi, Adriana Valerio, Paolo Viti, Donald Weinstein, Mary Westerman Bulgarella, Blake Wilson, Raffaella Maria Zaccaria, and many others. Their presentations, articles, and conversation made my research on Savonarola that much more exciting and rewarding.

In Florence I owe special thanks to Ludovica Sebregondi and Mario Ruffini, who not only gave me constant and reliable scholarly advice, but also brought me into their home and family, thereby immensely facilitating my work and incrementing a thousand fold my pleasure at being in Florence. Thanks to them, Florence has become a home to me and Savonarola 'il Nostro.'

Across the pond and as far as the antipodes, I have been blessed with colleagues whose advice on this project has been invaluable. I am particularly grateful to Lorenzo Polizzotto and Donald Weinstein for encouraging me in this work and suggesting texts to translate, for reading some of my work before publication, and for offering constructive and enlightening insights to clarify difficult areas. Along the same lines, I have benefited tremendously from the expertise of scholars and friends such as William R. Bowen, Paul F. Grendler, Sandra Parmegiani, Antonio Ricci, and Nicholas Terpstra. Milton Kooistra was instrumental in the final re-reading of the entire typescript, while Gerald Dunlevie helped me resolve some recalcitrant Latin cruxes.

Although I hope no great errors have slipped past me, I do fear otherwise—neither Savonarola nor scholarship are easy business. So I beg the reader who should come across any wayward words or faulty facts to bring them home to me and lay them at my doorstep.

I would like to close by thanking the Senate Research Committee of Victoria University in the University of Toronto for its generous financial support in the publication of this project and the Centre for Reformation and Renaissance Studies (Victoria University) for its willingness to publish it.

This book is dedicated to my mother and father, Ivetta and Erich Eisenbichler, who have always been my guide to righteous living.

Konrad Eisenbichler
Victoria College
University of Toronto

Introduction

Konrad Eisenbichler

On 23 May 1498 the Dominican friar Girolamo Savonarola was hanged to death on the main square of Florence. His body was then burned on a pyre already erected under the scaffold (fig. 1). When the flames had died away, the ashes were carted to the Arno River, a block away from the piazza, and unceremoniously dumped in it so as not to provide his followers with relics. Thus ended the meteoric career of one of the most controversial figures of the Italian Renaissance.

Savonarola's preaching had at first fascinated the Florentine population. They had come by the thousands to hear him deliver his spell-binding sermons from the pulpit of his convent church of San Marco or from that of the immense Florentine cathedral of Santa Maria del Fiore—at that time the largest church in all of Christendom (fig. 2).[1] His words had galvanized the Florentine masses into a powerful force for reform. He spoke of a new society, solidly grounded on strict Christian ideals and set on a millenarian path that saw Florence as the New Jerusalem. From the reform of children to that of government itself, little escaped the friar's attention in the four years (1494–98) when, though unable to hold elected office because of his non-Florentine roots, he managed nonetheless to influence dramatically the city's public life. Little,

---

[1] The cathedral of Santa Maria del Fiore was built between 1296 and 1436 on a project by the architect Arnolfo del Cambio. From the very beginning it was meant to be the largest church ever built, and so it remained for more than two centuries, when it was eventually surpassed in size by the new basilica of St Peter's in Rome (built in 1506–1606 by a series of architects including Bramante, Raphael, Giuliano da Sangallo, and Michelangelo) and then by St. Paul's Cathedral in London (built in 1675–1710 by Sir Christopher Wren).

that is, except for the innate Florentine penchant for factional strife—something that the Florentine poet and exile, Dante Alighieri (1265–1321) had decried already in the early 1300s and that the powerful hand of Lorenzo de' Medici (1449–92) had barely managed to rein in for just over a decade in the immediate past (1479–92). Ironically, in a matter of days in April/May 1498, this congenital factionalism that Savonarola himself had not been able to resolve—in fact, if anything, he aggravated it—abruptly changed the political climate of Florence once again and brought the friar's career and life to a sudden, violent end. His millenarian dreams of a New Jerusalem thus went up in smoke on a bonfire not unlike the 'bonfires of the vanities' he had sponsored on that same square during the previous two Carnivals (1497 and 1498).

Girolamo Savonarola was born on 21 September 1452 in Ferrara, the son of a middling local businessman and the grandson of Michele Savonarola, a noted physician and medical writer at the Este court. In this elegant and worldly city, steeped in a rich secular tradition, Girolamo received a humanist education aimed at preparing him for a profitable career in his father's or his grandfather's footsteps. He received his first schooling directly from his learned grandfather; he then attended grammar school, where he read the ancient Roman classics; and he went on to study at the University of Ferrara.[2] Then, much to his family's surprise, in late April 1475, at the age of twenty-two the young man ran away from home, crossed the border south into the Romagna, and entered the Observantist Dominican convent of San Domenico, in Bologna. Here, in the second largest city in the Papal States, home to a world-class university renowned for its program in canon and civil law, the young Savonarola made his profession into the Dominican Order and prepared himself for the ministry.

The church and convent of San Domenico were, themselves, an important centre for the Dominican Order. They were home to an influential Dominican *studium* and were the final resting place of the founder of the Order, St Dominic, who had died in Bologna in

---

[2]On Italian universities in general see Paul F. Grendler, *The Universities of the Italian Renaissance*: Baltimore and London: Johns Hopkins University Press, 2002. For Savonarola and the University of Ferrara see in particular Armando Verde, 'Studenti e professori fra l'università di Ferrara e l'università di Firenze' in *'In supreme dignitatis ...' Per la storia dell'università di Ferrara, 1391–1991*, ed. Patrizia Castelli (Florence: Leo S. Olschki, 1995).

1221. The presence of his corpse in one of the side chapels of the church must have been an inspiration for the young Savonarola who, in his own way, was soon to emulate his Order's founder in his quest for divine truth and spiritual renewal.

In a letter to his father composed on 25 April 1475, the day after his flight from home, the run-away Girolamo tried to explain the reasons for his sudden departure and the motivations behind his drastic change in life plans (see pp. 35–37 in this volume). In this brief, but important document we can easily discern the dramatic, not to say troubled, nature of Girolamo's vocation for the religious life and some of the fundamental beliefs that would guide him throughout his life. First among them stands his understanding that the world around him was steeped in sin and had become woefully degenerate, a view he elaborated poetically in his two early *canzoni* 'On the Ruin of the World' and 'On the Ruin of the Church' (see pp. 61–68). In both the letter and the poems it is clear that Girolamo's assessment of the state of the world and of the Church was not restricted to a concern for local, Ferrarese worldliness and decadence, but encompassed all of Italy and, by extension, all of European Christendom. The young man's troubled evaluation of the current situation is self-evident, as is also his belief that such a dismal state was certainly the sign of an imminent apocalyptic conflagration. The *canzone* 'On the Ruin of the Church' is especially rich in apocalyptic overtones and references, many drawn directly from the Book of Revelations. It is also profoundly indebted to Dante, himself a strong critic of his times and of the internecine wars that plagued Italy at the turn of the thirteenth century.

In his search for an escape from the moral quagmire that surrounded him, the young Savonarola found his salvation in Jesus, whose teachings he could not ignore nor deny. Compelled as he was to answer His calling, Savonarola abandoned his family and assumed the role of 'knight militant' for Jesus (p. 36)—a role very much in line with the Dominican Order's original mission of fighting against heresy and ignorance.[3] As Donald Weinstein explains,

> Spiritual exiles from the world were not unknown among Dominicans, but the followers of St. Dominic were especially renowned as fighters

---

[3]Savonarola's use of the term 'knight militant' is strongly reminiscent of Dante's description of Sts Francis and Dominic from *Paradiso* 12.

against heresy and religious ignorance—they were the 'Domini cani,' or
hounds of the Lord, great theologians and mighty preachers. By joining
the Dominicans, or Order of Friars Preachers, Savonarola was thus not
so much choosing a haven from worldliness as a citadel from which to
wage spiritual warfare upon it.[4]

In Girolamo's world view, the alternatives were suddenly
clear—'either you love me or you do not'; and the choice was
obvious —'would it not have been a great ingratitude on my part
to have prayed God to show me the straight road on which I must
walk, and then when he deigned to show it to me, for me not to
have followed it?' (p. 36). Moved, therefore, by this clarity of vision
and by this uncompromising commitment, Girolamo followed Jesus'
exhortation to abandon one's own earthly family and to follow him
(Mt 10:35–38). Though simple, such a decision was clearly not
easy—in his letter to his father, Girolamo admitted to having
agonized over it. However, it was a decision he simply had to make
in order to save his soul because, as he says, 'I am made of flesh
as you are, and sensuality is repugnant to reason: and so I must
fight fiercely so that the devil does not jump on my back' (p. 37).
This devil, ready to pounce on Girolamo's back or on that of any
unsuspecting sinner, would become a recurrent figure of danger
and eternal damnation in Savonarola's writings. It would also appear
in many of the woodcut illustrations that graced contemporary
editions of some of Savonarola's writings (see figs. 7–10).

Some years later, once his preaching ministry had taken him to
various northern Italian cities, we read in a letter addressed to his
mother Elena how Girolamo's original view of himself as a 'knight
militant' had changed. Responding to her motherly desire for letters
and even for a visit from him, Girolamo answered saying first that
he had been too busy to write, then that he had not had access to
a courier to Ferrara, and then finally by restating, very significantly,
two Biblical comments about prophets in their own country: that
they are not believed there and that they should not preach there
(p. 39). This letter thus gives us an insight into Savonarola's
growing awareness of a higher calling, a calling to be not just a
preacher, but a prophet. This vocation would culminate for him in

[4]Donald Weinstein, 'Girolamo Savonarola: Piety, Prophecy and Politics in
Renaissance Florence' in *Girolamo Savonarola. Piety, Prophecy and Politics in
Renaissance Florence* (Dallas, TX: Southern Methodist University, 1994), p. 1.

post-Medicean Florence, where it would eventually lead him to suffer a martyr's death on the scaffold. For the moment, however, Girolamo merely hinted at the fate that awaited him and advised his mother not only to accept whatever lay in store for him, but to take comfort in the knowledge that 'God has deigned to elect one of your fruits and to give him such an office' (p. 39).

In 1490, the same year in which he penned this revealing letter, Savonarola was re-assigned by his superiors to the convent of San Marco, in Florence. He had already been there in 1482–87 as a lecturer in theology, but he had not attracted much attention from the Florentines at that time. His return in 1490, however, was different. His presence had been requested by none other than Lorenzo de' Medici, the de facto ruler of Florence (r. 1469–92), on the recommendation of the young philosopher prince Giovanni Pico della Mirandola (1463–94), an admirer of Savonarola's learning and spirituality. Back in Florence it became suddenly clear that Girolamo was a changed man and a much more effective speaker. His years of itinerant preaching in northern Italy and his further studies had prepared him better for the challenge of what was, without a doubt, the most intellectually vibrant city in all of contemporary Europe (fig. 2). He had also grown in the belief that he had been called to be an 'apocalyptic preacher of penitence and Christian renewal.'[5]

Renewed, refreshed, and inspired, Savonarola quickly began to attract quite a lot of attention and consistently drew a large crowd of listeners to his public sermons. The following year, when he was elected prior of San Marco (July 1491), he quickly set himself to bringing his community of friars back to the strict observance of the Order's founding rule of 1215. His uncompromising reforms and his stirring sermons led to a dramatic increase in vocations to the convent of San Marco and to its growing visibility in the spiritual and devotional life of Florence. This, in turn, allowed Savonarola to parley his success into a papal decree for the separation of San Marco from the Lombard congregation of the Dominican Order and to its redesignation as the mother house of the newly formed Tuscan Congregation of Observant Convents, soon renamed the Congregation of San Marco, with himself as the Congregation's Vicar General (1493).

---

[5]Weinstein, 'Girolamo Savonarola,' p. 2.

Savonarola's success on his return to Florence was also due in part to his own peculiar oratorical skills which made him stick out as something quite unusual among contemporary Florentine preachers. 'His rough manners, his lack of rhetorical elegance, his constant recourse to Scripture, his lack of any references to ancient authors or to contemporary poets, which was the custom in contemporary preaching, made him appear "new" to the eyes of his listeners, who were starting to become ever more interested in this new prophet.'[6]

Savonarola's success was also due in part to the respect he garnered from influential members of the ruling Medici elite, and especially from the young philosopher Giovanni Pico della Mirandola, who had sought his return; the brothers Girolamo and Domenico Benivieni (1453–1542 and 1460–1507 respectively), who would remain life-long devotees of the friar; the humanist Marsilio Ficino (1433–99), translator of all of Plato's works, whose complete devotion to the pagan classics would, eventually, lead him to withdraw from Savonarola; the humanist and poet Angelo Poliziano (1454–94), a close personal friend of Lorenzo de' Medici and tutor to his children; the painter Sandro Botticelli (1444/45–1510); and many other. As a member, and then as the prior of the premier convent patronized and richly endowed by three consecutive generations of Medici rulers, Savonarola owed much to the current head of the household, Lorenzo de' Medici, not the least of which was the opportunity to have access to men of intellect and influence in Florence.[7] Some of these cultural, political, and economic leaders even converted to Savonarola's teachings and took the Dominican habit at San Marco from Savonarola's own hands (Malatesta Sacramoro, d. 1511, and Giorgio Antonio Vespucci, d. 1514); others

---

[6]Adriana Valerio in her introduction to G. Savonarola, *Fede e speranza di un profeta. Pagine scelte.* Introduction, translation and notes by Adriana Valerio (Milan: Paoline Editoriale, 1998), p. 14 (my translation).

[7]San Marco was given to the recently arrived Reformed Dominicans of the Lombard Congregation in 1435 by Pope Eugenius IV, then resident in Florence, at the insistent request of Cosimo 'the Elder' de' Medici. Cosimo then proceeded to underwrite extensive reconstructions, renovations, and redecorations at the convent and at the church. His son Piero 'the Gouty' and grandson Lorenzo 'the Magnificent' continued Medicean patronage well into Savonarola's time, something later Medici rulers would also do until the family's extinction in 1737.

heard his words assiduously and lived by them in their private lives (Giovanni Pico della Mirandola, Francesco Valori, d. 1498); others still chose to be interred in San Marco wearing the habit of the Dominican Order as a sign of their hope for a resurrection from the womb of the mother church of Savonarolan reform (Angelo Poliziano). In short, the élites of Laurentian Florence soon began to pay close attention to the fiery Dominican friar from Ferrara and to follow his teachings.

Savonarola's preaching met with such an enormous success that he was soon obliged to move his pulpit from the convent church of San Marco to the Medicean basilica of San Lorenzo and eventually to the immense cathedral church of Santa Maria del Fiore (fig. 3). Huge crowds came to hear him. In 1495 the Ferrarese ambassador to Florence estimated that there must have been about 20,000 persons at a recent sermon by Savonarola.[8]

These crowds consisted, for the most part, of the Florentine middle and working class, and especially of women. The latter not only came eagerly to hear Savonarola preach, but also constantly sought him out for spiritual counselling and advice. It is not surprising, therefore, that Savonarola's first published work was directed at women: *The Book on the Life of the Widow* (Florence, 1491). The work met with great interest from the reading public and quickly underwent several editions. By 1496 it had been published four times in Florence (1491, 1492–93, 1494, 1496). After Savonarola's death, when a strong underground Savonarolan movement was still active in Florence and spreading across northern Italy, the treatise was published another eight times in Venice (1504, 1511, 1512, 1535, 1538, 1547) and Milan (1510, 1516)— though not again in Florence.

Savonarola's many subsequent treatises and his numerous letters to women testify to his abiding interest in ministering to them (figs. 4–6). There may well be a practical reason for such an interest; as Maja Ryslavy points out,

> It is likely that, as a newcomer to Florence, Savonarola strove to target the portion of his audience which would give him the most enthusiastic support for his future endeavours. It was not a coincidence that he chose

---

[8]Natalie Tomas, *'A Positive Novelty': Women and Public Life in Renaissance Florence* (Victoria, Australia: Monash University, 1992), p. 52, n. 71.

the religious widows of Florence: they were appealing to Savonarola because their numbers were not insignificant and because they were less bound to act according to the dictates of the family and the broader community than any other social group. Indeed, widows later probably formed a sizeable and significant part of Savonarola's following. In support of this claim, suffice it to mention that in Pseudo-Burlamacchi's Trattato de' miracoli, out of four lay women who were reported to have brought Savonarola's presumed miracles to public attention, thus contributing to the propagation of his cult, three were widows (Caterina, widow of Agostino da Sexto from Lucca; Cassandra Acciaiuoli, widow of the Florentine Iacopo Ridolfi and an anonymous widow from Prato).[9]

After Savonarola's death, his teachings were kept alive in many women's convents where, incidentally, a veritable cult of him as a saint developed and further attested to the strong ties between the preacher and his female devotees.[10]

Many of the texts in this collection do, in fact, owe their origin to Savonarola's ministry to women—from the treatise on widowhood to the exposition on the 'Hail Mary,' from many of the letters to several of the poems. They reflect in part Savonarola's own

---

[9]Maja Ryslavy, *Women in an Earthly Kingdom: Girolamo Savonarola and the Rhetoric of the Female*. Ph.D. thesis, Department of Italian, The University of Sydney, Australia, 1995, vol. 1, p. 166. For the reference to the Pseudo-Burlamacchi, see his *Trattato de' miracoli* in *La vita del Beato Ieronimo Savonarola, scritta da un anonimo del sec. XVI e già attribuita a Fra Pacifico Burlamacchi*, ed. Piero Ginori Conti (Florence: Leo S. Olschki, 1937), pp. 216, 220 and 240. For the entire question of widows in fifteenth-century Florence, see Richard C. Trexler, 'A Widows' Asylum of the Renaissance: The Orbatello of Florence' pp. 66–93 in Richard C. Trexler, *The Women of Renaissance Florence*. Power and Dependence in Renaissance Florence, vol. 2 (Binghamton, NY: Medieval & Renaissance Texts & Studies, 1993); and Konrad Eisenbichler, 'At Marriage End. Savonarola and Widows in Late Fifteenth-Century Florence' forthcoming in *The Medieval Marriage Scene: Prudence, Passion and Policy*, eds. Cristelle Baskins and Sherry Roush (New York: Boydell & Brewer, 2003).

[10]For the role of women in the Savonarolan movement after the friar's death, see Lorenzo Polizzotto, 'When Saints Fall Out: Women and the Savonarolan Reform in Early Sixteenth-Century Florence' *Renaissance Quarterly* 46 (1993): 486–525; see his *The Elect Nation. The Savonarolan Movement in Florence 1494–1545* (Oxford: Clarendon Press/New York: Oxford University Press, 1994).

feelings for women, which may well partly lie behind his admission to his father that 'because I am made of flesh as you are, and sensuality is repugnant to reason [...] I must fight fiercely so that the devil does not jump on my back' (p. 37). They also reflect the Dominican Order's own abiding interest in, and devotion to the Virgin Mary, which we see reflected in Savonarola's several poems to her (pp. 73–74) and in his *Exposition on the Prayer to the Virgin* (pp. 227–40). Not surprisingly, one of Savonarola's projects was to effect a 'reform of women' in Florence that would, in part, have granted them some personal control over their lives. In spite of his extensive efforts to promote such a reform, Savonarola's attempts from March 1496 to January 1497 to get the Florentine government to enact the necessary legislation met with complete failure on all four occasions when it came to a vote in the Consilio Maggiore (Great Council). Clearly, his views on the role of women in society were not shared by the Florentine political class, not even when that class was clearly on his side.[11]

The *Exposition on the Prayer to the Virgin* was composed at the request of some nuns from a convent in Ferrara and was meant to explicate for them and for the young girls in their care the words and the meaning of the angelic salutation, the 'Hail Mary' (ill. 5).[12] The language is therefore simple and colloquial, with plenty of repetition for the sake of instruction—a standard pedagogical technique. The examples Savonarola adduces are drawn from contemporary life and would be immediately meaningful for the young girls—see, for example, his discussion of the term 'lord' and his references to lords of earthly states as opposed to the Lord of heaven (p. 231). Mario Ferrara, its modern editor, says that it is 'full of that tenderness and filial devotion that the Friar always professed for the Virgin Mary.'[13]

---

[11]On this entire episode, see Polizzotto, 'Savonarola, savonaroliani, e la riforma della donna.' On the problems faced by women in Renaissance Florence see (among the many works available), Richard C. Trexler, *The Women of Renaissance Florence.*

[12]The work was composed from notes Savonarola had made in 1483–84, but was first published only after April 1496; see Ferrara's 'Note critiche' to his edition in Savonarola, *Operette spirituali,* vol. 2, p. 293.

[13]Mario Ferrara in his 'Nota critica' to G. Savonarola, *Operette spirituali,* ed. Mario Ferrara (Rome: Angelo Belardetti Editore, 1976), vol. 2, p. 293.

One must be careful, however, not to overestimate Savonarola's devotion to the Virgin Mary or his ministry to women. As Adriana Valerio perceptively notes, 'If Savonarola's preaching is essentially biblical and Christocentric, this does not mean it lacks a heartfelt affection for the Virgin Mary, something that was particularly lively in Dominican spirituality. The friar, however, is very careful not to foster vain sentimentality, passionate languor and false devotions, often present in contemporary Marian cult. He sees Mary as a strong woman, as a model of Christian life, and he perceives her to be intimately united to the crucified Christ because she shares in his redeeming and intercessory work.'[14]

In reading Savonarola's works one must also be especially careful not to misinterpret as misogyny his negative comments about women's abilities and roles. Lorenzo Polizzotto, who has studied extensively Savonarola's works in light of his ministry to women, is absolutely correct when he points out that 'There is no doubt that Savonarola shared in the misogyny of his contemporaries. Just like his fellow friars and his followers, he was convinced of the "lower nature" of women, of their intellectual and moral inferiority in comparison to men, and of the need, therefore, to lead them on the right path and to preempt, in this manner, their potential for evil.' At the same time, however, Polizzotto points out that 'Without meaning to make of Savonarola a feminist *ante litteram*, I would say that, contrary to other preachers who drew upon him, he continued to believe and to preach that women could contribute significantly to the redemption and salvation of humanity.'[15] Perhaps for this reason women flocked to his sermons, as they had flocked to those of earlier popular Observant preachers such as the Blessed Giovanni Dominici (1357–1419) or St Bernardine of Siena (1380–1444), 'because, though berated rather than flattered, they found in them dignity and tenderness, the suggestion

---

[14]Adriana Valerio in her introduction to G. Savonarola, *Fede e speranza di un profeta. Pagine scelte.* Introduction, translation and notes by Adriana Valerio (Milan: Paoline Editoriale, 1998), p. 35 (my translation).

[15]Lorenzo Polizzotto, 'Savonarola, savonaroliani, e la riforma della donna' in *Studi savonaroliani. Verso il V centenario*, ed. Gian Carlo Garfagnini (Florence: SISMEL Edizioni del Galluzzo, 1996), p. 232 (my translation). Similar views on Savonarola's attitude to women are expressed by Donald Weinstein in his 'Girolamo Savonarola: Piety, Prophecy and Politics in Renaissance Florence,' p. 11.

of a new responsibility, the awareness of not just fulfilling a social function, but of being individuals who controlled their own destiny: in the intangible culture of inferiority, they rediscovered their spiritual freedom.'[16]

Savonarola was also keenly interested in the physical and spiritual well being of his fellow Dominicans. This is evident in the reforms he instituted at San Marco and in the advice he offered to his friars. His short, but frank treatise *On the Prudent and Judicious Way of Living in the Order* (pp. 181–85) is a case in point. This work began as an exhortation delivered by Savonarola at the meeting of the chapter of San Marco on 14 September 1496. It seems there had been some grumbling among the friars on account of the stringent regulations imposed by Savonarola in his attempt to bring the convent back to the Order's original regulations. Some friars clearly considered these regulations too severe for their own physical well being. Savonarola responded by uncompromisingly pointing out from the start that: 'The great care friars have for the health of their own body and the one superiors have for their subjects is a temptation of the devil who seeks in this way to undo the Order little by little.' (p. 181) To toughen his friars and to ensure that their bodies and their spirits were fit for the task he encouraged them to adhere strictly to the Rules, to be steadfast in their fasts, to resist temptation, and to pray assiduously.

Although strict in his desire to live by his Order's Rules, Savonarola could also be very understanding and even lenient in dealing with his disciples or in offering advice. He recognized, for example, that the young may not be as strong, and so they must be more moderate in their fasting (p. 181). Similarly, in a letter to the noblewomen Giovanna Carafa Pico and Eleonora Pico della Mirandola he advised the two sisters-in-law not to torment themselves with worries about their venial sins, but to put their hearts at rest, for 'even though [Jesus] wants us to refrain as much as we can from sinning even venially, nonetheless He also likes it that when one has fallen because of human frailty one should not be so upset as to lose peace of mind over it, but should instead look immediately to His great sweetness and say: —My kind Lord will

---

[16]R. De Maio, *Donna e Rinascimento* (Milan: Il Saggiatore, 1987), p. 14 (my translation); also cited in Polizzotto, 'Savonarola, savonaroliani, e la riforma della donna' p. 233.

offer satisfaction on my behalf—' (p. 48). To the indomitable virago Caterina Sforza, Duchess of Imola and Forlì, who had written seeking his counsel, he responded urging her to confess her sins, to do good works, to be just towards her subjects, and to pray God for His enlightening grace—balanced and understanding advice for a woman who was meant to rule and who, a few years later, would display immense courage and military savvy defending her possessions against the formidable Cesare Borgia. Even his treatise on widowhood, which may seem extremely severe in the advice it offers to widowed women, is, in fact, couched in a careful and deliberate classification of different levels of widowhood because, as he puts it, 'There are many different types of widows' (p. 196). Savonarola's words are thus meant not for the weak or disinclined, but for those women who are prepared to be 'widows' in all aspects of their lives (pp. 197–99).

Sometimes, however, the constant requests Savonarola received for advice or the many invitations to preach elsewhere elicited a curt, perhaps even abrupt answer from him. Busy as he was with taking care of his own spiritual needs, with the management of his convent and his Dominican Province, with the counsel he offered to the Florentine government, not to mention with his own extensive writings, it is not surprising that the friar might respond curtly to what he considered to be unnecessary intrusions. This is evident in a letter to the nuns of the convent of Annalena in Florence, who had asked him to come preach to them or to send them an exhortation for them to read (pp. 53–58; fig. 3). Savonarola responded saying that he had already written enough exhortations in the vernacular and saw no point in writing any more because this produced only tedium. In fact, Savonarola added, one should not waste one's time reading a lot, but one should read just a little and act on it, for this is better than to read a lot and then not act on it (pp. 55–56). Action, in other words, is better than meditation, doing is better than reading.

This revealing letter on the role of reading and meditation was published in October 1497 together with Savonarola's *Ten Rules to Observe in Times of Great Tribulations* (pp. 177–79). The first five rules apply to tribulations about to descend on the faithful, the second five to tribulations already afflicting them. These ten rules are taken directly from two Latin sermons Girolamo preached, one on 13 March 1494, the other on 15 March 1494. Given the dates of their delivery and the date of their publication, Mario Ferrara concludes that Savonarola's advice on how to deal with great tribulations was meant to help Florentines deal with two very specific and immediate situations at two different points in time. In the sermons of 1494, the rules were aimed at helping Florentines prepare for the imminent and much feared invasion by King Charles VIII of France, while in their published versions of 1497–98 they were aimed at helping them deal with the civil strife and the papal excommunication that had thrown Florence into a state of profound turmoil.[17] Whatever the immediate motivation might have been, the advice Savonarola proffered was both systematic and profoundly dependent on prayer.

During his incarceration in the tower of the Palazzo della Signoria (18 April to 22 May 1498), Savonarola relied on prayer and meditation, and he also continued to write. For his own comfort and sustenance he composed two meditations on Psalms 31 and 51 that were soon smuggled out of prison and published, quickly becoming two of Savonarola's best known works not only in Italy, but in England as well, where they enjoyed at least sixteen different editions in English translation in the sixteenth century alone (pp. 28–29). During those same days of incarceration Savonarola also composed a short treatise, *A Guide to Righteous Living*, aimed at a general readership and intended to be his last pastoral statement to the lay world outside. The chronicler Simone Filipepi, brother of the painter Sandro Botticelli, recalls the context for this work, saying that:

> While Fra Girolamo was in prison ... no-one could ever speak to him except his opponents, who went there to mock him or to insult him, all of which he suffered with great patience. And the turnkey who kept guard over him told me that he never saw him get upset because of anything that was said or done to him, but that at times he would say: 'Look to live righteously.' And I heard this from other people who went there. And the said turnkey was assigned to him because he had been one of his persecutors. However, as it pleased God, while he was with him in that room called the *Alberghettino* [the little hotel], he was converted by Savonarola and thereafter was always one of his support-ers. ... And Savonarola wrote for him a short work of his, in his own

---

[17]Mario Ferrara, 'Nota critica', pp. 313–17 in G. Savonarola, *Operette spirituali* (Rome: Angelo Belardetti, 1976).

hand, but with great difficulty because of the torture, a guide to righteous living, which the said turnkey kept concealed at that time, but which later was published.[18]

The treatise illustrates very well Savonarola's unflinching belief in the efficacy of grace and summarizes his message of salvation in three simple steps: the need for every person to acquire grace, to increase it, and to persevere in it (p. 187). As in other cases, the first step towards grace is founded on meditation upon death. Such meditation will inspire the faithful to carry out a thorough spiritual self-examination which, in turn, will lead to repentance for sins committed and to a full confession, followed thereafter by communion, that is, by re-union with God. Having obtained grace, the faithful then increases it by emotionally distancing himself from earthly affections and desires, which are all transitory and vain. Lastly, he perseveres in grace by physically distancing himself from all occasions from sin, thereby making sure that he follows unimpeded the path to salvation.

Savonarola's views on death and on the importance of meditating on its eventuality are clearly expressed in his sermon of 2 November 1496, popularly known as the sermon *On the Art of Dying Well* (pp. 119–48). The work is number 28 in a cycle of sermons traditionally known as 'Sermons on Ruth and Micah' delivered from the pulpit of the Florentine cathedral of Santa Maria del Fiore from 8 May to 27 November 1496. The series was first given this title in the sixteenth century possibly because the majority of its sermons, nineteen out of twenty-nine, take their cue from the two Old Testament books of *Ruth* and *Micah*. While the Book of Ruth is a 'timeless story about vulnerable people in society,' the Book of Micah is 'a denunciation of the wrongdoing in the nation, especially by the ruling classes'.[19] By extension, the cycle based on these books may well have been intended by Savonarola as a call to charity and to service and as an indictment

---

[18]Cited in *Scelta di prediche e scritti di Fra G. Savonarola con nuovi documenti intorno alla sua vita*, ed. Pasquale Villari and Eugenio Casanova (Florence: Sansoni, 1898), pp. 500–1 (my translation); and in G. Savonarola, *Operette spirituali*, ed. Mario Ferrara (Rome: Angelo Belardetti Editore, 1976), vol. 1, p. 331.

[19]*A Dictionary of the Bible*, ed. W.R.F. Browning (Oxford: Oxford University Press, 1996), pp. 328 and 251 respectively.

of contemporary evils. Delivered during a period of political tranquillity, when neither the pope nor Savonarola's Florentine opponents were particularly active against him, these sermons represent a concerted effort on Savonarola's part to answer calmly those who doubted or challenged him and, at the same time, to comfort his followers.[20]

Such tranquillity, however, gave way to a sense of urgency and impending doom with the two November feast days for the dead. On 1 November 1496, the feast of All Souls, as the cycle was drawing to close, Savonarola delivered a sermon based on three fantastic visions he claimed to have had. In the first, he described how he had seen a chapel in a church and had held a conversation with the blessed in heaven who answered his questions and offered him advice for the spiritual and temporal renewal not only of Florentines, but of all Italians and of the entire Church. In the second vision he had seen the tribulations of the Church of his time, and in the third the destruction of the wicked and the beginning of the *renovatio*, the renewal or reformation so much awaited by the true Church. The following day, 2 November 1496, the feast of All Saints, Savonarola engaged his listeners instead in a 'conversation, at times plain, at times elevated' on how to prepare oneself for the inevitability of death and on how to ensure that that fateful moment on which the eternal happiness of the soul hinged was both positive and profitable. The sermon ends with two terrifying examples of death—one good, one bad—taken from the *Dialogues* of St Gregory and depicted by Savonarola 'in vivid tones and with a firm hand.'[21]

By focusing on the 'good death' Savonarola is thus very much following the medieval tradition of treatises and manuals on the *buona morte*, that is, on the art of dying well. He was probably also responding to an immediate crisis, for Florence in those days was gripped by a high rate of mortality precipitated by famine and aggravated by plague.[22] The admonitory woodcuts that Savonarola

---

[20]Vincenzo Romano in his 'Nota critica' to G. Savonarola, *Prediche sopra Ruth e Michea*, ed. Vincenzo Romano (Rome: Angelo Belardetti Editore, 1962), vol. 2, pp. 480–81.

[21]V. Romano in his 'Nota critica' to G. Savonarola *Prediche sopra Ruth e Michea* (Rome: Angelo Belardetti Editore, 1962), vol. 2, p. 483.

[22]Lorenzo Polizzotto, '*Dell'arte del ben morire.* The Piagnone Way of Death

insisted should accompany the published version of this sermon illustrate amply the friar's strong awareness of a lurking evil presence, ready to attack the unsuspecting believer at the first sign of weakness (figs. 9–10). They also reflect the type of images Savonarola suggested people should keep in their houses to remind them of the inevitability and unexpectedness of death. On the title page of the post-1497 edition of this sermon a sinister figure of Death flying over the corpses of men and women, lay and religious, strewn on the ground holds a banner aloft that reads 'EGO SUM'—'I am' (fig. 8). Inside the book, another such figure speaks to a young Florentine man and gives him a choice 'O QVA SU' 'O QVA GIV'—'Either up here' 'Or down here', it says, pointing up to heaven or down to hell (fig. 7). In Savonarola's world view, as in Niccolò Machiavelli's, all human action is based on dichotomies, on a choice between two alternatives. As he had occasion to point out in his April 1475 letter to his father, for Savonarola that choice was clear, 'either you love me or you do not,' and its speaker was a Christ not unlike the figure of Christ the Judge that Michelangelo, who had heard Savonarola preach, would later paint at the Vatican on the altar wall of the pope's private chapel, the Sistine Chapel.

Notes to Savonarola's Poems

Savonarola's poetry is not particularly accessible to modern readers, partly because of its contents and partly because of its structure. The notes that follow are meant to serve as a guideline to students not familiar with poetic forms and contents. Each one begins with a description of the poem's form and versification; this is followed by a brief summary of the poem; and then by a few explanatory notes that will help the reader to contextualize and interpret the poem.

Canzone I.   'On the Ruin of the World'

The poem is a canzone consisting of six stanzas and an envoy. The stanzas are made up of eleven verses each and are rhymed ABBAACcDdEE (where capital letters indicate hendecasyllables and lower case letters septenaries). The envoy consists of five verses rhymed aBbCC. This is the same pattern used in the following canzone, 'On the Ruin of the Church.' The title of the poem is given in Latin, but the verses themselves are in Italian.

The author decries the corruption of the Church and the miserable state in which the world finds itself at that time. He particularly disapproves of one eminent cleric whom he accuses of various sins.

The poem is a product of Savonarola's youth. Its editor for the 'Edizione nazionale delle opere di Girolamo Savonarola' ('National Edition of Girolamo Savonarola's Works'), Mario Martelli, accepts the dating of 1472 found on a manuscript copy made by Fra Benedetto da Firenze (*ad saeculum* Luschino Betuccio) directly from Savonarola's lost original.[23] Such a date would place the work in those formative years before April 1475 when the young Savonarola was still struggling to find his way in the world and to deal with his religious vocation. To support such a dating still further, Martelli points to the well known corruption of the recently elected Pope Sixtus IV Della Rovere (r. 1471–84), and then to Savonarola's own analysis of the world as voiced in the famous letter to his father (25 April 1475):

> the reason why I entered into a religious order is this: first, the great misery of the world, the wickedness of men, the rapes, the adulteries, the thefts, the pride, the idolatry, the vile curses, for the world has come to such a state that one can no longer find anyone who does good; so much so that many times every day I would sing this verse with tears in my eyes: *Alas, flee from cruel lands, flee from the shores of the greedy.* I did this because I could not stand the great wickedness of the blind people of Italy, especially when I saw that virtue had been completely cast down and vice raised up. (pp. 35–36)

Other critics have suggested a later dating, more towards the mid 1490s, saying that the poem refers to the times of Pope Alexander VI Borgia (r. 1492–1503)—a favourite *bête noire* for all sorts of people. Valentino Piccoli, who hears echoes in the poem of some of Savonarola's later sermons in Florence, dates it to 1495 or shortly after, a time when Savonarola was, in fact, preaching

---

[23]M. Martelli, 'Nota critica' to G. Savonarola, *Poesie* (Rome: Angelo Belardetti Editore, 1968), pp. 199–203. Subsequent references to this 'Nota critica' will be given in abbreviated form (page number only) within the body of the text.

against the corruption of the Borgia pope.[24] He is followed in this by Domenico Coppola.[25] Martelli, however, argues convincingly against this critical tradition of a later date.

Canzone II.   'On the Ruin of the Church'

The poem is a canzone consisting of seven stanzas and an envoy. The stanzas are made up of eleven verses each and are rhymed ABBAACcDdEE. The envoy consists of five verses rhymed aBbCC. This is the same pattern used in the previous canzone, 'On the Ruin of the World.' The title of the poem is given in Latin, but the verses are in Italian.

As in the previous canzone 'On the Ruin of the World,' Savonarola is lamenting the corruption and decadence of the Church of his day. Using a rich array of images, comprehensible only to himself, but with clear echoes both to Dante and to the Book of Revelations, the poet identifies problems and solutions. He concludes with the realization that he can do nothing and must keep silent—an inherent contradiction both in the nature of the beast and in the glosses that Savonarola would later append to the poem.

In Fra Benedetto da Firenze's manuscript collection of Savonarola's poems, this canzone carries the date 1475. Martelli (p. 206) accepts it as the likely date of composition, following the same logic and arguments he had used to accept the date of 1472 for the previous canzone 'On the Ruin of the World.' This would place the work at a time when the twenty-two-year-old Savonarola, strongly disenchanted with the world, sought refuge and consolation in a vocation for the religious life. Savonarola in fact entered the Dominican convent of San Domenico in Bologna in 1475.

The glosses that accompany this poem are by Savonarola himself, who was asked to elucidate the images in this difficult work. They date from the mid-1490s when we find Savonarola complaining in his sermons, as he does in the glosses, against those who are 'lukewarm' in their faith (Martelli, p. 209). They were made by Savonarola himself directly onto the so-called 'Borromeo' manuscript, which has now been lost. Fortunately, Guasti-Capponi transcribed them into their edition of Savonarola's works. I will

---

[24]Valentino Piccoli in his edition of G. Savonarola, *Poesie* (Turin: UTET, 1926), pp. 8–9.

[25]Domenico Coppola, *La poesia religiosa del secolo XV* (Florence: Olschki, 1963), pp. 154–55.

report them in the footnotes to the poem indicating their provenance simply as Savonarola/Borromeo.

Canzone III. 'Song to Saint Catherine of Bologna'

This poem is a canzone consisting of six stanzas and an envoy. The stanzas are made up of twelve verses each and are rhymed ABCBCAaDEeDD. The envoy is a tercet rhymed aBB. The title of the poem is given in Latin, but the verses are in Italian.

In the canzone Savonarola sings the praises of the Blessed Caterina de' Vigri (1413–63), founder and abbess of the Poor Clares convent of Corpus Domini in Bologna.

The poem was sent by Savonarola directly to the nuns of Corpus Domini with a note asking them to pray for him and to recommend him to the Blessed Caterina (Martelli, p. 240). Although the autograph copy has been lost, there exists a transcription made by the Blessed Illuminata Bembo, a nun at that convent and Caterina's first biographer. Since Illuminata died in 1483, Savonarola's poem must clearly date from before that year. Martelli (p. 212) suggests a date somewhere around 1475–79, to coincide with the time when Savonarola was still residing at the convent of San Domenico in Bologna.

St Caterina de' Vigri (Bologna, 1413–63), also known as St Catherine of Bologna, was born into a noble family. At ten years of age her father sent her to Ferrara to be a companion to the young Margherita, illegitimate daughter of Duke Niccolò d'Este, and to be educated at court. When Margherita married Roberto Malatesta of Rimini, the nineteen-year-old Caterina entered into an Augustinian convent, which she soon convinced to re-align itself with the Franciscan second order, the Poor Clares. In 1456 she founded her own convent of Poor Clares in Bologna, the Corpus Domini, and served as its abbess until her death in 1463. A mystic, throughout her life Caterina claimed to have visions and revelations—she claimed, for example, that on Christmas 1445 the Virgin Mary had appeared to her and had let her hold the Baby Jesus in her arm; other times she claimed that St Francis had appeared to her, or St Thomas à Becket. Caterina was also a prolific writer. She composed a Latin biography of Jesus in 5596 verses using the fifteen mysteries of the Rosary as her inspiration and aptly titled it *Rosarium*. Her chief work, however, is in Italian: *Le sette armi necessarie alla battaglia spirituale* (The Seven Weapons Necessary for the Spiritual Battle), which contains not only spiritual advice directed, for the most part, to novices, but also a description of her own struggle towards spiritual perfection.[26] Her first biographer was her fellow nun, the Blessed Illuminata Bembo, whose *Specchio di illuminazione* is not only a narrative of Caterina's life, but also an autobiography of Illuminata herself and, as its recent editor Silvia Mostaccio called it, a treatise on the observant monastic life.[27] Caterina was canonized by Pope Benedict XIII in 1712. Her feast day is celebrated on 9 May. Her uncorrupted body is still preserved in the chapel of her Poor Clares convent of Corpus Domini in Bologna.

The Blessed Illuminata Bembo (ca. 1410–93) was the daughter of a Venetian noble, Lorenzo Bembo. In her manuscript collection of Savonarola's sonnets she is identified in a later hand as 'a holy nun, and a companion of this our Blessed Virgin Caterina from Bologna' (Martelli, pp. 115–16).

Sonnet I.   'On the Lord's Ascension'

The poem is a Petrarchan sonnet consisting of fourteen hendecasyllabic verses divided into two quatrains and two tercets. The verses are rhymed ABBA ABBA CDE CDE.

The poet imagines how, at his ascension into Heaven, Jesus rose past all the spheres, entered into the Empyrian, and proceeded to the most exalted seat within it, from whence, in the physical body of a man, he now rules the universe. The motif is further illustrated through the image of the eagle.

In classical times, the eagle was a symbol of imperial power, both earthly (the emperor) and heavenly (Jupiter). In a Christian context, it is most often associated with John the Evangelist. In applying it to Christ, Savonarola is recalling the medieval belief that the eagle soars higher than any other bird or animal; an idea which he then develops in a Christological vein.

---

[26]The work was recently published as *Le sette armi spirituali*, ed. Antonella Degl'Innocenti (Florence: SISMEL Edizioni del Galluzzo, 2000). It was translated into English in 1926 by A.G. McDougall as *Spiritual Armour*. For Caterina's letters and poems see *Laudi, trattati e lettere*, ed. Silvia Serventi (Florence: SISMEL Edizioni del Galluzzo, 2000); for her sermons see *I Sermoni*, ed. Gilberto Sgarbi (Bologna: G. Barghigiani, 1999).

[27]For subsequent biographical work on Caterina see: Emilio Nannetti, *Vita di S. Caterina Vigri, detta da Bologna* (Bologna: Marsigli, 1841) and Anastasio Curzola, *Caterina Vigri: 'La Santa'* (Milan: Vita e Pensiero, 1941).

In following Christ's ascent through the spheres, Savonarola mentions in particular the fourth sphere, which is that of the Sun; the fifth, which belongs to Mars; and the eighth, where the fixed stars are located. In so doing, the poet follows the Ptolemaic conception of the universe, but seems also to be alluding to Dante's re-conception of the system along Christian lines. In fact, in his *Divine Comedy*, Dante had added Christian values to the Ptolemaic spheres—thus in his *Paradiso* the sphere of the Sun (Apollo), symbolized the light of divine knowledge and contained the blessed who were meritorious because of their wisdom; the sphere of Mars, the pagan god of war, exemplified courage in the faith and contained those who had fought for their faith; the sphere of the fixed stars, who firmly stay in their place, held the Church Triumphant. The Empyrian, which exists beyond the spheres of the Ptolemaic universe, is the 'real' world where God himself abides and thus where the Trinity and all the elect actually do reside. Savonarola's metaphor for the ascension thus adheres to Dante's construction.

Because of its strong Petrarchan echoes—compare it especially to Petrarch's sonnet 31 'Questa anima gentil che si diparte' ('This gentle soul that now departs')—, Martelli (p. 210) attributes the sonnet to Savonarola's youth, dating it possibly to ca. 1472–75. This is a time, Martelli argues (p. 212), when the young Savonarola lacked a truly independent and original voice, so in his poetic writings he adhered closely either to the example of Petrarch for sonnets and canzoni or of Feo Belcari for laude.

Sonnet II.   'On the Assumption of the Virgin Mary to
            Fra Giovanni from Asula, O.P.'

The poem is a Petrarchan sonnet consisting of fourteen hendecasyllabic verses divided into two quatrains and two tercets. The verses are rhymed ABBA ABBA CDE EDC.

In the sonnet the poet sings the praises of the Blessed Virgin Mary whose ascension to heaven is celebrated on 15 August. Savonarola imagines that as Mary ascends to heaven Jesus descends towards her to greet her and to crown her Queen of Heaven. Savonarola ends his poem with an expression of regret for not being as capable of singing Mary's praises as the angels and the blessed do in heaven.

This sonnet is also to be assigned to Savonarola's youth. Martelli dates it to ca. 1475, again on the grounds of its strong Petrarchan elements and its clear allusions to Petrarch's 'Triumph of Death' (p. 210).

Fra Giovanni da Asula was a Dominican friar who, in 1475, resided at the convent of San Domenico in Bologna and participated in its Chapter meeting (Martelli, p. 210).

Sonnet III.   'To the Virgin'

The poem is a Petrarchan sonnet consisting of fourteen hendecasyllabic verses divided into two quatrains and two tercets. The verses are rhymed ABBA ABBA CDC DCD.

In the sonnet the poet sings the praises of the Virgin and begs her to turn her eyes towards him and to help him find the straight path to heaven.

The poem is inlaid with echoes to the famous canzone to the Virgin that closes Petrarch's *Canzoniere*, 'Vergine bella che di sol vestita' ('Beautiful Virgin dressed with the sun', poem 366). Because of this, Martelli attributes it to Savonarola's youth, dating it possibly to the period 1472–75 (p. 210).

Lauda I.   'Omnipotent God'

This short lauda consists of eight verses rhymed aBaBcDcD. The last verse is in Latin.

In the lauda the poet asks God to pierce him with His love. Requests of this sort are fairly common in the poetry of Christian mystics.

The work dates from before May 1492, when it was first published as an addendum to the Miscomini edition of Savonarola's *Operetta dell'amor di Gesù*.

Lauda II.   'Song of Praise to the Crucifix'

The lauda consists of ten stanzas, each followed by the same refrain. Each stanza is made up of four septenaries rhymed abab. The refrain, on the other hand, is a tercet made up of two four-syllable verses and one hendecasyllable rhymed aaA. The rhyme, the short verses and the steady rhythm of this lauda produce a very strong rhythmic beat; the poem is thus clearly meant to be sung in a lively, upbeat rhythm.

In the lauda the poet expresses his love for the crucified Christ and asks to climb on the cross with him.

The work dates from before 1492, when it first appeared in print in the Miscomini edition of Savonarola's *Operetta dell'amor di Gesù* (published on 17 May 1492). Martelli points out that the lauda is strongly indebted to the Florentine lauda tradition, so much so that it faithfully echoes in both metre and rhyme words Feo Belcari's lauda 'Vergine tu mi fai' ('Virgin, you make me', p. 199).

Of all of Savonarola's poetic works this lauda is, without a doubt, the one that enjoyed the greatest popularity both in the friar's lifetime and after.

Lauda III.   'My heart, why do you stay here?'

The lauda consists of ten six-verse stanza rhymed ababbc and a refrain made up of a triplet rhymed ccc. The verses in the stanzas are all septenaries, while those of the refrain are two five-syllable verses followed by a septenary. The entire metric construct suggests that the lauda was meant to be sung to a lively, bouncy tune and may be intended to reflect, structurally, the joy of someone disgustingly happy in love.

The theme of the lauda is, in fact, the devotee's rapturous rush to the love of Christ and the ensuing embrace with the divine beloved. In a way, it connects well with the mystical and the charismatic traditions of Christianity documented from as early as St Paul (who claimed to know someone—himself—who in ecstasy had been rapt to the third heaven; 2 Cor. 12:2–4).

The work is undated, but we can safely attribute it to Savonarola's earlier production (1470s–80s).

Translation and Editorial Standards

The works in this collection have been translated from the standard and definitive 'National Edition of Girolamo Savonarola's Works,' as will be indicated below.[28] They have not been edited for translation, but are rendered fully, respecting the completeness of the text and adhering, as much as is possible in a translation, to the linguistic tonalities of the original. Savonarola's occasional words and phrases in Latin have also been translated into English; they are indicated in the text by italic script.

In translating Savonarola's poems, I have not maintained the rhyme scheme, but I have indicated it in the notes to the poems

---

[28]The 'National Edition of Girolamo Savonarola's Works' consists of over twenty volumes published between 1955 and 1984. Its editors are some of the most eminent Renaissance scholars in Italy.

(see above) using the standard Italian system of upper case letters for eleven syllable verses (hendecasyllables) and lower case letters for shorter verses (generally, septenaries). In order to retain the sense of a poetic line, I have rendered the Italian hendecasyllable with an English pentameter verse, and the Italian septenary or octonary with trimeters. In the laude, the steady beat and at times bouncy rhythms detectable in the English version are also to be found in the Italian originals; they may sound silly to our ears, but the reader should remember that the laude were meant to be sung, often to a lively tune with a definite beat and rhythm to it.

In the texts, biblical references have been indicated in square brackets. It should be noted that Savonarola cited biblical passages from memory and that he was not necessarily always referring to the 'standard' Vulgate edition (in fact, the Catholic Church would not declare St Jerome's translation of the Bible to be its official Latin version until the Council of Trent, long after Savonarola's death). As a result, some of Savonarola's citations vary from St Jerome's rendering; for example, his citation of Galatians 2:14 in the sermon *On the Art of Dying Well* reads *Tu iudeus cum sis, et gentiliter vivis, quare rogis gentiles iudaizare?* while the Vulgate version reads *si tu cum Iudaeus sis gentiliter et non iudaice vivis quomodo gentes cogis iudaizare*. In translating such citations I have therefore translated the Latin text as Savonarola provided it, but I have then given its location by referring back to the Vulgate. In most cases the variance in the words is not significant, so I have not felt the need to point it out to the reader. In referring to the Psalms, when the Vulgate and Revised Standard Version differ in the computation of the Psalms or of the verses, I have given the Vulgate numbering followed by the RSV version in parentheses; e.g.: Ps 136(137):1 or Ps 59:5(60:3). For the names for biblical books I have used the Vulgate version.

Savonarola, and the Italian language as a rule, use a generic that is gendered masculine—*omo*, *chi*, etc. The connotations of such a grammatical construct are not, strictly speaking, masculine nor masculinist; however, in current English usage they may appear to be so. In order to avoid such an unfortunate misreading of Savonarola's intentions, I have sought to translate these Italian words using English that was not gender specific. When, however, it was not possible to do so elegantly or quietly, I have retained the masculine generic forms used by Savonarola.

In arranging the translated texts, I have not set them out in chronological order, but in groups by genre that are more reflective of my own idiosyncratic thinking than any true scholarly rationale. I have started with Savonarola's early letters to his parents explaining his vocation and his mission; I have followed them with his letters to women (in chronological order) so as to remain within the genre and illustrate his pastoral work through his correspondence; his poems, all of which date from his early years, come next; they are followed by his sermons; these are followed by assorted pastoral works that offer advice on dealing with times of tribulation and on living righteously. The volume ends with an explication of the *Ave Maria*. Having said this, I will add that the readers are free to approach these texts in whatever sequence might be more suitable or convenient to them.

Abbreviations

The following abbreviations have been used in the apparatus to refer to books of the Bible:

Col	= Colossians	Macc	= Maccabees
Cor	= Corinthians	Mk	= Mark
Dan	= Daniel	Num	= Numbers
Deut	= Deuteronomy	Mt	= Matthew
Eph	= Ephesians	Pet	= Peter
Ex	= Exodus	Phil	= Philippians
Ez	= Ezekiel	Prov	= Proverbs
Gal	= Galatians	Rev	= Revelations
Gen	= Genesis	Rom	= Romans
Heb	= Hebrews	Prov	= Proverbs
Hos	= Hoseah	Ps	= Psalms
Is	= Isaiah	Sam	= Samuel
Jas	= James	Tim	= Timothy
Jh	= John	Thes	= Thessalonians
Lam	= Lamentations	Tob	= Tobias
Lk	= Luke	Wis	= Wisdom

For the sake of clarity, Ecclesiastes and Ecclesiasticus have been written out in full. I have not abbreviated Amos, Job, Joel, or Kings.

Source Texts for the Translations

The letters are translated from G. Savonarola, *Lettere*, eds. Roberto Ridolfi, Vincenzo Romano, and Armando F. Verde, O.P. *e Scritti apologetici*, eds. Vincenzo Romano and Armando F. Verde, O.P. (Rome: Angelo Belardetti Editore, 1984), pp. 3–20, 101, 137–38, 145–46, 154–56, 159–60, 181–82, 207–16; 'Nota critica' pp. 339–400.

The poems are from G. Savonarola, *Poesie*, ed. Mario Martelli (Rome: Angelo Belardetti Editore, 1968), pp. 3–41; 'Nota critica' pp. 55–269.

The sermons are taken as follows:

On Haggai, Sermon No. 1 'Do penance' is from G. Savonarola, *Prediche sopra Aggeo*, ed. Luigi Firpo (Roma: Angelo Belardetti Editore, 1965), pp. 1–23.

On the Psalms, Sermon No. 3 'Behold the sword of the Lord' is from G. Savonarola, *Prediche sopra i Salmi*, ed. Vincenzo Romano (Roma: Angelo Belardetti Editore), vol. 1, pp. 37–62.

On Ruth and Micah, Sermon 28 'On the Art of Dying Well' is from G. Savonarola, *Prediche sopra Ruth e Michea*, ed. Vincenzo Romano (Rome: Angelo Belardetti Editore, 1962), vol. 2, pp. 362–97, 479–525.

On Exodus, Sermon No. 1 'Renovation Sermon' is from G. Savonarola, *Prediche sopra l'Esodo*, ed. Pier Giorgio Ricci (Roma: Angelo Belardetti Editore, 1955), vol. 1, pp. 3–36.

Ten Rules to Observe in Time of Great Tribulations is from *Operette spirituali*, ed. Mario Ferrara (Rome: Angelo Belardetti Editore, 1976), vol. 2, pp. 171–76; 'Nota critica' pp. 313–19.

On the Prudent and Judicious Way of Living in the Order is from G. Savonarola, *Operette spirituali*, ed. Mario Ferrara (Rome: Angelo Belardetti Editore, 1976), vol. 2, pp. 149–55, 'Nota critica' pp. 301–4.

A Guide to Righteous Living is from G. Savonarola, *Operette spirituali*, ed. Mario Ferrara (Rome: Angelo Belardetti Editore, 1976), vol. 2, pp. 187–94; 'Nota critica' pp. 331–35.

The Book on the Life of the Widow is from *Operette spirituali*, ed. Mario Ferrara (Rome: Angelo Belardetti Editore, 1976), vol. 1, pp. 9–62; 'Nota critica' pp. 299–329.

Exposition on the Prayer to the Virgin is from *Operette spirituali*, ed. Mario Ferrara (Rome: Angelo Belardetti Editore, 1976), vol. 2, pp. 125–47; 'Nota critica' pp. 293–97.

Other Translations into English of Works by Savonarola

A small number of Savonarola's works have already been translated and published in English. They are as follows:

Some of Savonarola's letters were translated as: *Spiritual and Ascetic Letters of Savonarola*, ed. B.W. Randolph, intro. Henry Scott Holland. London: A.R. Mowbray/New York: T. Whittaker, 1907.

English translations of some of his laude can be found in: *Savonarolan Laude, Motets, and Anthems*, ed. Patrick Macey. Madison, Wisc.: A-R Editions, Inc., 1999 [these include the original lyrics, Macey's translations, and scores in modern notation for Savonarola's songs].

So far only one of Savonarola's sermons has been rendered into English—the one delivered on 13 January 1495. It appeared in an abridged version on pp. 4–15 of John C. Olin, *The Catholic Reformation: Savonarola to Ignatius Loyola. Reform in the Church 1495–1540* (New York: Harper & Row, 1969) in a translation by Alfred E. Vecchio with the title: *On the Renovation of the Church*.

The treatise on the government of Florence, the *Trattato del reggimento e governo della città di Firenze*, has appeared as *Liberty and Tyranny in the Goverment [sic] of Men*, trans. Carlo Maria Flumiani. Albuquerque, NM: American Classical College Press, 1976 [1984, 1986].

The treatise *De simplicitate Christianae vitae* was rendered into English in the seventeenth century as *The Felicity of a Christian Life*. London: [n.p.], 1651.

The treatise *De Triumpho Crucis*, on the truth of the Christian faith, also first appeared in English in the seventeenth century and has enjoyed several translations as:

The Verity of Christian Faith. London: by R. Daniel, 1651.

The Truth of the Christian Faith, or, The Triumph of the Cross of Christ. Cambridge: by John Field, 1661.

The Triumph of the Cross, trans. O'dell Travers Hill. London: Hodder and Stoughton, 1868.

The Triumph of the Cross, trans. John Procter. London: Sands & Co./Dublin: H.H. Gill & Son, 1901.

With at least twenty different editions in English (sixteen of which in the sixteenth century alone), the works of Savonarola most available in English have been, by far, his two meditations on Psalm

31 'In te, Domine, speravi' and Psalm 51 'Miserere mei Deus' that the friar composed while imprisoned in the *Alberghetto* (as his cell in the belltower of the Palazzo della Signoria was ironically called). Their first English translation appeared in a collection of prayers and meditations entitled:

Prayers of the Bible taken out of the olde testament and the newe ... An exposicyo[n] upo[n] the Psalme of Miserere and upon the Psalme of In te domine speravi made by freer Hierom Savonarole of Ferrarie ... London: Robert Redman, [1535?].

The printer re-issued the collection again in 1537? and 1539. They also appeared in English from a number of other presses, both in primers to be used by schoolchildren and in collections of devotional works published both in England and in the Netherlands (in English) as follows:

The prymer of Salysbery use, bothe in Englyshe and in Laten ... A meditacyon of Ierom de fararia vpon the Psalme of in te Domine sperui [Antwerp: Widow of C. Ruremond for Iohan Gowghe, 1536].

A goodly prymer in Englysshe newely corrected and prynted, with certeyne godly meditations [and] prayers added to the same ... [London: by T. Gibson for W. Marshall, 1538?].

Certeine prayers and godly meditacyons very nedefull for euery Christen. Malborow [i.e. Antwerp]: per me Joannem Philoponon [i.e. H. Peetersen van Mideelburch?], 1538.

An exposicyon after the maner of a co[n]te[m]placyo[n] vpon ye .lj. Psalme called Miserere mei De[us] whiche Hierom of Ferrarye made at the latter ende of hys dayes [and] *A medytacyon of the same Jerome upon the Psalme of In te Domine speraui ...* [Rouen]: Nicolas le Roux for François Regnault in Paris, 1538.

Thys prymer in Englyshe and in Laten is newly translated after the Laten texte. Rouen: [Nicolas le Roux?], 1538.

The primer in Englishe and Laten: set oute at length with the exposicion of the Miserere and In Te Domine speraui ... London: By John Mayleer at the signe of the whyte Beare in Botulph Lane, [1540?]; then again London: by Thomas Petyt, c.1540; London: by [Richard Grafton for] Roberte Toye, 1542; London: by Thomas Petyt, 1543.

An exposicyon after the maner of a contemplacion, vpon Psalme called Miserere mei Deus whiche Hierome of Ferrary made at the latter ende of hys days. London: by John Herforde, for Robert Toye, [1542?]; then again [Antwerp?: n.p., 1545?].

An other meditatio[n] of the same Hieronimus Sauanorola vpon the xxxi Psalme of Dauid. Emden: E. van der Erve, [1555?].

An exposicion after the maner of a contemplacion vpon the .li. Psalme called Miserere mei deus ... Exposition in Psalmum In te Domine speravi. London: by Thomas Marshe for Michel Lobley, 1558.

A Pithie Exposition upon the 51 Psalme ... Also a godly meditation upon the 31 Psalme ... Newly augmented and amended by Abraham Fleming.: London: T. Dawson, 1578.

A goodly exposition vpon the XXX. Psalme in te domine speraui. London: J. Byddell for W. Marshall, [1635?].

An exposition of the psalm Miserere mei Deus, trans. F.C. Cowper. Milwaukee, Wis.: The Young Churchman, 1889.

Meditations on Psalm LI and part of Psalm XXXI, trans. E.H. Perowne. London: C.J. Clay and Sons, 1900.

Prison Meditations on Psalms 51 and 31, trans. John Patrick Donnelly. Milwaukee: Marquette University Press, 1994.

Select Bibliography in English

Biographies

The reputable biographies of Savonarola available in English are:

Ridolfi, Roberto. *The Life of Girolamo Savonarola,* trans. Cecil Grayson. London: Routledge & Kegan Paul/New York: Alfred A. Knopf, 1959; 6th ed. 1981.

Villari, Pasquale. *Life and Times of Girolamo Savonarola,* trans. Linda Villari. London: T.F. Unwin / New York: C. Schribner's, 1988; rpt St Clair Shores, Mich: Scholarly Press, 1972.

The following fundamental biographies are, unfortunately, still not available in English:

Burlamacchi (pseudo). *La vita del Beato Ieronimo Savonarola scritta da un anonimo del sec. XVI e già attribuita a Fra Pacifico Burlamacchi,* ed. Piero Ginori Conti, intro. Roberto Ridolfi. Florence: Leo S. Olschki, 1937.

Luschino, Benedetto. 'Cedrus Libani ossia vita di fra Girolamo Savonarola' ed. Vincenzo Marchese, in *Archivio storico italiano,* appendix VII (1849): 39–95.

Schnitzer, Joseph. *Quellen und Forschungen zur Geschichte Savonarolas,* 4 vols. Munich: Verlag der J.J. Leutnerschen Buchhandlung, 1902.

Schnitzer, Joseph. *Savonarola. Ein Kulturbild aus der Renaissance.* 2 vols. Munich: E. Reinhardt, 1924; Italian translation: *Savonarola*, trans. Ernesto Rutili. 2 vols. Milan: Treves, 1931.

Readers are advised not to bother with William H. Crawford's *Girolamo Savonarola. A Prophet of Righteousness* (Cincinnati: Jennings and Graham / New York: Eaton and Mains, 1907), which is academically weak and outdated, nor with George Eliot's *Romola*, 3 vols (London: Smith-Elder, 1863), which is mostly a fictionalized account of Savonarola's love life and is not to be taken seriously.

Assessments of Savonarola by his Own Contemporaries

For assessments of Savonarola by his own contemporaries or near-contemporaries available in English, see in particular:

Guicciardini, Francesco. 'History of Florence' chapts. 12–16 in his *History of Italy and History of Florence*, trans. Cecil Grayson, ed. John R. Hale. New York: Twayne Publishers, 1964, pp. 34–38, 47–50. See also F. Guicciardini, *The History of Italy*, trans. Sidney Alexander. New York: The Macmillan Company, 1969, pp. 83–85, 127–31, and *passim*.

Landucci, Luca. *A Florentine Diary from 1450 to 1516*, trans. Alice de Rosen Jervis. London: J.M. Dent and Son, 1927, *passim*.

Machiavelli, Niccolò. *The Discourses*, I.11, I.45, I.56, III.30.

Machiavelli, Niccolò. *The Prince*, chapt. 6.

Machiavelli, Niccolò. Letter of 9 March 1498 to Ricciardo Bechi and letter of 17 May 1521 to Francesco Guicciardini in *Machiavelli. The Chief Works and Others*, trans. Allan Gilbert, 3 vols. Durham, NC: Duke University Press, 1965, vol. 2, pp. 886–89, 972.

Bibliographic Overviews

For a brief overview in English of recent scholarship on Savonarola, see:

Eisenbichler, Konrad. 'Savonarola Studies in Italy on the 500th Anniversary of the Friar's Death' *Renaissance Quarterly* 52 (1999): 386–94.

Weinstein, Donald. 'Hagiography, Demonology, Biography: Savonarola Studies Today' *Journal of Modern History* 63:3 (1991): 483–503.

There are also two useful and extensive bibliographies in Italian:

Ferrara, Mario. *Bibliografia savonaroliana. Bibliografia ragionata degli scritti editi dal principio del secolo XIX ad oggi.* Florence: Leo S. Olschki, 1958.

Ferrara, Mario. *Nuova bibliografia savonaroliana*. Vaduz: Topos Verlag, 1981.

Scholarly Studies in English

The most important historical work in English on Savonarola and on Savonarolism has been carried out by Donald Weinstein and Lorenzo Polizzotto. Their books and articles are of fundamental importance, and in particular the following:

Polizzotto, Lorenzo. 'Domenico Benivieni and the Radicalisation of the Savonarolan Movement' *Altro Polo* 7 (1982): 99–117.

Polizzotto, Lorenzo. 'Confraternities, Conventicles and Political Dissent: The Case of the Savonarolan *Capi rossi*' *Memorie domenicane* n.s. 16 (1985): 235–83 [on Savonarolism in a confraternity in the 1530s].

Polizzotto, Lorenzo. 'Confraternities, Conventicles and Political Dissent: The Case of the Savonarolan 'Capi rossi'. Documents' *Memorie domenicane* n.s. 17 (1986): 285–300 [documents pertaining to the preceding article].

Lorenzo Polizzotto, *'Dell'arte del ben morire*. The Piagnone Way of Death 1494–1545' *I Tatti Studies. Essays in the Renaissance* 3 (1989): 27–68 [on testamentary donations to the convent of San Marco during and after Savonarola].

Polizzotto, Lorenzo. 'When Saints Fall Out: Women and the Savonarolan Reform in Early Sixteenth-Century Florence' *Renaissance Quarterly* 46 (1993): 486–525 [on the Savonarolan movement in women's convents and on two 'holy women' in Tuscany in the early sixteenth century].

Polizzotto, Lorenzo. *The Elect Nation. The Savonarolan Movement in Florence 1494–1545*. Oxford: Clarendon Press/New York: Oxford University Press, 1994.

Polizzotto, Lorenzo. *Children of the Promise. The Confraternity of the Purification and the Socialization of Youths in Florence, 1427–1785*. Oxford: Oxford University Press, 2003 [see chapt. 3, 'In the Shadow of Savonarola, 1494–1530' for Savonarola and youth confraternities; I thank the author for kindly having let me see a pre-publication copy of his work].

Weinstein, Donald. *Savonarola and Florence. Prophecy and Patriotism in the Renaissance*. Princeton, NJ: Princeton University Press, 1970 [a fundamental work on Savonarola as a prophet].

Weinstein, Donald. 'Savonarola—Preacher or Patriot?' *History Today* 39 (Nov. 1989): 30–36 [an article aimed at a general readership].

Weinstein, Donald. 'The Art of Dying Well and Popular Piety in the Preaching and Thought of Girolamo Savonarola' pp. 88–104 in *Life and Death in Fifteenth-Century Florence*, eds. Marcel Tetel, Ronald Witt, and Rona Goffen. Durham and London: Duke University Press, 1989.

Weinstein, Donald. 'Girolamo Savonarola: Piety, Prophecy and Politics in Renaissance Florence' pp. 1–16 in *Girolamo Savonarola. Piety, Prophecy and Politics in Renaissance Florence* [exhibition catalogue]. The Elizabeth Perkins Prothro Galleries, 20 March–30 July 1994. Bridwell Library. Dallas, TX: Southern Methodist University, 1994.

Weinstein, Donald. 'Girolamo Savonarola' vol. 5, pp. 406–10 in *Encyclopedia of the Renaissance*, ed. Paul F. Grendler. New York: Charles Scribner's Sons, 1999 [an excellent scholarly overview of Savonarola, his works, and his influence].

Among the many other works in English on Savonarola, see in particular:

Brown, Alison. 'Savonarola, Machiavelli and Moses: A Changing Model' pp. 57–72 in *Florence and Italy. Renaissance Studies in Honour of Nicolai Rubinstein*, ed. Peter Denley and Caroline Elam. London: Committee for Medieval Studies, 1988.

Brucker, Gene. 'Savonarola and Florence: The Intolerable Burden' pp. 119–33 in *Studies in the Italian Renaissance: Essays in Memory of Arnolfo Ferruolo*, ed. Gian Paolo Biasin, Albert N. Mancini, and Nicolas J. Perella. Naples: Società Editrice Napoletana, 1985.

D'Accone, Frank. 'Sacred Music in Florence in Savonarola's Time' pp. 311–54 in *Una città e il suo profeta. Firenze di fronte al Savonarola*, ed. Gian Carlo Garfagnini. Florence: SISMEL Edizioni del Galluzzo, 2001.

Eisenbichler, Konrad. *The Boys of the Archangel Raphael. A Youth Confraternity in Florence, 1411–1785*. Toronto: University of Toronto Press, 1998 [see pp. 49–55 for Savonarola and youth confraternities].

Erlanger, Rachel. *The Unarmed Prophet. Savonarola in Florence*. New York: McGraw-Hill, 1988.

Fenlon, Iain. 'The Savonarolan Moment' pp. 355–70 in *Una città e il suo profeta. Firenze di fronte al Savonarola*, ed. Gian Carlo Garfagnini. Florence: SISMEL Edizioni del Galluzzo, 2001 [music and Savonarola].

Goff, F.R. 'The Four Florentine Editions of Savonarola's *Predica dell'Arte del Bene Morire*', *New Colophon* 3 (1950): 286–301.

Hall, Marcia. 'Savonarola's Preaching and the Patronage of Art' pp. 493–522 in *Christianity and the Renaissance. Image and Religious Imagination in the Quattrocento*, eds. Timothy Verdon and John Henderson. Syracuse, NY: Syracuse University Press, 1990.

Kent, F.W. 'A Proposal by Savonarola for the Self-Reform of Florentine Women (March 1496)' *Memorie domenicane*, n.s. 14 (1983): 335–41.

Macey, Patrick. 'The *Lauda* and the Cult of Savonarola' *Renaissance Quarterly* 45 (1992): 439–83 [Savonarola and music].

Macey, Patrick. *Bonfire Songs. Savonarola's Musical Legacy*. Oxford: Clarendon Press, 1998 [a prize-winning book, complete with a CD of the laude recorded by the Eastman Capella Antiqua in April–June 1997 in Christ Church, Rochester, NY, under the author's direction].

Meltzoff, Stanley. *Botticelli, Signorelli and Savonarola. 'Theologia Poetica' and Painting from Boccaccio to Poliziano*. Florence: Leo S. Olschki, 1987.

Pugliese, Olga Zorzi. 'A Last Testimony by Savonarola and His Companions' *Renaissance Quarterly* 34:1 (1981): 1–10.

Savonarolan Laude, Motets, and Anthems, ed. Patrick Macey. Madison, Wisc.: A-R Editions, Inc., 1999. [lyrics, translations, and scores in modern notation for Savonarola's songs].

Steinberg, Ronald M. *Fra Girolamo Savonarola, Florentine Art and Renaissance Historiography*. Athens, OH: Ohio University Press, 1977.

Tomas, Natalie. '"A Preacher for Women?" Savonarola and the Women of Florence' pp. 38–57 in her *'A Positive Novelty': Women and Public Life in Renaissance Florence*. Monash Publications in History, 12. (Victoria, Australia: Monash University, 1992).

Trexler, Richard C. 'Lorenzo de' Medici and Savonarola, Martyrs for Florence' *Renaissance Quarterly* 31:3 (1978): 293–308.

Wilson, Blake. '*Hora mai sono in età*: Savonarola and Music in Laurentian Florence' pp. 283–309 in *Una città e il suo profeta. Firenze di fronte al Savonarola*, ed. Gian Carlo Garfagnini. Florence: SISMEL Edizioni del Galluzzo, 2001.

The World of Savonarola. Italian Elites and Perceptions of Crisis, ed. Stella Fletcher and Christine Shaw. Aldershot, UK, and Burlington, VT: Ashgate, 2000 [17 articles from the Warwick conference of 29–31 May 1998].

In the last ten years, on the occasion of the 500th anniversary of Savonarola's death, a number of excellent collections and studies have appeared, many of them the product of international conferences held in Florence, Ferrara, and elsewhere. Readers of Italian or French may thus consult some of the following:

Garfagnini, Gian Carlo. *'Questa è la terra tua'. Savonarola a Firenze*. Florence: SISMEL Edizioni del Galluzzo, 2000 [20 articles, most previously published elsewhere].

Girolamo Savonarola da Ferrara all'Europa, eds. Gigliola Fragnito and Mario Miegge. Florence: SISMEL Edizioni del Galluzzo, 2001 [articles from the Ferrara conference of 30 March–3 April 1998].

Il santuario di Santa Maria del Sasso di Bibbiena dalla protezione medicea al Savonarola. Storia, devozione, arte, eds. Armando F. Verde, O.P. and Raffaella M. Zaccaria. Florence: SISMEL Edizioni del Galluzzo, 2000 [12 articles from the Bibbiena conference of 8–9 May 1998].

Savonarola. Democrazia, tirannide, profezia, ed. Gian Carlo Garfagnini. Florence: SISMEL Edizioni del Galluzzo, 1998 [14 articles from the Pistoia conference of 23–24 May 1997].

Savonarola e la mistica, ed. Gian Carlo Garfagnini. Florence: SISMEL Edizioni del Galluzzo, 1999 [5 articles from the Florence conference of 22 May 1998].

Savonarola e la politica, ed. Gian Carlo Garfagnini. Florence: SISMEL Edizioni del Galluzzo, 1997 [14 articles from the Florence conference of 19–20 October 1996].

Savonarola rivisitato (1498–1998), ed. Massimiliano G. Rosito. Florence: Città di Vita, 1998 [22 articles and documents; also published as vol. 53, issue 2–3 (1998) of the journal *Città di vita*].

Savonarole. Enjeux, débats, questions, eds. A. Fontes, J.-L. Fournel, M. Plaisance. Paris: Université de la Sorbonne Nouvelle, 1997 [17 articles from the Paris conference of 25–27 January 1996].

Studi savonaroliani. Verso il V centenario, ed. Gian Carlo Garfagnini. Florence: SISMEL Edizioni del Galluzzo, 1996 [30 articles from the Florence conference of 14–15 January 1995].

Una città e il suo profeta. Firenze di fronte al Savonarola, ed. Gian Carlo Garfagnini. Florence: SISMEL Edizioni del Galluzzo, 2001 [30 articles from the Florence conference of 10–13 December 1998].

Verso Savonarola. Misticismo, profezia, empiti riformistici fra Medioevo ed età moderna, eds. Gian Carlo Garfagnini and Giuseppe Picone. Florence: SISMEL Edizioni del Galluzzo, 1999 [5 articles from the Poggibonsi conference of 30 April 1997].

Letters

Letter 1
To his father, Niccolò Savonarola, in Ferrara
25 April 1475

Savonarola explains the reasons for his sudden and secret departure to
Bologna, where he has entered a Dominican convent, and seeks to
console his father.

*To the noble and illustrious man Niccolò Savonarola, a most
excellent parent. In Ferrara.*[1]

Jesus Christ

My honourable father,

Without a doubt, you are suffering greatly because of my departure,
and especially because I departed secretly from you. With this letter
I want you to understand my state of mind and my desires so that
you may be comforted and understand that my action is not as
juvenile as other people think. First, I want from you, as I would
from a strong man who spurns transitory things,[2] to follow truth
and not passion, as simple women do, and to judge rationally
whether I should have fled the world to pursue this wish of mine.
First, the reason why I entered into a religious order is this: first,
the great misery of the world, the wickedness of men, the rapes,

---

[1]Here and elsewhere, italic script indicates that Savonarola is writing in
Latin.

[2]Savonarola uses the phrase *uomo virile* (lit.: 'a manly man') to indicate a
man whose character is not weakened by feminine or other non-manly
influences, then, in the next phrase, contrasts it with *le feminule* (lit.: 'the small,
insignificant women'). In other words, Savonarola wishes to speak with his
father 'man to man', rationally, and does not want him to be influenced by
'womanly' passion, that is, by emotion.

the adulteries, the thefts, the pride, the idolatry, the vile curses, for the world has come to such a state that one can no longer find anyone who does good; so much so that many times every day I would sing this verse with tears in my eyes: *Alas, flee from cruel lands, flee from the shores of the greedy*.[3] I did this because I could not stand the great wickedness of the blind people of Italy, especially when I saw that virtue had been completely cast down and vice raised up. This was the greatest desire I could have in the world; for this I prayed the Lord Jesus Christ every day to remove me from this sludge; and so I constantly recited a short prayer to God with great devotion saying: *Teach me the way I should go, for to thee I lift up my soul.* [Ps 142(143):8] Now, when God was pleased to do so, in His infinite mercy He showed me the way and I have accepted it, though I am unworthy of so much grace. Answer me, therefore: is it not a great virtue to flee the filth and iniquity of this world in order to want to live as a rational [human being] and not like an animal among the swine?[4] *Also*, would I not have been most ungrateful to have prayed God to show me the straight road on which I must walk and then, when He deigned to show it to me, not to have followed it? Alas, my Jesus, better a thousand deaths, than for me to be so ungrateful towards you. So, *sweetest father*, you must thank the Lord Jesus and not cry: He gave you a son and then sustained him very well till he was twenty-two years old; and not only this, but He also deigned to make him His knight militant. Alas, do you not consider it a wondrous grace to have a son who is a knight of Jesus Christ! *Or, in a few words,* either you love me or you do not. I know very well that you would not say you do not love me. If, then, you love me, *seeing that* I have two parts, that is, a soul and a body, either you love my body more or my soul. You cannot say the body, because you would not love me if you loved the baser part of me. If, then, you love my soul more, why do you not also seek the good of my soul? For, certainly, you must rejoice and celebrate this victory. But *I know* very well that it is impossible for the flesh not to suffer a little; however, one must restrain it with one's reason, *especially* wise and generous men such as yourself.

Don't you know that it grieved me deeply to separate myself from you? I definitely want you to believe me [when I say] that never,

---

[3]Virgil, *Aeneid*, Bk. 3, v. 44.

[4]A clear reference to the parable of the Prodigal Son (Lk 15:11–32).

since I was born, did I suffer more, nor did I agonize more, seeing myself abandon my own blood and go among unknown people to offer my body in sacrifice to Jesus Christ, and to sell my own will into the hands of those I did not know; but then, considering that God was calling me, and that He did not disdain to become a servant among us little worms, I never would have dared not to bend myself to His sweetest and so pious voice: *Come to me, all who labor and are heavy laden, and I will give you rest. Take my yoke upon you* [Mt 11:28–29] etc. Since *I know* that you complained about me, that I had departed so secretly, and that I had nearly run away from you, know that in my heart the grief and pain at having to leave you were so great that, if I had indicated this to you, I really believe my heart would have broken before I could have left; and my thoughts would have prevented my action. So, do not be surprised that I did not tell with you. I did, in truth, leave some papers behind the books leaning against the window that informed you about my affairs.

I beg you, then, my dear father, stop crying and no longer make me sad and give me pain, as I have had: not out of grief for what I have done, for certainly I would not undo it [even] if I thought I would become greater than Caesar, but because I am made of flesh as you are, and sensuality is repugnant to reason: and so I must fight fiercely so that the devil does not jump on my back: all the more when I hear about you. Soon these days when the wound is still fresh will end and then I hope that you and I will be comforted in this world with grace and then in the next with glory. I have nothing more to say except to beg you, for the man that you are, to comfort my mother. I pray that she and you will grant me your blessing; and I will always fervently pray for your souls. *From Bologna, the 25th day of April 1475.*

I recommend all my brothers and sisters to you, and especially Alberto;[5] have him educated, for it would fall upon your shoulders and it would be a great sin if you allowed him to waste his time.

Girolamo Savonarola, your son.

---

[5]Alberto was a younger brother of Girolamo; he never married, but followed his father and grandfather in the medical profession.

Letter 2
To his mother, Elena Savonarola, from Pavia
25 January 1490

On his way from Brescia to Genoa, Savonarola writes to his mother from Pavia explaining why he has not written to her recently and why he must travel so much, adding that a prophet is not honoured in his own land.

Honourable Mother,

The peace of Christ be with you.

I know you wonder why I have not written to you for so many days already. It is not because I have forgotten you, but for lack of couriers, for I have not found anyone during this time going from Brescia to Ferrara. Admittedly, one of our men did come here after Christmas, but I was so busy with the celebrations that I forgot to write to you, for which I am very sorry. Then, when Friar Iacomo da Pavia, who had been prior in our convent of the Angeli before being prior of the one where he is now, came here, he told me about you and how you complained that I had not written; and I, not having couriers available, answered him that the road between Brescia and Ferrara is out of the way and so one cannot have a regular courier. But since I was going to Genoa, he told me that when I would get to Pavia I would find couriers every day, and that I should write to you from Pavia. So, obeying the command to go preach in Genoa this Lent, and having arrived in Pavia, I write to you as I had planned, letting you know that I am well, and I am happy in my mind and healthy in my body, though I am tired from the journey and I still have a long way to go before I reach Genoa.

I do not know what else to tell you, except that I know well that I have not had any letters from you since I last saw you, as far as I remember, nor news of you, except from the aforementioned Friar Iacomo. I can well imagine that you are troubled and so, as much as my frailty lets me, I constantly pray God for you. I do not know what else to do: if I could help you in any other way, I would. Once upon a time, when I was free, I made myself a servant out of love for Jesus, and this beloved of mine[6] made Himself man and

---

[6]That is, Jesus. Savonarola has suddenly changed the meaning of the phrase

became a servant in order to free me [Phil 2:7]; then, in everything He sought the glory of the freedom of the children of God. And so, as much as I can, I seek to serve Him, and not to withdraw from these labours for any earthly or carnal affection, but to work instead willingly in His vineyard in various cities out of love for Him, so that I not only save my own soul, but *also* that of others, in great fear of His judgement should I not do this, because, since He has given me the talent, I must spend it in the way He wants me to.

So, my most beloved Mother, do not let it burden you if I wander far from you or if I go to various cities to speak, for I do all this for the salvation of a lot of souls, preaching, exhorting, confessing, reading and advising. I never go from one place to the other for any other reason. This is *also* the reason why my superiors always send me. And so you should take comfort from the fact that God has deigned to elect one of your fruits and to give him such an office. You should know that if I were to stay in Ferrara all the time, I would not reap such a harvest as I do when I am away, because no religious, or very few, ever produces a harvest of holy life in his own country, and so Holy Scripture always urges us to go away from our country [Gen 12:1], and *also* because one does not lend as much faith to someone from one's own country as one does to a foreigner, be it in preaching or in counsel. And so our Saviour says that no-one is a prophet in one's own country [Lk 4:24], so much so that even He was not accepted in His own country. Therefore, since God has deigned to elect me out of my sins to such an office, for which I thank Him an infinite number of times, be happy that I am in the vineyard of Christ, away from my country, where I know and can touch with my hands, and where I know from experience that, without comparison, I can reap a greater harvest for my soul and for that of others than I would in Ferrara. If I were there and wanted to do as I do in other cities, I know I would be told what was said to Christ by His own countrymen who, when He preached, would say: 'Is this man not a carpenter,[7] and the son of a carpenter, and the son of Mary?' [Mk 6:3, Mt 13:55] And they did not deign to listen to Him. The same

---

to refer to Jesus himself and not to his love for Jesus.

[7]Savonarola uses the word *fabbro* (smith); I have translated it using the more usual English word for this biblical passage, 'carpenter.'

they will say of me: 'Is this man not master Girolamo who committed such and such sins, who was like us? We know very well, now, who this man is.' And they would not listen devoutly to my words. For this reason I was told many times by some people in Ferrara who see me going from city to city, that our friars must be short of men, as if to say: 'If they use you, who are so base, to do so much, they must certainly be short of men.' But outside my country people do not say such things to me; on the contrary, when I want to leave, they cry, both the men and the women, and they greatly appreciate my words.

I do not write this because I seek human praises, nor because I take pleasure in praise, but to show you why I stay away from my country, so that you may know that I stay away gladly because I know that I do something much more pleasing to God and much more profitable for me and for the soul of my neighbours. I so much prefer these profits to all earthly treasures which, compared to my profits, seem like mud to me [Wis 7:9]. And so, my most honourable Mother, do not grieve for this, because the more I make myself pleasing to God, the more my prayers for you will gain merit with Him. And do not think that you have been abandoned by Him because of your tribulations. On the contrary, believe rather that you have abandoned Him and not that He has abandoned you, because with His scourges He forces you to draw towards Him. Perhaps in this way He wants to save you and your children and He wants to listen to my prayer in which I do not pray that He give you wealth, but that He give you His grace, and that He lead you to eternal life through whatever path He likes.

I thought I would write a few words, but love has let the pen run on and I have opened my heart to you more than I thought I would. So, be assured in the end that my heart is more than ever set on exposing my soul and my body, and all the knowledge God has given me, and all His grace for the love of God and for the salvation of my neighbour. Because I cannot do this in my country, I will do it away from it. So I pray you not to obstruct me in this path and rest assured that whenever I might be able to help you in anything, I will do it. When it will be necessary, it will not burden me to come to Ferrara; but when it is not necessary, I consider it a great sin to set aside God's work, which He has given me, for the sake of trifles.

I encourage you to be patient in everything, and to console my sisters, who should know that God has provided for them much more than they believe, because if, perhaps, He had dealt with them differently, giving them wealth and honour and marrying them off, they might have fallen into a variety of grave sins that they know nothing of, and they might be more involved in the world than they are.[8] I would want them to open their eyes and to recognize the grace God has granted them; they should recommend themselves to Him with all their heart, for He never abandons those who trust in Him. Encourage my brothers and the entire company to live righteously. Today, after I have eaten, I will continue my journey towards Genoa. Pray God that He keep me safe and that He allow me to reap a great harvest among that people. Remember me to my uncle and my aunt and my cousins. God be with you in grace, and keep you from evil for love of our Lord Jesus Christ. Amen.

Written in Pavia, in a hurry, the day of the Conversion of St Paul the Apostle, 1490.

Your son,
Friar Girolamo Savonarola

Letter 3
To Elena Savonarola on the death of her brother Borso
5 December 1485

God scourges us in order to draw us to Him. One should not place one's joy and heart in things of this world because they are transitory. Savonarola urges his mother and sisters to devote themselves to Jesus.[9]

Most honourable and most beloved Mother,

May divine peace and consolation be with you. Having learned from one of your letters that our uncle Borso, your brother, has died, I began to think in my heart what might be God's providence towards our house; because the more I pray and have prayed to

---

[8]For further negative comments on married life, see below, his treatise *On the Life of the Widow*, pp. 192–95.

[9]The autograph copy of this letter is at the Rosenbach Museum and Library in Philadelphia, PA, with shelf mark Ms. f 810/30. It has recently been brought to the attention of scholars and described by Victoria Kirkham in her article 'Two Letters Relocated: Savonarola and Castiglione at Philadelphia's Rosenbach' *Lettere italiane* 38:4 (1986): 514–24.

Him for it, the more He has struck it every day. I certainly thank the most wise and most kind Creator and Redeemer for our souls, for He does more for us than we know or might ask or think. I see that my prayers are heard more and much better than I should have thought, because, praying for the salvation of your souls, I see this salvation drawing nearer to you, if only you would know how to draw near to it. For, the more our soul is tied to earthly things, the more it is distant from its eternal goal. So, in order to raise your spirit towards heavenly things, God shows you clearly in this way[10] that human hopes are blind and false.

Your Creator is striking you often in order to wake you up from the deep slumber in which you have slept a long time, loving the present life more than the future one. These, Mother, are most powerful voices from Heaven, as you yourself know in the depth of your heart. They call out to you loudly urging you to withdraw your affection from earthy and passing things, and drawing you towards the love of Jesus Christ. Believe me, my dear Mother and sisters and my beloved brothers all, that the most sweet Jesus and our most kind Saviour follows you calling out to you: —Come to my kingdom, leave behind this world full of wickedness and iniquity.— And because you are asleep, He, like someone who longs for your well being, strikes you in order to wake you up. Open, therefore, your eyes, and do not be ungrateful. Consider whether in the world, from its beginning to its end, any servant of God ever lived without temptation, persecution, or tribulation. God scourges His children so that they should not place their hope on things of this earth. He cuts their every hook, every root and everything they trust, so that, seeing themselves abandoned by the world, finally, finding no other recourse, they throw themselves into His arms. Oh kind God! Oh infinite mercy! Oh inestimable charity! He follows us as if He had great need of us! Come, tell me, I ask you, what rich man, what famous man on this earth, on whom this perverse age smiles, what man exalted and raised to great heights by the world does good things? Which one serves God with all his heart? Do you not know that Jesus cannot lie? Now, He says that it is very difficult and nearly impossible for a rich man to be saved [Mt 19:23–24], and He has sanctified the poor of spirit [Mt 5:3]. Do you not know now how the world turns? If you hope in the world, this is how it treats you, this is how, when it falls, it will make you

---

[10]That is, by the death of her brother Borso de' Bonaccossi.

fall as well. Whoever hopes in God, however, will not be abandoned [Ps 33:23 (34:22), Hebr 13:5], because that man does not seek the things of this world, but eternal life, to which one arrives through many tribulations. One must not lay down foundations in this world. The dead teach us how little the acquisition of wealth, a life of riches, dressing elegantly, honours, glory and the pleasures of the present are worth, when we possess them for such a short time.

Last Wednesday, in the church of Santa Liberata, here in Florence, a young, vigorous, healthy youth suddenly fell dead, to everyone's surprise. Not two days ago a young woman, a singer who was the greatest delight of all of Florence because of her wonderful singing abilities and the sweetness of her voice, who alone surpassed all the great singers, died with great pain while giving birth, carrying with her the pain of her sin, not without great grief on the part of the noble citizens of Florence. If she had followed the path I once showed her, she would not have come to this. Now, what use are all these pleasures to them? Where are the melodies? Where is the delicate food? Do you not see that everything passes like the wind? And so one must answer God when He calls us and we must rest our hearts in Him. Let us seek Him, love Him, follow Him, and we will not lack anything we might need for the present life. Let us do what we can for our part and let us trust in Him and He will not abandon us, because He says: *I will never desert you, nor will I ever abandon you* [Heb 13:5]. If you say: —There is shame in being poor—, I answer you that no-one should be ashamed to be like Christ and the Virgin Mary were. Where is your faith? If we believe that the glory God promises for His lovers is immense, ineffable and eternal, and that the pains of Hell are horrible, and since we must go to one of these two places, what are we waiting for? Why are we not trying to flee Hell and reach Paradise? We cannot stay very long on this earth; but the next life is without end. What is the point, then, of labouring vainly on this earth? What is the point of enjoying the moment and then being tormented for eternity? It is better, therefore, to tolerate patiently our brief tribulations so as to have eternal joy and peace and glory everlasting. Remember the martyrs of the past. Where are their sufferings now, their torments, their great tribulations so much greater than yours? All over now, and they are in glory and there they will always rejoice, and the tyrants who struck at them suffer eternal punishment and cannot hope ever to be freed.

Oh most beloved Mother, if we were to think, with all our heart, and ponder deeply, and believe without a doubt, that we are pilgrims on this earth and that we are walking towards heaven or hell, we would not place much value in this world nor in its riches and pleasures, not in its tribulations. But today people are blinded and do not think about this, but about building on land they cannot own. Oh foolish and blind and miserable mortals, God has promised you so much if you keep His commandments, and so much pain if you do not keep them. You know from experience that you cannot dwell long in this world, and you think about everything else but this! Oh immense blindness, oh miserable condition of ours, for we think only about the present and faith is annihilated and so is charity, and every virtue extinguished. True faith laments only for sin and weeps only for offenses against God. A firm faith does not fear tribulations, it is not bewildered by death! This is that virtue that gave the martyrs of the past joy in their torments. But why do we, today, have no faith, why do we seek this world and not value the next life? When we are deprived of our wealth or of our relatives and friends, why do we lament much more than when sin deprives us of the grace of God? Everyone speaks well about the righteous life, everyone praises and extols virtue, but few follow it. What will you say now?

Well, I have spent a lot of time saying these things to you and I have opened my heart to you so as to be a helper to God, who is calling you to Him. From now on I will begin to stimulate you and invite you to the love of Jesus Christ. Give yourself completely to Him and rush to Him in your tribulations, and thank Him for every thing, and especially that He might deign to call you to Him. No longer value the things of this world, for they do not exist, but work only to cleanse your conscience and to prepare for death. If anything should intervene that you do not like, commend yourself to Him with good patience, so that your conscience is never harmed. If you keep it immaculate, believe me [when I say] that your tribulations will sadden you very little or not at all. Do not worry about your daughters. See that they be good, not only according to the goodness praised by the world, but also according to the goodness that God likes; that is, that they be devout, committed to prayer, fasts and holy sermons, like brides of Christ. Be assured that, without you, God will take care of them and will lead them to a better goal than they might even know to ask for, because, although they are not in a monastery, nonetheless they can serve God even in this world and be brides of Jesus.

I pray you, therefore, sisters and my spiritual daughters, Beatrice and Chiara, that you give yourselves completely to prayer and leave aside all vanities, not only in your works, but also in your affections. Give yourselves to solitude, to holy lessons, to prayer. Do not care for company, nor to see anyone or to be seen. Contemplate Jesus Christ and His passion and His life step by step. Do not stay among men, but let your heart be constantly with Jesus Christ and He will console you more than you can think. If you draw near to Him with a clean conscience, you will experience heavenly joy and disdain this world, and you will consider all other women vain, unhappy. Oh how many delights come from prayers offered by a pure conscience, and especially by the conscience of virgin brides of Christ, whom He loves tenderly! Therefore, be united in Christ in charity with your mother and serve her in poverty, and have no doubt that He watches over you, and you will not think that He is treating you worse than other women for, if you will learn to know your times, He will have made you better. Saint Paul says, or rather the Holy Spirit says through Saint Paul's words, that those who marry do not sin, but will have tribulations [1 Cor 7:32, 34], as you can see in the case of our mother; and whoever does not marry does better, and that a virgin who serves God in this way will be more blessed because she will be holy in mind and in body. So, seek a holy life and prayer, for, if you will taste the sweetness of Jesus, I know well that you will scorn every worldly pleasure.

I have not been able to have copies done of what I wanted you to have, because I have had to give the copyist a lot of other things that were more urgent, so yours have suffered a delay; but I will see to it that they are copied.

Now I return to you, Mother, and pray you that you forget this world by now. This is what I wanted to say in my other letter when I wrote to you saying that you should consider me dead, for I would like you to love Jesus so much that you cared no more for your children than is necessary. I would want your faith to be such that you could watch them die and be martyred without shedding a tear for them, as that most holy Hebrew woman did when seven of her saintly children were killed and tortured in front of her and she never cried, but instead comforted them in their death [2 Macc 7:1–41]. Saint Felicity, in the New Testament, did the same.[11] I did

---

[11]There is no such saint or event in the New Testament. Savonarola is referring, instead, to the legend of St Felicity (feast day 10 July) narrated, among others, by Jacopus da Voragine in his *Golden Legend* (New York: Arno

not say that because I did not want to offer you comfort, for this would be contrary to charity, but in order to lessen your suffering, so that, if it should happen that I die, you will not suffer much pain.

Nor does it bother me that you write to me often while I cannot write to you as often, especially long letters such as this one — which, because of my many duties, I had to leave and pick up five times before I could finish it. Write often, then, in the name of God, and I will try to answer you, briefly or at length.

I will say no more about our uncle, except that I will say some Masses for his soul.

Comfort my brothers to live righteously and to persevere, and [comfort] my aunt Margarita[12] on my part and tell her that I am sorry about her situation, but if she puts herself in God's hands and gathers up her life in His love, she will find comfort, otherwise she will find nothing but trouble in this world.

The peace and charity of God be always with you. Amen.

From Florence, 5 December 1485.

Your son Friar Girolamo Savonarola *wrote this.*

To the venerable lady Elena Savonarola, my honourable mother.

Letter 4
To Giovanna Carafa Pico
15 December 1495

Savonarola congratulates Giovanna Carafa Pico, wife of Count Gianfrancesco Pico, for her wish to die rather than sin.

Magnificent lady and beloved in Christ Jesus,[13]

I drew great pleasure from your letter, reading that you would wish to die rather than offend God. This shows that you are in His grace and you have already received His mercy and the remission of your sins. If you will persevere in this good wish of yours, distancing yourself from the love of worldly vanities and giving yourself often to holy prayers, considering with a lively faith that soon this life will

---

Press, 1969), p. 347.

[12]Borso's widow.

[13]In Renaissance Italian, the term *Magnifico* has connotations of generosity, as well as splendour, majesty, and grandeur.

pass and the glory of the blessed is eternal, constantly searching and sighing for it, I hope you will find plenty of consolation, especially when you consider the love our Saviour Jesus Christ bore and bears for us. For I have no doubt that in this way you will fall in love with Him and you will go joyfully into eternal life. Amen. I will pray God for you that it may be so. *The grace and peace of our Lord Jesus Christ be with your spirit. Amen. From Florence, the 15th day of December 1495.*

Friar Girolamo of Ferrara

Letter 5
To his sister, Beatrice Savonarola
3 November 1496

Savonarola sends his sister a lauda in honour of St. Mary Magdalene as a souvenir of himself and consoles her saying it is better for her not to have married.

Most beloved sister,

May the grace of Jesus be with you.

Because of my many duties I cannot satisfy your wish by writing, so I send you with the courier of this letter a small office that I have composed in praise of Saint Mary Magdalene, for the preservation of mental and corporal chastity, and to beseech for the remission of sins, so that you have it to remind you of me. This will be in lieu of the letters I should write you. This does not mean that I will stop writing to you when necessary. I encourage you to recite it and to give yourself completely to the Lord God. Believe me, it was better for you to remain as you are, than to have taken a husband because in this state you will be better able, if you so wish, to work for your salvation. Keep yourself from dangerous conversations and give yourself completely to righteous living and recommend me to Chiara.[14]

May the grace of Jesus be always with you.

In Florence, 3 November 1496.

Friar Girolamo Savonarola, your brother.
To our most beloved sister in Christ Jesus, Beatrice Savonarola. In Ferrara.

---

[14]Savonarola's other sister.

Letter 6
To Giovanna Carafa Pico and Eleonora Pico della Mirandola
3 April 1497

Savonarola tells them not to worry about venial sins because Jesus wants a tranquil heart and it is counterproductive to worry about every small sin.

Most beloved in Christ Jesus,

Since your lord and mine, Count Gianfrancesco,[15] has asked me to write a few words in my own hand to Your Benevolences, I write in the name of our Saviour [to say] that you should make an effort to taste and know how good and sweet our Lord Jesus Christ is, who, although He does not want us to follow the wide road of sin, also does not request from us a conscience so narrow that we see every straw as a beam. Our Saviour likes a serene conscience, tranquil and at peace, one that places so much hope in His goodness and in His blood that it believes that our tiny sins are easily absolved by the depth of His goodness. And even though He wants us to refrain as much as we can from sinning even venially, nonetheless He also likes it that when one has fallen because of human frailty one should not be so upset as to lose peace of mind over it, but should instead look immediately to His great sweetness and say: —My kind Lord will offer satisfaction on my behalf—, always resolving oneself to serve Him eagerly, because anyone who worries more than is necessary about everything shows that he has little faith in divine mercy, which asks nothing of us but what we can do. We cannot live without committing venial sins; however, to turn these venial sins into

---

[15]Gianfrancesco Pico della Mirandola (1469–1533), prince of Mirandola and Concordia. He was the husband of Giovanna Carafa Pico and the nephew of the Neoplatonic philosopher Giovanni Pico della Mirandola. A staunch supporter of Savonarola, Gianfrancesco was a prolific defender of the friar. As Donald Weinstein puts it, 'Gianfrancesco Pico alone wrote [a polemical tract] for practically every Piagnone crisis, including Savonarola's excommunication, his imprisonment, and the first public reports of his confession.' (*Savonarola and Florence*, p. 232). In 1530 Gianfrancesco wrote a biography of Savonarola, *Vita R.P. Hieronymi Savonarolae*, eventually edited for publication by Jacques Quétif (Paris: Ludovicus Billaine, 1674), 2 vols. On Gianfrancesco, see the standard monograph by Charles B. Schmitt, *Gianfrancesco Pico della Mirandola (1469–1533) and his Critique of Aristotle* (The Hague: Martinus Nijhoff, 1967).

mortal sins is a way of upsetting oneself and of turning a Christian life, which by the grace of God is a life of special freedom, into a life of servitude, and to turn the law of love into a law of fear. Give your heart to our Lord Jesus Christ and leave behind your love for the world and serve Him with real love, because He is such a lover that He never gets angry and, in fact, seeks those who do not love Him and constantly re-establishes His love for His bride.[16] So, walk cheerfully in His path and think often of the eternal happiness He has prepared for His beloved.

May the grace of Jesus be with you. Amen.

From Florence, 3 April 1497.

Letter 7
To Polissena Petrati and Lucrezia de' Rana (?)
24 May 1497

Savonarola congratulates the two women for wanting to enter a convent.

Most beloved in Christ Jesus,

Since you have elected to become brides of our Lord Jesus Christ, I praise your decision most highly, for it surpasses all other. In order to please this groom, so glorious and so great, one must fall in love and be completely enraptured with Him and forget everything else, for perfect love does not admit anything extraneous. And this is right, because, in wanting to receive such a lord, He must not find the house sullied by vile things, but tidy and devoid of any earthly affection. Finding it so, He will dwell most sweetly with you. I will gladly have prayers said for you, and I will also pray our Lord Jesus Christ that He accept you and confirm you in His grace. And you also pray God for me, and the peace and grace and consolation of the Father and the Son and the Holy Spirit be always with you. Because of my endless work, I cannot write to you at greater length. *Be well in the Lord.*

From the convent of San Marco in Florence, 24 May 1497.

---

[16]In this case, the 'bride' is the people, or the 'church' of God.

Letter 8
To Angela Sforza d'Este
24 May 1497

Savonarola encourages Angela Sforza d'Este to continue praying and to listen to God's voice.[17]

Most beloved in Christ Jesus,

The wish you express in your letters to please God and to be helped by our prayers (though they are unworthy), can come from nothing else but divine inspiration and a good mind. While you have this wish, you can rest assured that God is near you and knocking at your door [Rev 3:20]. I am certain, therefore, that if you open to Him He will come to dwell deep inside your heart and He will enlighten you every day the more you seek, with good works and with a purged mind, to draw near to Him. If you consider how everything else is smoke in the wind and how the glory of this world will soon turn to dust and ashes, you will disdain more easily these vain and transitory things and you will draw near that infinite and highest good that fills every devout mind with incredible joy and sweetness, and lets it be happy and at peace even in times of tribulation.

This is the way to righteous living: love God above all else and keep yourself from whatever might displease Him, as the beloved bride does with her spouse, because love teaches us to do everything. Therefore, I will constantly pray our Lord Jesus Christ to inflame you with His love, since He deigned to come into the world in human flesh so that His creatures may contemplate Him visibly and may more easily come to know His infinite goodness, through which He has redeemed us with His precious blood.

Because of the many benefits He has given us and because of the immortal life and infinite glory He promises us in return for the short breadth of time we spend in His service, it is right, therefore, that we follow Him willingly, and that we keep our mind's eye always fixed on eternal things, as a sailor or the owner of a ship does when he keeps it fixed on the port. In this way, remembering

---

[17]Angela Sforza (1479–97) was the daughter of Carlo Sforza, count of Magenta, and Bianca Simonetta. In 1491 she married Ercole d'Este, Lord of San Martino in Rio (d. 1514).

the shortness and uncertainty of this life, and the eternal suffering of the damned, and the perpetual glory of the blessed, you will abhor evil and delight in good works. I am so busy I cannot be more prolix, but I will remember Your Ladyship in my prayers, which will be all the more acceptable to God if you will help them along with your own prayers for me and with your good and praiseworthy works. I recommend myself to your husband and to Your Ladyship.

1497. *From the convent of San Marco in Florence, 24 May.*

Letter 9
To Caterina Sforza, Duchess of Imola and Forlì
18 June 1497

In response to Duchess Caterina Sforza's request for advice, Savonarola tells her to confess her sins, do charitable work, administer justice righteously, and pray to God.[18]

Most illustrious and distinguished Lady, honourable Lady,

In Your Ladyship's desire, as you indicate in your letters, to seek refuge in God and to be helped by Him, especially in the dangerous

---

[18]An indomitable woman, Caterina Sforza (c.1463–1509) was born the illegitimate daughter of Galeazzo Maria Sforza, future duke of Milan. Legitimized by him, she was married and widowed three times: first to Girolamo Riario, nephew of Pope Sixtus IV (1477); then to Iacopo Feo (1490), captain of one of her castles; and then, after the latter was murdered in front of her eyes, to the Florentine ambassador Giovanni di Pierfrancesco de' Medici (1496 or '97). From this last union was born Giovanni delle Bande Nere whose son, Cosimo I de' Medici, would become duke and then grand duke of Florence and founder of the Medici dynasty that ruled Florence and Siena until 1737. Caterina Sforza was famous in her own time and still is for her stalwart defence of her duchy (with force of arms as well as with fierce determination); for her uncompromising stand against the assassins of her first two husbands (1488 and 1495 respectively); for her stand against the invading Cesare Borgia (Dec. 1499–Jan. 1500); not to mention for her seizure of Castel Sant'Angelo, in Rome, during the conclave that elected Pope Innocent VIII Cibo (1484) in a single-handed effort to sway the results of the conclave in her favour. See the standard monograph by Ernst Breisach, *Caterina Sforza. A Renaissance Virago* (Chicago and London: Chicago University Press, 1967).

times that are upon us when not an iota of what was prophesied will fail to come to pass, I believe you are well advised and moved by God, from whom every good inspiration proceeds. So, to put this into effect, I encourage Your Ladyship to be good and to be truly contrite of your sins, redeeming them with works of charity, that is, by giving alms to the poor, because alms giving extinguishes sins just as water extinguishes fire [Tob 12:9], and above all take every care and be prompt in administering justice to your subjects and have recourse with all your heart to the most merciful God, praying Him constantly to enlighten you to carry out His will, because in so doing and in refraining from sin without a doubt Your Ladyship will be answered and you will know better, day by day, the greatness of divine goodness. Then, if you consider the misery and brevity of this life, and the fact that soon we will have to present ourselves in front of a Judge who will examine all our past deeds, I am certain you will seek His favour while you can obtain it easily, because everything else is vanity. And thus I comfort Your Ladyship as much as I can. I thank Your Ladyship for your good disposition towards me. When it seems appropriate, perhaps I will send you some of my disciples and brothers for your consolation. At present it would not be opportune, but I will constantly pray God for Your Ladyship, to whom I offer and recommend myself.

From the convent of San Marco, 18 June 1497.

An unworthy servant of Jesus Christ, Friar Girolamo Savonarola, Order of Preachers, etc.

*To the most illustrious and most excellent honourable
lady, Lady Caterina Sforza, Lady of Imola and Forlì.*

Letter 10
To Giovanna Carafa Pico
13 August 1497

Tribulations merely prepare our way to salvation. Many suffer tribulations at San Marco and in Florence, but see them as a way to God and die joyfully.

Magnificent and most beloved Lady in Christ Jesus,

I took comfort from your last letter thinking of your good mind and ready willingness to live righteously and to persevere in this, and *even* of your healthy and firm faith, which is not founded on human reason nor on things that can be seen, but, instead, is a gift from God, because it does not fail in times of tribulation or persecution, which we constantly have. There is no need, therefore, for Your Ladyship to fear you will not be able to withstand tribulations should God please to give them to you, because the one who has given you faith and good intentions will also give you fortitude and joy in tribulation. At present, we have remarkable examples of this constantly in front of our eyes in this city, both among the laity and the clergy. One cannot describe with what joy believers live amid these tribulations, so much so that they often say to me: —Father, we no longer know what tribulation is—. And those who die with so much devotion and joy depart from this life in such a way that no-one who sees their passing has any doubts they are going to eternal life. Up to this point they have not been few in number, but there has been a great number of men and women, which I do not cite so as not to be wrong. Unbelievers are unhappy now and cannot help but show their unhappiness on their faces. And so we already see that God's elect will be wonderfully consoled in these tribulations with hope for the next life, which God has promised us, where everyone who enters it will live in joy *for ever and ever.* Amen. May the grace of Jesus be with you. I recommend myself to your prayers, illustrious Lady, and to those of your sister-in-law.

Florence, 13 August 1497.

I pray and will pray constantly for you and *also* for your entire house, as I promised our lord Count Gianfrancesco.

Letter 11
To the nuns of Annalena[19]
17 October 1497

Responding to their request that he come preach at their convent or
send them an exhortation for them to read, Savonarola tells the nuns of
the Annalena convent in Florence that he has written enough exhortations in the vernacular and there is no point in writing more because
this only causes tedium. He then adds that one should read little and
act on it, rather than read a lot and not act on it.

Friar Girolamo of Ferrara, an unworthy servant of Jesus Christ, to
the nuns of the Third Order of Saint Dominic, popularly called of
Annalena, who live in the monastery of Saint Vincent in Florence,
and to all other nuns and devout persons wishing exhortatory
letters from him, grace and peace and joy in the Holy Spirit.

Most beloved in Christ Jesus,

Since your father confessor has expressed to me your desire to
hear one of our exhortations, or at least to have an exhortatory
letter from me, I answered him that I cannot fulfil the first request
at present and I do not think the second is necessary. Nonetheless,
since he insisted with this second one and partly to satisfy your
desire, leaving aside our other worries, I will write something that
will *also* satisfy other persons who ask the same thing from me as
you have done.

   You must know, then, that the Sacred Gospel, which contains all
the perfection of spiritual life, was not written on tablets of stone
or other matter, nor on paper or on sheets, but on human hearts
by the finger and the power of the Holy Spirit, who found the heart
of the apostles purged of all sin and earthly affection; and through
their ministry it was written on the hearts of other believers whom
they converted to the faith. So, the apostle Paul said to the
Corinthians: 'You will be the epistle of Christ enunciated and written
by us not with ink, but with the Spirit of the living God, not on
tablets of stone, but on the tablets of your human heart' [2 Cor 3:3],
that is sweet, soft and flexible. Christ's books, therefore, were the

---

[19]The Florentine convent of San Vincenzio d'Annalena was founded in 1454
to house Dominican tertiaries. It was suppressed in 1786 and converted to
secular use.

apostles and the other saints, written by the hand of the Holy Spirit. However, because our Saviour knew that, because of sin, men would lose the Spirit and their evil would grow, and so that the holy doctrine written in the hearts of the apostles would not fail, but would spread *even* among those who were not present and would be kept for those who would come after them, and so that evil men might not debase it, He wanted the Gospel to be written down on paper as well. And although Sacred Scripture contains most abundantly everything that pertains to spiritual life, nonetheless, because of its elevated and obscure nature, God then sent the holy doctors who have explained it and have delved more deeply into the specifics, so that the uneducated might gather some benefit from it. At present, however, since Christians have dedicated themselves to the study of the pagans, many who today are called wise deceive simple and unlettered persons under the guise of a doctrine that is vain and inflated and hides the truth of righteous Christian living. So, to remedy this error, not only I, but *also* many devout men, both in orders and lay, have composed in the vernacular language various treatises for unlettered persons on the perfection of righteous Christian living, writing nothing else but what is written in Sacred Scripture and in the doctrine of the holy Church and of the holy doctors. Since we have written 'On the simplicity of the Christian life,' 'On charity,' 'On humility,' 'On prayer,' 'On the Ten Commandments,' and 'Rules for the perfection of people in orders,' and many other things pertaining to the perfection of spiritual life, it seems to me not necessary but superfluous to compose other exhortations in the vernacular since the aforementioned works have been printed and distributed everywhere, and they are enough for someone who wants to live righteously. If some particular situation were to develop — such as the need to put out some error that had newly arisen or to bring concord where discord had entered, or in other particular cases such as these — then one would have to write or compose something as required by the time and needs of such a case. But to write down and repeat those same things is nothing more than to create tedium and not bear fruit.

Writing is one thing, preaching another. Since what is preached does not remain on paper, and because people generally either have short memories or are negligent in their works, then in preaching the same thing must be brought back into people's memory, be it to remind those who have forgotten it, or to teach it to those who were not present the previous times, or to rekindle the negligent, for the spoken voice moves the audience greatly, *even* when one says things they know and have heard other times, for there is a big difference between hearing something and reading it, and there is also a big difference between hearing something said in one way or another.

Therefore, you who seek new written exhortations but have no specific need for one, beware lest you be among those who always read and never learn and do even less. It is useless to read sacred things if one does not then purify one's heart so that the Holy Spirit might write on it what one can read on the outside, for one knows only as much as what is written in one's heart. And so, if anyone wants to reap fruits from spiritual lessons and understand Sacred Scripture, first of all he must purge his heart well, not only of every mortal sin, but *also* of every affection of self love, and not read only in order to teach, but in order to learn for oneself about righteous living. And every time he goes to read, he must first pray God to enlighten him in that lesson about the way of truth, and then read diligently, not rushing, but considering the sentences and memorizing them. And he must always return to his own conscience as women do when they want to adorn themselves—they go to the mirror not to see what is around the mirror, nor to see everything that appears in the mirror, but to look at their face and their head to see if there is anything that is not suitable. In the same way the soul should approach the lesson of Sacred Scripture as if she were looking at the face of conscience and at the head of reason and to see whether in reason or in conscience there is anything amiss or any spot that needs to be cleaned up in order to make herself pretty in the presence of the eternal groom. And then, when one has read and carefully considered how the lesson applies to him, he must return to his prayers and pray God to forgive him those things in which he sees he has failed, and to give him the grace to do what he has learned from this lesson, so that it might be of benefit to him and *also* to his neighbour. Those who study and read in this manner do not need so many books to edify themselves. I say to edify themselves, because the doctors and those who have been placed in a position to teach others, after they have edified themselves on the spiritual life, need to discuss it by way of many other books so as to defend the truth from its adversaries, and to instruct others more clearly and more efficiently.

Now, however, let us speak of the lesson one follows in order to edify and increase and maintain spiritual life in oneself. I warn you in this lesson that someone who reads one page in the way we have just described reaps greater benefits than someone who skims over all of Scripture without pleasure and without prayer. It was more profitable for Saint Anthony to hear the reading of those few words our Saviour said to a certain youth: —if you want to be perfect, go and sell everything you own and give it to the poor and come and follow me—, [Mt 19:21] than for many great theologians to read and turn around all of theology. Similarly, it served Saint Francis better to hear that passage from the Gospel where our Saviour says to the disciples that on the road they should not carry either a stick, or a bag, or shoes [Mt 10:10, Lk 10:4], than the lesson and study of all the books in the world might serve someone who reads them but does not act on them. One must then read sacred matters carefully and meditate on them, and follow through with action what one has read. Your Benevolent selves should realize that nothing makes someone grow more lukewarm than to read and to treat the things of God without reverence and without works. Experience shows this, because people in orders and secular priests who deal all day with sacred matters and live badly are all tepid and incorrigible. If someone who lives on delicate food and always nourishes himself with it should became ill, nothing can be found to restore his health; in the same way, these people, who have been nourished with delicate spiritual food and have mixed it with the foulness of pride and other sins, both spiritual and corporal, can no longer be revived by preaching or by exhortation, because they have grown accustomed to reading such words and hearing them alongside their evil works. Thus they always hear them in one way, because their custom follows their nature and they cannot separate themselves from it. So, most beloved, guard yourselves very much from this vice so that you do not become tepid and beyond conversion. Read little, therefore, and observe it, rather than much and not observe it.

We read that when Saint Paul the Simple[20] asked a monk to teach him a psalm, the monk began to teach him that psalm that starts: *Dixi, custodiam vias meas ut non delinquam in lingua mea* [Ps 38:2 (39:1)]; and when he had learned this first verse he asked him what it meant, and the monk answered: —It means this: I have sworn

---

[20]St Paul the Simple was an Egyptian monk, disciple of St Anthony the Abbot (4th cent.). On discovering his wife in a compromising situation, Paul preferred not to create an uproar but to withdraw into the monastic life. He entered into the monastery of St Anthony and soon distinguished himself for his simplicity of life and his ability to cast out devils.

and decided to guard my ways so that I do not offend with my tongue—. At which Saint Paul said: —I want to learn more of it, but first I want to do what this first verse says and then I will return to learn the rest—. And for many years he did not come back, and one day when the aforementioned monk found him again he said to him: —What does it mean that you did not return to learn the rest of the psalm?— Saint Paul answered: —Because I have not yet carried out what the first verse says—. So it seems that to read profitably one must follow the lesson with action, or at least commit oneself firmly always to follow it. Therefore, most beloved, since you have so many works in the vernacular that are enough not just for your salvation, but for that of the entire world, one must not multiply books or letters needlessly. Read, instead, what you have in the manner I have told you, and that will be enough. And so, I encourage you to read what is written and to follow it through with your actions, especially since you live together in charity and humility and in constant prayer and good works. And constantly pray God for me and for His works, so that He might deign to open the hearts of men to His truth and grace; which may always be with you and lead you to the kingdom of the blessed. Amen.

Dated in Florence at San Marco, 17 October 1497. Amen.

Letter 12
To Giovanna Carafa Pico
6 November 1497

Savonarola advises Giovanna Carafa Pico to set aside her scruples of conscience and live more cheerfully; and if she has questions or doubts, she should seek her husband's counsel.

Magnificent and most beloved in Christ Jesus,

Knowing that your good mind is turned to God, I urged myself to write you these few words to comfort you and support you in your good intentions, exhorting you to know the great benefit that is worth more than all the treasures of the world and is given to few, and especially to few who are rich. Grow, therefore, in spirit and in truth, always placing the love of our Lord Jesus Christ before all else in this world, *even* before yourself, always resolved to die rather than to fall back because of mortal sin. Do not, however, be overly scrupulous with your conscience, because our Lord is liberal and kind and does not look at every speckle. Charity extinguishes all sins; you must live cheerfully in it and walk the middle path and not fear to the point of losing hope, nor have so much hope that you lose your fear. And if you do not know how to walk the middle path like this, lean rather towards too much hope than too much fear, for our God is sweet and inclines more willingly towards mercy than justice. You will be more pleasing to Him if you live cheerfully, not thinking about scruples, but always keeping yourself in the love of His goodness. And if your conscience still troubles you, take the counsel of good and discreet men, and follow their advice. You have your husband, the Count Gianfrancesco, to whom you can go for counsel; you may and you must have faith in his advice, because I know that he will counsel you well. By humbling yourself to believe him, you will do something pleasing to God, and from this humility you will obtain grace and tranquillity of mind and you will serve God with joy.

Every day I will pray especially for you and you, likewise, pray for me. There is nothing else.

The grace of Jesus be always with your spirit. Amen.

Florence, 6 November 1497.

Your Ladyship should read the letter I wrote to Lady Lionora[21] and she should read yours, because what I write to the one on this matter of easing one's conscience, which I know is too strict in you, I also write to the other. I pray you to recommend me to Her Ladyship.

Friar Girolamo, in his own hand.

---

[21]Eleonora Pico della Mirandola.

SIC TRANSIT GLORIA MVNDI.

Figure 1: 'Sic transit gloria mundi'. The execution of Savonarola and his two companions. Woodcut from *Processo di Savonarola*, n.p., n.d. [Venice, 1498], frontispiece.

Figure 2: 'View of Florence in the 1490s.' Woodcut from Bernardino, *Le bellezze e i casati di Firenze*, Firenze, n.d.

Poems

Canzone I
On the Ruin of the World

Though it is true, and I do so believe
Your Providence to be, Lord of the World,
Forever boundless (nor could I believe
Its opposite, because *experience* proves it)
At times it does seem colder still than snow   5
When I behold the world turned on its head,
And lifeless on the ground
Lies every virtue, every custom fair.
I find no brilliant light,
Or even someone shamed by all his sins,   10
Some men deny you, others say you sleep.

But, Lord Most High, I think you linger still
Because of your great pity for its faults,
Or else you wait because you know that day
Is drawing near when hell will quake with fear.   15
Your Mercy will not always turn towards us:[1]
The enemies of God are here revealed;
Now Cato is a beggar;[2]

---

[1] I have translated *virtù* as 'Mercy'; already in Dante *virtù* was a synonym for God (see *Purg.* 3, v. 32; *Par.* 13, v. 80; *Par.* 26, v. 84). In the context of these verses, it seems that *virtù* may well be intended to indicate God's mercy.

[2] Marcus Porcius Cato (95–46 BC). "In an era when public morality was rapidly disintegrating, Cato stood out for his uncompromising rigor and his conspicuous Stoic virtue" *Encyclopedia Americana* (1966), 6:58. In referring to Cato, Savonarola is probably thinking of the *Disticha Catonis* (*Distichs of Cato*), a late classical/early medieval compilation of moral proverbs attributed to the Roman moralist and used as a textbook in medieval and Renaissance schools; on this work and its use in the Renaissance, see Paul F. Grendler,

The sceptre has come into pirate hands;[3]
Saint Peter is laid low;   20
Here lustfulness and every prey abounds,
And I know not why heaven is not baffled.

     Do you not see that satyr gone quite mad,[4]
How full of pride he is, a font of vices
That makes my heart consume itself with scorn?   25
Oh! Look at that debauched effeminate,
That panderer in purple dress, a clown
The rabble follow and the blind world loves!
Are you not moved to scorn
When you see how that lustful swine delights,   30
And wrests your highest praises
With sycophants and parasites about him,
While your men are expelled from land to land?

     Now those who live from theft are all content,
And those who feed the most on others' blood,   35
Who rob from widows and from swaddling babes,
And those who rush to ruin the paupers, too!
A gentle and most special soul is one
Who now with fraud or force can gain the most,
Who mocks our Lord and heaven, too,   40
And always seeks to bring someone to ruin;
This man the world esteems,
Whose books and papers are replete with swindles,
And those who best are skilled in evil deeds.

Schooling in Renaissance Italy. Literacy and Learning 1300–1600 (Baltimore and London: Johns Hopkins University Press, 1989), pp. 197–99 and *passim.*

[3]Pope Sixtus IV Della Rovere who, having been born in a small town outside Savona and coming from old Genoese nobility, was quickly labelled a pirate, a taint often used to smudge the sea-faring Genoese and other Ligurians. Not by chance, the verse that follows mentions St Peter, both because he was the first pope and because Jesus called him to be 'fisherman of souls' (Mt 4:18–19, Mk 1:16–17), a rather different sort of man of the sea than the pirate pope Sixtus IV.

[4]According to Martelli (p. 204), this stanza refers to Cardinal Pietro Riario, the young and dissolute nephew (some say son) of Pope Sixtus IV Della Rovere.

The earth is so oppressed by every vice   45
That never by itself it will unload,
And Rome, its head,[5] is crawling on the ground,
And never will return to its great office.
Fabritius, Brutus, how you both must grieve
If you have heard of this great further ruin!   50
Catilina is not enough,
Nor Silla, Marius, Caesar, Nero too,
But here all men and women,
Each one does what he can to do her harm.
Those times once chaste and pious are long past.   55

    — Poor virtue, you never spread your wings —
The rabble and the wicked hordes cry out;
And usury now is called philosophy.
All men now turn their backs on doing good;
No-one is on the straight path any more.   60
So now the little worth I have grows cold,
But for a little hope
That will not let it go away completely,
For I know in the next life
It will be clear to all which soul was gentle   65
And who did raise his wings to a lovelier style.

    Canzone, do be careful
Not to lean against a purple colour,[6]
Flee palaces and loggias
And tell your thoughts to just a little few,   70
For you will be a foe to all the world.

---

[5]A clear reference to the classical epithet for Rome, *caput mundi*, head of the world.

[6]Purple is the colour of the bishops. Savonarola is saying that the canzone cannot trust the high prelates of the Church.

Canzone II
On the Ruin of the Church[1]

— Virgin chaste,[2] though an unworthy son,
I am still made in body like your Spouse:
So I am grieved a lot to see the loving
Ancient times[3] and their sweet dangers[4] gone
From us, and no advice seems to come forth   5
On how to bring them back or maybe dare to;
The ancient burning voice[5]
No longer knows the Greek or Roman people;
The light of earlier years
Has now returned to heaven with its Queen[6]   10
And, alas for me, no longer bends towards us.

Where are, alas, the jewels[7] and diamonds[8] fine?
Where are the burning lamps[9] and sapphires fair?
Oh what great pity, oh what tears, what sighs!
Where are the stoles[10] so white and songs[11] so sweet?   15
Where are the horns[12] now and the holy eyes,

---

[1] The so-called 'Borromeo' manuscript of Savonarola's works carries autograph glosses by Savonarola explaining many of the images in this canzone. I will include them in this translation and refer to them simply as: Savonarola/Borromeo.

[2] Savonarola/Borromeo: 'He speaks to the Virgin Church because the Faith was never corrupted in her.'

[3] Savonarola/Borromeo: 'The time of the fervour of past saints.'

[4] Savonarola/Borromeo: 'When the saints were persecuted and cheerfully went to their martyrdom.'

[5] Savonarola/Borromeo: 'Of past preachers.'

[6] Savonarola/Borromeo: 'With the Church triumphant.'

[7] Savonarola/Borromeo: 'The saints, full of virtue.'

[8] Savonarola/Borromeo: 'Just men, most strong in all tribulations.'

[9] Savonarola/Borromeo: 'The charitable doctors.'

[10] Savonarola/Borromeo: 'The holy virgins.'

[11] Savonarola/Borromeo: 'Of the holy clerics.'

[12] Savonarola/Borromeo: 'The holy bishops mitred with the New and Old Testament with which they fanned the entire world, winning over their enemies.'

The golden continents[13] and spotless steeds,[14]
Three, four, five lofty ones,[15]
And the great wings,[16] the eagle[17] and the lion?[18]
One finds the coal[19]   20
Is barely warm among the burning ink!
I plead with you to show me all your tears! —

    Thus spoke I to our ancient, pious Mother[20]
Out of my great desire always to weep;
And She,[21] whose eyes seem never to be stern,   25
With face bent down[22] and with a modest soul
Took me by hand and led me to her poor
Cave[23], all the while weeping as we went;
And here she said: — When I
Did see that haughty woman[24] enter Rome,   30
Who goes among the flowers[25] and the grass
With great assurance,[26] I withdrew so much
That now I lead my life in constant weeping. —

---

[13]Savonarola/Borromeo: 'The continent and chaste.' Savonarola is playing with the double meaning of 'continent' to mean both 'area' and 'restrained.'

[14]Savonarola/Borromeo: 'Preachers intrepid in war.'

[15]Savonarola/Borromeo: 'The twelve Apostles, who preached the faith of the Trinity throughout the four corners of the world to carnal men who delighted in the five senses of the body.'

[16]Savonarola/Borromeo: 'Contemplation of the New and Old Testament, that is of the spiritual and temporal power.'

[17]Savonarola/Borromeo: 'The contemplative clergy.'

[18]Savonarola/Borromeo: 'The most Christian empire.'

[19]Savonarola/Borromeo: 'The religious, who are in the fire of holy things, and have failed in charity, and declined in holy and fiery Scripture, and are made lukewarm.'

[20]Savonarola/Borromeo: 'The Church.'

[21]Savonarola/Borromeo: 'The true Church, that is the congregation of true Christians who always weep for the sins of others and lament such a great downfall.'

[22]Savonarola/Borromeo: 'Out of shame for so many sins.'

[23]Savonarola/Borromeo: 'He says this because there are few good people and they are poor, and they hide and weep because they can neither speak nor appear in public.'

[24]Savonarola/Borromeo: 'The ambition for ecclesiastical honours.'

[25]Savonarola/Borromeo: 'Carnal pleasures.'

[26]Savonarola/Borromeo: 'Because she does not believe that God will wreak vengeance for this.'

Then: — Look, — said she — my son, what cruelty! —
The stones would weep at what she here unveiled.[27]   35
I saw no hyacinths[28] here, nor marigolds,[29]
Not even a spotless glass.[30] Oh! What sorrow!
Oh Silla! Marius! Where are your swords?
Why does evil Nero not rise up?
The earth, the air, the sky   40
Call forth for vengeance of this honest blood:
The milk,[31] I see, is spent
And broken is the breast a thousand times,[32]
No longer meek and holy as it was.[33]

She walks in poverty,[34] her limbs uncovered,[35]   45
Her hair[36] dishevelled and her garlands[37] broken;
She finds no bees,[38] but on the ancient acorns[39]
With hunger great, alas, she throws herself.
The scorpion[40] bites her and the snake[41] perverts her

---

[27]Savonarola/Borromeo: 'An infinite number   of grievous sins that are committed in secret.'

[28]Savonarola/Borromeo: 'Men filled with heavenly contemplation and with angelic conversations.'

[29]Savonarola/Borromeo: 'Men of living faith.'

[30]Savonarola/Borromeo: 'A pure heart.'

[31]Savonarola/Borromeo: 'The preaching of the New and Old Testament that nourishes those who are not perfect.'

[32]Savonarola/Borromeo: 'Because they are full of philosophy and logic and of various opinions.'

[33]Savonarola/Borromeo: 'Because the new doctors [of the Church] are divided in a thousand different opinions; because today the preachers and the doctors of the Church are full of pride.'

[34]Savonarola/Borromeo: 'Of virtue.'

[35]Savonarola/Borromeo: 'Because they are no longer ashamed of their sins, not even the clergy.'

[36]Savonarola/Borromeo: 'The vain thoughts for the things of the world.'

[37]Savonarola/Borromeo: 'The virtues that keep the heart composed.'

[38]Savonarola/Borromeo: 'The sweet things of Jesus in Scripture.'

[39]Savonarola/Borromeo: 'To the poets, rhetoricians and philosophers.'

[40]Savonarola/Borromeo: 'The hidden heretics.'

[41]Savonarola/Borromeo: 'The demon.' The reference is to the devil who, in the form of a snake, tempted Eve and led her and Adam to sin (Gen. 3).

And all the locusts[42] seize the tender roots;[43]   50
And so she crawls on earth
The crowned one[44] and her holy hands,[45]
Cursed by the dogs,[46]
Who swindle all the sabbaths and the calends.[47]
Some can not[48] and some perceive not.[49]   55

     Weep now, fourfold six white heads,[50]
You four beasts[51] and holy trumpets seven;[52]
Weep now, my zealous stable master,[53]
Weep now, you blood-red pilgrim waters;[54]
Oh living stones,[55] most lofty and divine,   60
Let every planet, every star now weep.[56]
If the news has reached
Up there, where each of you resides in joy,
I think (if I can say)[57]

---

[42]Savonarola/Borromeo: 'False brothers, who claim to fly high and to be Christians, and yet they dwell on the earth.'

[43]Savonarola/Borromeo: 'They do not let the grass grow, that is, the good people; on the contrary, they seek to mislead them, or to gnaw away at the root of grace: and they do this even to their own children.'

[44]Savonarola/Borromeo: 'The Church.'

[45]Savonarola/Borromeo: 'The holy works.'

[46]Savonarola/Borromeo: 'By the Infidels, who say: if she were the true Christian Faith, Christians would not live in this manner.'

[47]Savonarola/Borromeo: 'Because today the feasts belong more to the devil than to God.'

[48]Savonarola/Borromeo: 'Help her.'

[49]Savonarola/Borromeo: 'How or when God should help her.'

[50]Savonarola/Borromeo: 'The twenty-four elders mentioned in the Apocalypse, who represent the twelve patriarchs and the twelve apostles.'

[51]Savonarola/Borromeo: 'The four evangelists.'

[52]Savonarola/Borromeo: 'All holy preachers.'

[53]Savonarola/Borromeo: 'Paul the Apostle with all fervent [people] like him.'

[54]Savonarola/Borromeo: 'The martyrs.'

[55]Savonarola/Borromeo: 'All the angels of the heavens and all the Saints who are its edifice in the heavenly city.'

[56]Savonarola/Borromeo: 'Let them show some sign of grief.'

[57]Savonarola/Borromeo: 'He says this because there is not and there cannot be grief in Heaven; but some grievous consequences at times lead men to grieve.' In other words, Savonarola is underlining the fact that his imagined grief in heaven is merely a human verbal construct.

That you do grieve a lot from so much harm: 65
The temple is laid low,[58] the chaste house too.

    — My Lady, — said I, then — if you don't mind,
My soul would gladly weep along with you.
What power is this that takes your kingdom from you?
What haughty person so disturbs your peace?   70
She answered with a sigh: — One false,
And haughty prostitute,[59] Babylon. —
And I: — By God, Lady,
If one could only break those mighty wings?[60] —
And She: — A mortal tongue   75
Can not,[61] nor may, nor could it raise a weapon.
Weep and be silent, this seems the best to me.

    Canzone, I think nothing
Of the scorpion's bite.[62] Do not engage:[63]
That you be understood   80
Is perhaps better; be happy with the *point*.
Since by necessity it is, so be it.

---

[58]Savonarola/Borromeo: 'The holy minds are prostrate in vice and few good people can be found.'

[59]Savonarola/Borromeo: 'That is, pride, lust, and avarice.'

[60]Savonarola/Borromeo: '*That is*, break the spiritual and temporal power so that evil people should not have it in their hands.'

[61]Savonarola/Borromeo: 'Speak about this.'

[62]Savonarola/Borromeo: 'That is, I do not care if bad things are said about me or if I am stung.'

[63]Savonarola/Borromeo: 'That is, do not engage in disputes, as if you wanted to defend yourself from what blind people say, [that is] that these things are not true and that tribulations will not come; but be at peace.'

Canzone III

Song to Saint Catherine of Bologna

Fair soul, when you went up to heaven
You left your holy limbs behind on earth
As proof for us of that far better life;
Now that at last your war is finally over,
Where never once you faltered in the fight   5
Nor ever walked away from your fair Groom,
You stand before His presence
With spotless heart and with a mind most pure,
Rejoicing in your victory so great
In glory everlasting,   10
Where now secure in Christ you will reside
Far from this bitter, blind, and cruel life.

Your sacred body demonstrates to all
How God exalts you in his highest Heaven,
And by its virtue,[1] that we all can see,   15
It is, fair soul, a message to this world,
A heavenly flame for consciences grown cold,
And, oh, for those who grieve it is relief!
If one, devoutly weeping,
Should bend his head towards you, blessed virgin,   20
He will cast out a thousand mortal thoughts,
Because your merit in
The eyes of Christ, oh crowned bride, is known
By Heaven and by the world where you were born.

From a thousand places people rush   25
To look upon your body which, they hear,
Though it lie dead, it seems to be alive
And seems to recollect your spirit still;
They all can see it there, they all adore it,
And full of wonder they pay homage to it.   30
What heart is there so wild
That would not greatly weep with tears of joy
At these your holy works and humble face?
If, then, your body is

---

[1] The fact that it is incorruptible, as we read more clearly in the next stanza.

A paradise to men and is so dear,   35
What shall we say when we will see your soul?

      Oh happy soul, who never once removed
Your holy foot from its true rightful path,
Always disdaining what the worldly crave!
Oh heavenly spirit, most uncommon soul,   40
Who now beholds her Lord who loves her so,
Where often she would wander with her heart![2]
Oh! Well she understood
That far from him all things are weak and frail
And time breaks down all things beneath the Sky,   45
That all our greatness fades,
And always turns its back on this vain world;
And so she took the straight path up to Heaven.

      Oh wretched mortals, oh you blinded men,
Do you not understand this world is naught   50
And all your thoughts are quite futile and vain?
For if your soul is foul, what is the worth
Of jewels, sceptres, and the world's esteem,
And all your cravings bent on sordid gain,
If all will end at last   55
By Heaven's mighty hand, their charm all gone,
And humble people will forever rule?
For it is truly right
That those who live on earth in tears and pure
In Heaven should be exalted with the blessed.   60

      So, Virgin, full of hope I come to you
With hands now joined in prayer and bended knee:
Though I am but a worm, a little mud,
Your high and most uncommon virtues will,
I know, yet yield some wholesome fruit within me   65
And do a worthy deed in Heaven on high.
Ah! do beseech that kind
And pleasant Lord, your Bridegroom dear to you,
That he should lead me to the righteous path,
And take me from this evil,   70

---

[2] A clear reference to Catherine's mystical visions.

Crooked path, where I learn every vice,
And sin abounds, and what is good is scarce.

       Catherine, my sad heart
As contrite as I can I send to you:
My soul and body I commend to you.   75

72   Girolamo Savonarola

Sonnet I
On the Lord's Ascension[1]

This gentle Eagle that departs in flight
And rises, proud of victory, to heaven,
Will not, I know, once it has passed the fourth
Consider staying in the fifth with Mars.   4

And if I place my trust in Holy Writ,
The eighth such honour cannot hope to have,
For, crossing every rank of the Empyrian,
It will lay claim to its most blessed site.   8

Gentle spirit of the heavenly city,
What are you doing, tell me, thinking now,
Or looking at? You see our greatest hope.[2]   11

A man (who can deny it?), he rules the heavens
And gathers such a triumph from his sufferings[3]
That he outshines the cherubim in splendour.[4]   14

---

[1]The Christian feast of the Ascension of the Lord is celebrated forty days after the feast of the Resurrection of the Lord (Easter); it is thus a movable feast that falls on a Thursday in May or June.

[2]ie, the heavenly city.

[3]The Italian original, *martiri* could mean either 'sufferings' or 'martyrs' depending on which syllable is stressed. According to the rhyme scheme, the stress should fall on the penultimate, thus giving us *martìri* ('sufferings'); this, then, is the meaning I have used for the translation. However, if one were to stress the first syllable, as in *màrtiri* ('martyrs'), the verse could be read to mean: 'And brings along with him such a triumph of martyrs'. Savonarola is clearly playing with the ambiguity.

[4]Of the nine orders of angels (angels, archangels, thrones, domi-ations, virtues, principalities, powers, cherubim, and seraphim), the cherubim are the second highest and second closest to God. They are traditionally associated with knowledge (and paired with the seraphim who represent love). They are also often associated with the Dominican Order (while the seraphim are associated with the Franciscan Order).

Sonnet II

On the Assumption of the Virgin Mary
to Fra Giovanni da Asula O.P.[1]

This Woman, glorious and celestial,
Whom all could see had little of this earth,[2]
Rose on this day, I know, beyond the spheres,
And so the Church now speaks of her to us.   4

The One who made her queen above the angels
And took from her His true and human flesh,
Descends through all the heavens, sphere by sphere,
To honour her and place the crown upon her.   8

What praises and what triumphs, my sweet brother,
Ring out from joyful souls in highest heaven
As they behold her singular ascension.   11

Happy are they, Oh Queen, who can sing out
To you a hymn so sweet, which I cannot,
And with their hands can touch your blessed gown.   14

---

[1]Fra Giovanni da Asula was a Dominican friar who, in 1475, resided at the convent of San Domenico in Bologna and participated in its Chapter meeting (Martelli, p. 210).

[2]There was little that was earthly, or worldly, in Mary.

Sonnet III

To the Virgin

Hail, Holy Queen,[1] *glorious virgin,*
From whose brow the sun does take its light,
Mother of Him to whom all honour is due,
And of his Father sweet daughter and bride,   4

A triumph in heaven, a powerful lamp
That shines on earth and even in the depths,
A mighty power, as none the world has known,
A precious, heavenly jewel from the East.   8

Turn, Oh Virgin, your fair eyes towards me,
If ever you did welcome that first *Hail*
That came from heaven down to this low world.   11

Look not upon my failings, all so great,
But point me to that path that few men take,
For now at last I give you my heart's key.   14

---

[1]The first verse is in Latin and with it Savonarola echoes the salutation of the 'Salve Regina' (which, however, then continues with the attribute 'mater misericordiae' and not 'virgo gloriosa').

Lauda I

Omnipotent God
You know what I need to do my work
And what my longing might be.
I ask you not for a crown or a treasure,
Like that blind and grasping man,   5
Nor that a town or a fort be built for me,
I ask only, My dear Lord,
That you pierce my heart with your love.   8

Lauda II
Song of Praise to the Crucifix

Jesus, my highest comfort,
You are my only love
You are my blissful harbour
And saintly Saviour true.   4
    Oh mercy great,
    And piety sweet,
    That man is glad who lives as one with you.   7

How often have my soul
And dismal heart offended?
But you stretched on the cross
To save a wretch like me.   11
    Oh mercy great, etc.

Jesus, what did inspire
Your goodness without end?
Tell me! what love did lead you
To suffer so much harm?   15
    Oh mercy great, etc.

Never have I been grateful
Or passionate with you
But you instead were wounded
Most brutally for me.   19
    Oh mercy great, etc.

Jesus, you have most gently
Suffused the world with love
That is so sweet and joyous
It makes all hearts serene.   23
    Oh mercy great, etc.

Jesus, now let me perish
From this your living love;
Jesus, now let me suffer
With you, my Lord most true!   27
    Oh mercy great, etc.

Jesus, I wish I could be
Nailed to that tree so tall
Where I see how you suffer,
Jesus, my Lord so kind!   31
   Oh mercy great, etc.

Oh Cross, make room for me now
And take my body on,
For with your holy fire
You light my heart and soul.   35
   Oh mercy great, etc.

Inflame my heart completely
With your love so divine,
Till deep inside I'm blazing
As bright as seraphim.   39
   Oh mercy great, etc.

And in my heart be sculpted
the Cross and Crucifix
And may I dwell forever
In glory, where He's gone.   43
   Oh mercy great, etc.

Lauda III

My heart, why do you stay here?
My heart, why do you stay here?
Run off to your sweet love now.

That love is Jesus Christ
Who sweetly makes us burn,   5
He cheers the weary heart,
That sighs and craves for him.
Whoever loves him purely
Is purged of all his faults.
    My heart, why do you stay here?   10

If you should feel afflicted,
He is your comfort sweet,
He is that shore so pleasant
And that most welcomed port,
That I exhort you always   15
To love so fervently.
    My heart, why do you stay here?

No longer linger with me,
If peace is what you seek;
To Jesus go and stay there,   20
This world is full of flaws
And He no longer likes you
Unless you can forsake it.
    My heart, why do you stay here?

If here on earth you linger,   25
Your life will be quite harsh;
There's war in every corner
And faith and peace are rare;
If life is precious to you,
Then seek the holy light.   30
    My heart, why do you stay here?

Don't put your trust in others,
For every man is false;
But if you turn to Jesus,
Your burdens will be sweet,   35
And you will spend your lifetime

With honour and rewards.
    My heart, why do you stay here?

If you should find Him, humbly
Do recommend me to Him,   40
And see that you be fervent
In raising my request,
Till He extend His sweetness
Upon my grief so great.
    My heart, why do you stay here?   45

And when you will have reached Him,
Give Him a holy kiss;
His hands and feet above all
Embrace them all you can:
Ignite yourself in His love   50
And crave Him day and night.
    My heart, why do you stay here?

If by the hand He takes you,
Do not ever let go.
Whoever burns with His love   55
Won't suffer timeless woe;
If you remain beside Him,
You'll conquer every fear.
    My heart, why do you stay here?

My heart, reside with Jesus,   60
And let all men complain:
This is your God so tender,
Whom you must fully love,
And for whose love you suffer
The anger of this world.   65
    My heart, why do you stay here?

Go gather all your weapons,
You enemies of good,
For I no longer fear you,
And pain is sweet to me;   70
And this is right and fitting
When someone is in love.
    My heart, why do you stay here?

Figure 3. 'Savonarola preaching from the pulpit.' Woodcut from
G. Savonarola, *Compendio di Revelatione*. Florence: ad istanza
di Piero Pacini da Pescia, 23 aprile 1496, title page; also in
Predica dell'arte del ben morire, Berlin, 1926, p. [1]

Figure 4. 'Savonarola blessing a group of women in their
convent courtyard.' Woodcut from G. Savonarola, *Operetta
molto divota sopra e dieci comandamenti di Dio*. Florence,
1490s, f. 28r.

On Haggai

Sermons on the Book of Haggai
Sermon No. 1
(1 Nov. 1494)

'Do Penance'

Sermons of the Reverend Father Friar Girolamo from Ferrara delivered in Florence and in Santa Maria del Fiore in the months of November and December 1494.

Do penance: the kingdom of heaven is drawing near etc. [Mt 3:2, 4:17].[1]

My beloved in Christ Jesus, because God placed mankind on this earth between two extremes contrary one to another, that is between Paradise and Hell, and since in Paradise there is all that is good and in Hell all that is bad, mankind should lift up its mind's eye and seek with great care always to walk by way of good works

---

[1]This sermon was delivered on 1 November 1494, the feast day of All Saints when the Catholic Church honours all the faithful who have died and gone to heaven (on 2 November it honours instead All Souls, that is, all the faithful who have died and, presumably, are in Purgatory). At this time Florence was in a state of political uncertainty and lingered on the brink of political and economic collapse. King Charles VIII of France had invaded Italy and was camped in Tuscany, threatening Florence from near-by Pisa. Piero de' Medici, who had tried to appease him by ceding four Florentine fortresses to the French, was faced with a popular rebellion against him and had been obliged to flee the city. In the confusion that followed the flight of the Medici, Florence lay open to an outright French occupation. On 17 November 1494, three weeks after this sermon was delivered, King Charles VIII did, in fact, enter Florence— though he did so peacefully and without opposition on his way to Rome and Naples.

towards Paradise, where it can hope to obtain all that is good, instead of, by way of evil deeds, wanting to seek Hell, where it may fear to find every evil. And because the mean always partakes of the nature of the extremes, many find themselves drawing near, some more, some less, to one of these two extremes, that is, to Paradise or to Hell, with their good or depraved works.

But, alas, since one sees the majority of people lean more towards Hell than reach for Paradise, one should lament greatly for this foolish human creature that, placed between good and evil and given the freedom to choose what it wants, would sooner seek its own ruin than its eternal happiness, deceiving itself for the sake of a little of this world's vanity. But since mankind is closer to the centre of the earth, where Hell is, than to Heaven, where the blessed are, in its own little consideration it lets itself be drawn more easily towards the first, as if it wanted to partake of the closer of the two extremes, that is, Hell, than of Heaven, which is further away. Oh, how much greater is the number of the damned than that of the saved (*for many are called, but truly few are chosen*), as our Lord says in the holy Gospel! [Mt 22:14] *Mark this*: the more simple and less material a creature is, the more it leans up towards Heaven and spiritual things, and the more it has of matter the more it leans down towards the centre; the angels, who are more simple and more spiritual, were those who, in far greater numbers, remained in Heaven than those who chose to fall to the bottom; mankind does the opposite for, being more earthly, it seeks the earth, and so most people seek their damnation and so the majority will go to Hell, for in mankind one sees many more sins than merits or good works. Yet, thanks to God's mercy, which is very great, some people will be saved. Nor should one marvel at the small number that will be saved because, considering how low mankind is, it is still a great thing that God should raise it to such glory; one sees few people do penance, and if some do it, most of the time it is little, and *also* it is often not true penance, but many times it is simulated.

Therefore, anyone who seeks his bliss must force himself to do true penance in this life, and I never stop crying out: *Poenitentiam agite*! Do penance, for the kingdom of Heaven will draw near in you. And I have called everyone to enter into the ark, and in previous sermons I have said what the signs are that distinguish those who have made true penance. The first sign is the joy and delight of the mind; one always sees a true penitent happy in everything and patient. The second sign is enlightment, for he knows that simplicity and the life of Christ and of His true Christians is the highest happiness; and the true penitent is so enlightened that he knows that the entire world and all its pleasures are vanity. The third sign is praise, for one always sees him praising God, and he always speaks of divine things both to praise them and for the glory of God. The fourth sign is conversation with good people; you no longer see the true penitent talking with bad companions, nor with worldly persons, but with people who are modest, temperate, and devout.

Now then, my beloved, you know that we have built the ark and that many penitents and good people have entered it. This morning I want to give some documents to those who have entered it,[2] but it seems I am still not allowed to do so. I will tell you why.

But first I turn to you, my almighty Lord; I confess my ignorance to you; truly, Lord, you have conquered me and I am confused in your sight. I really thought, Lord, that you were most good and that your mercy was infinite, but my imagination could not fully conceive how merciful you truly are. I could see the great and grievous sins of many people and I thought them so obstinate in their hearts that I assumed that they could not receive from you, my Lord, any mercy at all, but could only await their punishment. And I thought one could tend only to those who had mended their ways and had entered into the ark of righteous living, and I wanted to give them those documents that were necessary for their survival, and I assumed that the earth would, as it were, open under these evil and obstinate people and swallow them up and that they could no longer find mercy from you. But I was told: 'Wait, speak to them again and call those who are rusty and full of sins to penance.' And so, my Lord, I said you had conquered me and my imagination could not rise so high.

And so, my most beloved, I will not preach this morning, but we will speak and call everyone to penance, should they want to return, whether sinner, or obstinate, or lukewarm, or anyone who is delaying till the end to repent. *Poenitentiam agite*: do penance, do it now, do not delay any longer, for the Lord is still waiting for

---

[2]Savonarola is extending a metaphor: the 'documents' would be the papers necessary to travel by sea (in the ark). In other words, he would like to offer his listeners (those who are already in the ark) further documentation necessary for their journey to salvation.

you and He calls you. Hear my words, not as if they came from
me, but from the Lord. I can do nothing else but say: *Do penance*;
see how good God is and how merciful and how He would like
to lead you to the ark and save you. Come, sinners, come, for God
calls you. I grieve and have great compassion for you. Come on
this feast of All Saints that we observe today and which, when I
think about it, increases my grief because, when I think about the
joy and bliss which today, on this feast, they find themselves in,
and then when I compare it with the misery you find yourselves
in, I can do nothing but grieve with all my heart for love of you.
And their bliss and happiness is so great that one cannot imagine
it, let alone speak about it. They enjoy and benefit from that healthy
good *the things that no eye has seen, nor ear has heard, nor human
heart has felt*, as St Paul said when he was raised to the third heaven
[1 Cor 2:9]. We, down here, see the things of God *as an image in
a mirror and we speak of God's high things, as we can, studdering*
[1 Cor 13:12].[3] Think, I say, oh sinners, about the bliss, the joy, the
eternal good you lose by your wilful, insane living. I say, let us
discuss this passage thoroughly, but first let us rest a little.

Natural [scientists] say that the objects of our senses are either
proper, common, or *accidental*.[4] Light is the specific object of the
eye. Heat is specific not only to the eye, but, because it has
quantity, it is also common to the sense of touch. With physical
things that are moved from place to place and which do not have
movement on their own, it is *accidental* if they are or are not
moved by others.[5] However, when I think about the light of the

---

[3]Savonarola is drawing on 1 Cor. 13:12, 'Now we see puzzlingly reflections
in a mirror,' and then adding the concept of speaking about the things of God
like a stuttering man found in several patristic and medieval writers, including
Pope Gregory the Great, Rabanus Maurus, and Hincmar of Rheims.

[4]See Aristotle, *De anima* 2.6 and Thomas Aquinas, *In de anima* 2.13. The
object of a sense is called a 'sensible'; a 'proper sensible' is perceived directly
by one sense only (e.g., colour is a proper sensible because it is perceived by
one sense only, sight); a 'common sensible' can be perceived by more than
one sense (e.g., size is a common sensible because it can be perceived by
sight and by touch); an 'accidental sensible' is not perceived directly by the
senses, but by some other cognitive faculty (e.g., a house is perceived as a
house by the virtue of cognitive processing of a variety of sense perceptions).

[5]The awkward, even colloquial structure of this sentence is such in the
original, so I have retained it to reflect the spontaneity of Savonarola's speech.

blessed, so resplendent and so clear on this feast day of theirs, I say to myself: 'Oh, how much greater is the light of God! It is an inaccessible light and an infinite light.' Then, when I think about the quantity of those blessed spirits and their great number, for they are more numerous than all other created things, I see how great God's power and wisdom is. And when I think about the peace and rest of the blessed, and I contrast it with the mutability of the heavens and their movements which, if they were to cease, suddenly there would be no movement at all, and seeing that down here in the universe every mutable thing is without any peace whatsoever, I exclaim and cry out: Oh, how great is the peace and tranquillity of the blessed! Oh foolish men, who by sinning wish to lose such peace and such rest, *poenitentiam agite*, do penance, return to God and you will find every kind of rest; repent of your errors, confess your sins, set your mind never to sin again, take communion with that holy sacrament that will make you, too, blessed.

When I look at those who have mended their ways and are on the road to righteous Christian living and confess their sins and take communion often, one sees in them something akin to divinity, a modesty, a spiritual joy. They have almost changed their face into that of an angel. Look, *on the contrary*, at the faces of the wicked and obstinate perverts, and especially at those of some clergymen when they are unrestrained in their vices, and you will see they are like demons and worse than lay people, and yet these clergymen partake of this sacrament every day. See how different the effects are: this sacrament sweetens the hearts of good people and leads them to every modesty; the opposite can be seen in the wicked. And so I was thinking and saying: 'If this sacrament, in which one believes what one does not see, gives so much joy to those who are well disposed to take it and to receive it, how much greater this joy will be, and is for those blessed spirits who see Him *face to face*, who enjoy Him, and who benefit from Him.' Oh human heart, why do you not break and melt in all this sweetness and love? But rest a while, let us consider a little better how great the joy of the blessed might be.

Oh Lord, what have I heard that leads me to know something else? I see the martyrs of the past, cheerful, joyous, and happy in the midst of their sufferings, all for love of Christ crucified, *not only* desirous of such suffering, but often not even forced or spurred towards it. I see how this Crucifix has changed people's hearts away from natural inclination, which would be to flee those things that afflict the body and to flee infamy and insults and rudeness, but these martyrs sought them and moved towards them. I see that the most stupid and frightening thing one could find at that time, that is, the cross, gave so much peace and so much happiness to these martyrs. For these reasons I was thinking and I came to realize what a great and more abundant consolation comes today, on this feast day, from the glory we can see them enjoying for having chosen to suffer out of love for their Lord. One cannot imagine it great enough, for it is greater still, *for it is something that no eye has seen, nor ear has heard, nor human heart has felt* [1 Cor 2:9]. So great is the prize Christ has prepared for those who love Him and follow Him, that no human heart can conceive it.

The other consolation that those who love God with all their passion have in this world is Holy Scripture, where all divine treasures and all that can satisfy the human heart are hidden. I declare *in the sight of God*, and *truly* I say that I would sooner have with me Holy Scripture and be hidden and locked up anywhere, than to be given and to have all the kingdoms of the world. Oh, how much sweeter it will be to see the book of books, that is, God, in whom one sees everything!

As I thought about this, my pain grew *and sadness filled my heart* [Jh 16:6]. First, because I am not there, where there is such joy; second, because I am not worthy to be there; third, because I can see it will be a long time before I can go there; fourth, because there are many dangers on the way that can prevent me from arriving there; fifth, because I see this time of ours is full of iniquities and wicked people, and the world is full of tribulations, and these things greatly afflict people's souls; last, oh my Lord, when I see and think about how good and full of all goodness you are, alas, if I were to lose you and such a kingdom and such good and life as well, what would I do? These are the things that afflict my heart and my soul. So, this morning of All Saints' I, full of pain and sadness, am not about to speak of their lives and sing their praises, but of our weeping, instead. Now listen.

By the rivers of Babylon, there we sat down and wept [Ps 136(137):1]. Lamenting and remembering their Babylonian captivity, those Israelites said: 'By the rivers of Babylon, there we sat down, there we wept.' And they remembered their homeland, from which they had been taken, and so they lamented and cried and said: '*We hung our instruments on the willows*' [Ps 136(137):2],[6] that is, we

---

[6]Savonarola says: *Applicavimus organa salicibus*; the Vulgate actually reads: *In salicibus in medio eius suspendimus organa nostra.*

will no longer sing and dance, but we have hung our musical instruments on the willows and we linger by the rivers of Babylon in tears. Oh Florence, you sit by the rivers of your sins. Shed a river of tears to wash them away, remember your heavenly homeland, where your soul came from. Seek to return to that homeland through penance, as these Israelites did. One cannot sing, but one must cry *in an alien land* [Ps 136(137):4], that is, in you, because on account of your sins you are alien to, and distant from God. When the world was in bloom, one did not cry, but now we must shed rivers of tears. Everything is devoid of spiritual gifts. Now tribulations are coming. We must change life and purpose. The tribulations you see laid out for you should lead you yet to change your habits.

Do you not know what is said of those first philosophers, *that because they were amazed, they began to philosophize?*[7] They admired the things of the universe and sought the causes of these effects. So you must look upon these tribulations, that you see readied for you, and seek their cause, and you will find that their cause is sin. If you linger in amazement, it is out of ignorance. Go seek the cause. You will see, I say, that the sins and wickedness of today's world produce this effect of tribulations. Seek, I say, *all people wish to know nature,*[8] everyone wants to know the reason, *especially*, when he sees something unusual, as those philosophers did when they saw the moon and the sun eclipse, and still, by seeking, they found the cause. And so will you, if you consider that God has created this world and takes care of it, and especially of mankind. And you will see that, with all the wickedness we see done and with God being just, He will want to punish mankind. And so you will come to know that God sends these tribulations, and that God is at the head of these armies, and that He leads them. And so you will do penance for your sins, if you are wise and want God to help you in these hardships.

---

[7]Aristotle, *Metaphysics* 1.2.9. The concept was then taken up by a multitude of thinkers, including: the Venerable Bede, *Sententia* (Sectio prima. Sententiae ex Aristotele collectae); Dante, *Quaestio de aqua et terra*, 20 ('unde propter admirari cepere physolophari'); and others.

[8]Aristotle, *Metaphysics*, 1.1.1.

And because I told you a long time ago that tribulations will come and God will send them to cleanse His Church of its many evils, you should by now believe me, because you see it happening. I tell you, these tribulations are not without cause; *nothing on earth is without a cause and no sorrow comes from the earth* [Job 5:6]. No sorrow rises from the earth. Strike it as much as you want, it does not feel anything and does not cry out in pain because it does not have any feeling, nor is there a cause that would give it pain. But if the sinner will cry in sorrow, that pain comes from sin, for it deserves to be punished with the pain of sorrow. So, your wickedness, oh Italy, oh Rome, oh Florence, your impieties, your fornications, your usuries, your cruelties, your iniquities bring on these tribulations. This is the cause. And if you have identified the cause of this evil, seek the medicine. Get rid of sin, for it is the cause of this evil, and you will be healed, *for, if you remove the cause, you remove the effect.*[9] If you do not do this, believe me, nothing else will help you. You deceive yourselves, Italy and Florence, if you do not believe what I tell you. Nothing else can help you, but penance. Do what you will, it will all be in vain without it. You will see.

Oh rich, oh poor, do penance. Rich people, give alms to the poor: *redeem your sins with alms* [Dan 4:24]. Oh you who fear God, do good and have no fear of tribulations, for God will console you greatly in them. Penance is the only remedy, and if you, just you, do true penance, you will remove a great part of these tribulations. *Do penance* and take away the sins that are the cause of tribulations.

Your ingratitude, too, oh Florence, is a cause of your tribulations. *Ingratitude puts out the fountain of divine pity,*[10] oh ungrateful Florence. And God has spoken and you did not want to listen to Him. If the Turks had heard what you have heard, they would have done penance for their sins. I have cried out so much and shouted out so much that I no longer know what to say. The angels do not speak with their voice among themselves, but in other spiritual ways; they understand one another and express their ideas and understand each other without voice and without tongue. This is

---

[9]Thomas Aquinas, *Summa theologiae* I.ii.3.

[10]Bernard of Clairvaux, *Sermones in Cantica Canticorum*, Sermon 51: 'Ingratitude is a strong wind that dries up the fountain of pity, the dew of mercy, and the stream of grace.'

not so with mankind, who expresses its ideas with tongue and with voice. I speak to you, Florence, and I do nothing but cry out in a loud voice: 'Do penance.' And *though* little, it benefits many. And even if it bears fruit in a few people, it is the Lord, not I, who has done this out of His mercy. *He who plants and waters does little, but God gives growth* [1 Cor 3:6]. Oh Florence, the Lord has spoken to you in many ways, and if God had not enlightened me, you would not be enlightened through my many sermons, and you have been enlightened more exclusively than any other place.

Do you not remember, Florence, how, not so many years ago, you stood in the things of God and in faith? Were you not like a heretic in so many ways? Do you not know what moved you to touch the faith with your hands, as it were? You dwelt in those external ceremonies of yours and you thought you were saintly, and God showed you how wrong you were and how those things are not worth anything without purity of heart and how a Christian life consists of things other than ceremonies.

Nor was this infinite gift of drawing you away from the darkness of ignorance enough for God, for He also chose to reveal His secrets to you, and He had the future predicted to you long in advance of it. You know that several years ago, long before anyone had heard the noise or smelled any of today's wars, moved by people from beyond the Alps, great tribulations were announced to you. You also know that not two years have passed since I told you: *'Behold the sword of the Lord falling on the earth quickly and swiftly.'*[11] Not I, but God predicted it to you. And, look, it has come to pass and it is here. You know, when I used to tell you: *'The Lord says this,'* you did not believe it. Now, instead, you are obliged to believe it, because you see it. Do you not remember, Florence, when, many years ago, I told you these words from God: *Ego, Dominus, loquor in zelo sancto meo, quod venient dies in quibus evaginabo ensem super te. Convertimini antequam compleatur furor meus. Nam superveniet tribulatio, et voles pacem et non invenies.*[12] That is, God was saying to each person: 'I speak to you

---

[11]This exact passage is not in the Bible, though it echoes a number of passages such as Isaiah 34:5 or Ezekiel 21:7. See Savonarola's third sermon on the Psalms (in this volume) for his extended use of this verse as a sermon motif.

[12]The entire passage is not in the Bible, but is very reminiscent of the exhortations and threats found in Isaiah, Ezekiel, and other prophets.

in my holy zeal; look, the day will come when I will draw my sword upon you; mend your ways,' God was saying, 'mend your ways before my wrath is complete, for tribulations will come and then you will seek peace and will not find it.' And, like this, I said many other things about you, oh Florence, when I said: '*The Lord God says this: Poenitentiam agite,* do penance, for there is no other remedy.' I could not have made it plainer to you that this is the last remedy, but those people who had closed their ears could not and did not want to hear. Behold, now, see how tribulation comes upon many people who did not want to change. Behold, behold, here is the day of the Lord, coming towards us, but you do not want it at all. You do not want the day of the Lord because it is written: *Veh desiderantibus diem Domini* [Amos 5:18]. Woe to those who wish for the day of the Lord. *Ad quid eum vobis?* [Amos 5:18] What good do you hope it can bring you? You deceive yourself. *Dies Domini tenebrae et non lux* [Amos 5:18]. That is, the day of the Lord is darkness and not light, as you imagine it. Oh, how many will be deceived! *Poenitentiam agite,* do penance, and tend to nothing else, for nothing else can help you. Believe this friar, for anything else is vain.

You will say to me: 'Father, when you used to say these words, I did not think they were coming from God.' And I answer, you should very well have thought they were, and you should have weighed them, for one should not hold the words of God in such little account, as you did. You know that it is written: *Prophetias nolite spernere* [1 Thes 5:20]. One must not spurn prophecies, but try them first and seize what is good in them.

If I told you: 'Do penance, for the sword is coming,' what do you lose in doing this? Nothing. You gain, instead, the redemption of your sins from this. Because of this, you will not be forgiven at all for your ingratitude in refusing to recognize this benefit of having been warned that you could flee your danger. You know I used to say to you: 'The time will come when you will not be able, even though you might want to.' And if you were to say: 'I suspected that you might have been mislead,' I answer you that I allayed all these suspicions of yours and I showed you with the most valid reasons that there could be no deception here. And you say that there still were those who told you the opposite. You know I used to show you that these lukewarm persons were deceiving you and I used to say to you: 'It would be better for you to believe rather than not to believe these things,' and that when the tribulations will come and you will have no more time, it will be better for you to have believed. You know I used to say to you: 'God will take away your soul and your wits, then, and you will seem like a drunk and you will not know what to do with yourself.' Oh Florence, how many things did God have announced to you that, had you believed them, you would have been blessed.

Moreover, and thirdly: do you not remember how often I said that God wants to renew His Church and His Christian people, and He will do it with the sword, and soon, and that God does not like these governments? Behold, see how everything is proceeding according to plan. I tell you that of all the things I have told *in the words of the Lord* [1 Thes 4:15] not one iota will fail. You know how much antagonism I encountered when I foretold the renewal of the Church and how, although I was greatly opposed, I never wanted to remain silent. And even though I made many enemies because of this, nonetheless I have always held firm, and so I remain, and I could not nor can I do otherwise, for I was certain and more than certain. And then you, that is, the lukewarm people, said that I would flee, and I told you that I intended to hold firmly to this truth even at the cost of my life, if necessary, for the love of Christ and of this truth. You also know that when I used to tell you: *'Behold the sword of the Lord falling on the earth quickly and swiftly,'* you used to mock me and say that I was a simpleton. And if I were to say to you now: *'Quickly and swiftly,'* even as things can be seen to be unfolding, you would say the same thing, obstinate and perverse as you are. I tell you: *'The Lord says this: turn to me with all your heart, with fasts, tears, and lamentation.'* [Joel 2:12] Turn to the Lord, for He still waits for you. Do true, not false penance, and do not do it because of human fear, but *with* all your heart, out of love of God, who can still forgive you and have mercy of your sins. Otherwise, I warn you, He will punish you in your soul, in your body, and in your life. Let us stop a little and we will follow with the rest.

I told you that this morning we would let be the documents I wanted to give to those who have come in, and that we would only need to call sinners to penance and to weep for their sins, otherwise, if you do not do it, I do not know whether the Lord will spare us, for we cannot tell you anything new. Let us first see whether you will do this penance.

You should know by now that I speak to you as a father to his children for your own good, and you should see that in this affliction God has given me as a father to you in order to show you the way to correct yourselves of your errors, so that you might deserve some forgiveness from the Lord. Oh fathers, oh mothers, oh sons, oh daughters, *do penance*, mend your ways, do penance, and God will have mercy on you. Although I am not worthy, the Lord, as you see, has given me to you as a father and as a mother in order to comfort you in this time of tears. And to show you that this is so, I kneel in front of God, your true and principal father and mother, who alone can help you and grant you salvation, and I say that He is the one who makes and has made all things, and we are His instruments, though unworthy, and He is the one who works all that is good. You can tell whether I am like a father to you because a father gathers for his child and shares with him all he has. I have done the same with you, Florence: all I have learned and struggled for in my entire life, be it about the truth of the faith or about righteous Christian living, I have poured out for you as a good father does for his beloved children. And, by God's will, through me you have shared more fully in God's secrets about the future. On the other hand, have I ever asked anything from you for all that I have toiled for you? Nor am I asking it now. We are satisfied with the mere bread God gives us for our fare, and if I could I would even do without it.

I know that you will accuse me of folly today: *in my foolishness I say all these things* [2 Cor 11:21], as Paul said. The zeal I have for you, Florence, makes me say what I am saying. I do not want the Lord to close the ark quite yet, but I want you to enter it by living righteously for your salvation. Oh Florence, am I not also like a shepherd to you? *For the good shepherd will risk his soul for his sheep* [Jh 10:11, 14–15]. A good shepherd will risk his life and honour and all he has for the well being of his lambs. For your salvation and because God wants this, I have exposed myself to disgrace, to derision, to the whispers of many, all for love of you, and I have never left you, and so I am here for you and not for me, nor for any profit to me, but because God has willed it like this. And He has taken a lowly and unsuitable man for this office, so that He might show that it is He who does this, and not a little friar. Even if I wanted to, I could not leave you and flee all these attacks and all these labours. *Far be this from me.* May it not please God that I should ever flee persecution for His truth. On the contrary, I have always prayed to God for those who persecute us, that the Lord might enlighten them, for they are blind.

Florence, am I also not to you like a mother to her little child? I have suffered and suffer many pains and many afflictions to give you birth and to lead you to Christ. I have also been like your wet-nurse in raising you and counselling you about what is good for you and about your health. Where, oh Florence, is my honour and that of my superiors? The honour and crown of a father is the righteous life of his children. Florence, if only you would live righteously; this is what I want from you, my daughter, and this should be my crown and yours, and nothing else. If only you would have pity on me, for I grieve so much for you and for your health. What else do I want from you, Florence, but that you be saved and that you live righteously, and nothing more. Other cities have told me that if I had said and done what I have said and done in your city, they would have become something else completely than what you are. So I pray all of you no longer to remain obstinate, but to turn to the Lord and do penance, and quickly, for I do not say this without a reason. *Turn to the Lord our God, for He is good and full of mercy* [Joel 2:13]. My children, be merciful towards each other and repent of your sins, and God will also be merciful towards you, and this penance is the sole, true, and only remedy, and there is no other. Now, think about this carefully, for it is right for you.

Do penance; the kingdom of Heaven draws near [Mt 3:2, 4:17]. See, my most beloved, how great is the goodness of God, whom you have much offended with your sins and for so long; and *yet* see how long He has waited for you and still waits for you, so that you might do penance and He need not punish you. Come, wait no longer, mend your ways at last and do penance, do not delay any longer.

But because till now I have spoken to all of you in general and I see that this does not help, so now I must be a little more specific. I have told you that God wanted me to be like a father to you, and so I will now speak to you more specifically, as one does to children, and all for your correction and your health. Oh priests, oh prelates of the Church of Christ, leave those benefices you cannot in justice keep, leave your ostentation, your banquets and dinners that you hold so splendidly. Leave, I say, your concubines and kept boys, for it is time, I say, to do penance, for the great tribulations by which God wants to fix His Church are coming towards us. Say your masses with devotion, otherwise, if you do not want to understand what God wants, in the end you will lose your benefices and your life. Oh monks, leave what is superfluous in habit, in silver, and in the great fat of your abbeys and benefices, give yourselves to simplicity and work with your hands, as the ancient monks, who are your fathers and ancestors, did, otherwise, if you do not do it willingly, the time will come when you will be forced to do it. Oh nuns, you, too, leave aside all that is superfluous, leave that simony of yours when you accept the nuns that come to stay in your monasteries, leave all the displays and ostentation you use when your nuns take their vows, leave your figured melodies, and instead weep, I say, for your flaws and your errors, because I tell you that the time is quickly coming for weeping, and not for singing and merry making, for God will punish you if you do not change your life and your habits. If you do not do it, do not be surprised, afterwards, when the slaughter will come and everything will be in danger. Oh my friars, to you I say: leave what is superfluous, your paintings, your frivolities. Do not cut your habits so large or from such thick cloth. Are you not aware that with your superfluous things you take away the alms for the poor? Oh brothers, oh children, it is necessary to speak openly in this manner so that no-one might then say: 'I did not know' and excuse himself. I am obliged to say this, and *woe to me if I do not preach the Gospel* [1 Cor 9:16], woe to me if I do not say it. I announce to you that if you do not listen to the voice of God, He will punish you. Oh merchants, leave your usuries, return your ill-gotten gains and other people's goods, or else you will lose everything. Oh you who have extra things, give them to the poor, for they are not yours. Bring them to the Company of St Martin so that they might distribute them to the shamed-faced poor who often die of hunger while you have so much extra.[13] Give them, I say, to the Good Men of St Martin, bring them there to them, not to me

---

[13]The confraternity of the *Buonomini di San Martino* (the Twelve Good Men of St Martin) was founded by the Dominican Fra Antonino Pierozzi (1389–1459), Savonarola's predecessor as prior of San Marco, and later archbishop of Florence. Pierozzi was canonized as St Antoninus in 1523 under the pontificate of Clement VII de' Medici. The aim of the confraternity was to collect alms and then to distribute them to the 'shamed-faced poor,' that is, to those who had unexpectedly fallen into need but were too shamed-faced to beg. In other words, the confraternity did not assist the chronic indigent, but those middle and upper class persons who were experiencing temporary economic distress. It was one of the very few confraternities to survive the general suppression of sodalities in 1785 and still survives and operates today (with continued great respect from the Florentine population) from its original chapel on the Piazza S. Martino.

nor to my friars, I tell you, for it is not our task to distribute alms to the poor. You, poor people, go to them so that they might distribute the city's alms and so that you might be assisted. I tell you that anyone who has something expendable should give it to the poor and I tell you, moreover, that the time has come to give more than just what is expendable. Oh priests, I must come back to you; I speak of bad priests, always keeping reverence towards good priests. Leave, I say, that unspeakable vice,[14] that damned vice that has so much provoked the wrath of God upon you, for woe, woe to you! Oh lustful people, put on a hair-shirt and do penance, because you need it. Oh you with your houses full of vain objects and dishonest pictures and things, and evil books, and the *Morgante*,[15] and other poems against the faith. Bring them to me so that we can burn them and sacrifice them to God.[16] And you, mothers, who adorn your daughters with so many vanities and superfluous things and hair-dos, bring all these things here to us so we can put them on the fire so that, when the wrath of God comes, it will not find these things in your house. And in this case I order you as your father to do this. If you do this, as I have told you, what you do will be enough to placate the wrath of God, otherwise I would not want to be the one to give you the bad

---

[14]This is now the second time in this sermon that Savonarola accuses priests of committing same-sex sodomy.

[15]A chivalrous romantic epic in Italian by the Florentine poet Luigi Pulci (1432–84), a member of the circle of artists and intellectuals around Lorenzo de' Medici. Although the work was commissioned by Lucrezia Tornabuoni (Lorenzo's mother), a woman of profound piety and devotion, it is replete with ribaldry, witticisms, and racy situations that parody not only chivalric, but Christian traditions as well (its opening octave, for example, is a parody of John 1:1 'In the beginning was the Word, and the Word was with God, and the Word was God'). Not surprisingly, Savonarola did not approve of this poem. The work was completed in 23 cantos sometime before 1470; it was then published in 1478 in an expanded version of 28 cantos known as *Morgante maggiore.*

[16]Such burnings would take place some years later, during the Carnivals of 1497 and 1498, when Savonarola organized the enormous bonfires in the Piazza della Signoria and had all sorts of 'vanities' burned as a sign of rejection of earthly values and temptations. The so-called 'bonfires of the vanities' were preceded by laud-singing processions through the city.

news. Now then, another four more words and then you may go home.

Vox dicentis: 'Clama.' [Is 40:6] A voice that says: 'Call out.' Oh Italy, *because of your sins these adversities are upon you.*[17] Oh all you cities of Italy, the time has come to punish all your sins. Oh Italy, because of your lust, your avarice, your pride, your ambition, your thefts and extortions many enemies will come your way, many scourges will come your way. *Vox dicentis: 'Clama,'* a voice saying: 'Call out'; *Oh Florence, because of your sins your enemies are upon you.* Oh Florence, oh Florence, oh Florence, because of your sins, because of your rapes, because of your avarice, because of your lust, because of your ambition many upheavals and many afflictions will still come your way. *A voice saying: 'Call out.'* And whom do you call? Oh tonsure, tonsure, tonsure,[18] *this storm has risen because of you,*[19] oh tonsure, you are the major reason for these enemies, because of your wicked ways this storm has come; because of your sins many tribulations have been prepared; woe, woe, I say, to those with a tonsure on their head. *Vox dicentis: 'Clama,'* a voice that still says: 'Call out.' And what more do I need to call out? *Clama, ne cesses, annuntia populo huic scelera eorum* [Is 58:1]. Call out, it says, do not stop at all: *annuntia populo huic scelera eorum*: announce to all the people of Italy that because of their wickedness, because of their blasphemies, because of their iniquities, tribulations will come upon them; *poenitentiam agite,* do penance.

Behold, the tribulation of Italy, that I announced to you many years ago, has begun. What do you say now, you lukewarm man, who derided and mocked my words so much? Oh lukewarm, at least weep now for your sins and recognize your error. But perhaps there is no more time for you, oh tonsure, for you are the reason behind all these scourges. Let everyone look inside himself and say: 'My sins are the reason for these tribulations.' Oh sinners, your iniquities, your sins have called forth and brought these tribulations

---

[17]The passage is not in the Bible, but clearly echoes the usual chastisements found in the prophetic books.

[18]Savonarola is addressing the clergy by referring to their ritually shaved head; at the time, it was standard practice for clergymen to have a tonsure, that is, to shave a circle on their head as a sign of humility. Savonarola's own large tonsure is clearly visible in his portraits.

[19]The passage is not in the Vulgate, but echoes passages such as Jer 23:19.

on. Let everyone think about himself and do penance, for you have no other remedy. I have often said it and often shouted it out. I have often cried for you, Florence. This should be enough for you.

Pray the Lord for me *that God might comfort me*. Oh Florence, I wanted to speak with you this morning and to each of you *specifically* and openly because I could not do anything else. And still the voice calls out: *vox dicentis: 'Clama,'* the voice of one who says: 'Call out.' And who else should I call? I have called everyone to penance: *Clama ad Dominum Deum tuum*, call out and shout to your Lord God. I turn to you, my Lord, you who were put to death because of your love for us and because of our sins. *Spare your people, Lord* [Joel 2:17]. Forgive, forgive, Lord, this your people, forgive, Lord, the Florentine people, who want to be yours, oh Lord, *ne des hereditatem tuam in obprobrium* [Joel 2:17], do not hand over your inheritance and your children, Lord, to these tribulations. If you have given me, Lord, to be their father, I recommend my sons and my daughters and my mothers to you, I recommend this people to you. We celebrate today the feast day of All Saints: I pray to you, glorious saints, for this festivity of yours, that you might pray to the Lord for this people. And you, my Lord, who have fed us with your sweetness on this day, *feed us with the wine of contrition on the feast day of All Saints* [Ps 59:5(60:3)], I pray, *by your tender mercy* [Lk 1:78], give this people true knowledge of Yourself and true repentance for its sins through the merits of your passion and for the merits of your most holy mother and for her prayers and those of all the saints and of the cherubim and seraphim and of all the choirs of angels and of all the hierarchies of your most holy angels and blessed spirits. And deliver them from this tribulation and quickly make a liar out of me, always safeguarding your honour, my Lord, *who are blessed for ever and ever. Amen.*

Figure 5. 'Savonarola giving one of his treatises to the abbess of the Dominican convent of the Murate in their chapel.' Woodcut from G. Savonarola, *Operetta molto divota sopra e dieci comandamenti di Dio*, Florence, Lorenzo Morgiani e Giovanni di Magona, ca. 1495, title page; also in *Predica dell'arte del ben morire*, Berlin, 1926, p. [8].

Figure 6. 'Savonarola leading a group of saintly women into heaven.' Woodcut from G. Savonarola, *Compendio di Revelatione*. Florence: ad istanza di Piero Pacini da Pescia, 1496,

On the Psalms

Sermons on the Book of Psalms
Sermon No. 3
13 Jan. 1495

Sermons of the Reverend Father Fra Girolamo from Ferrara delivered in Santa Maria del Fiore in the year 1494 according to the Florentine style[1] on various Psalms and Scriptures beginning on the day of Epiphany and following on the other Sundays, gathered by Ser Lorenzo Violi[2] from the spoken voice of the preacher.

---

[1]The sermon was delivered on 13 January 1495, on the octave of Epiphany. In Florentine style the year lags one year behind our common style (or common era) for all dates from 1 January to 24 March and then joins with common style on 25 March; this difference is caused by the Florentine practice of beginning the computation of the year from the feast of the Incarnation (25 March).

[2]The Florentine notary Lorenzo Violi (or Vivoli) was born in 1464 and died after 1549. A lay follower of Savonarola, he transcribed the friar's sermons as they were being delivered—beginning, in fact, with the 1495 cycle on the Psalms from which this current sermon is taken. In the late 1530s, long after Savonarola's death, the now elderly Violi composed one of the earliest defences of the friar, *Le giornate* (ed. Gian Carlo Garfagnini. Firenze: Olschki, 1986). In it, he comments on his first transcriptions saying that the sermons on the Psalms were 'the first he began to jot down, and that he did not take great pains to transcribe them precisely, word by word, but he transcribed their substance, more as an exercise for his own interests than for any other reason, never thinking that they would be printed and published, especially since in those early days he was not as devoted to the friar's mission as he later became' (*Le giornate*, 1986, p. 37; my translation). All in all, Violi would eventually transcribe five cycles of sermons: on the Psalms (1495), on Amos and Zechariah (Lent 1496), on Ruth and Micah (May–November 1496), on Ezekiel (Lent 1497), and on Exodus (Lent 1498). On Violi, aside from G.C. Garfagnini's introduction to *Le giornate*, see: Cesare Vasoli, 'Note sulle *Giornate* di Ser Lorenzo Violi' *Memorie domenicane* n.s. 3 (1972): 11–56; Armando F. Verde, 'Ser Lorenzo Violi "segretario" del Savonarola' *Memorie*

'Behold the sword of the Lord falling on the earth
quickly and swiftly'.[3]

Our intention, this morning, is to repeat all we have said and
preached in Florence these last years on the renewal of the Church,
which will happen *completely* and soon. We will repeat ourselves
so that those persons who did not hear it previously might hear
and know that the renewal will certainly take place and soon. And
those who heard it previously and believe it, might this morning
be reconfirmed of this; and those who did not believe and do not
believe, might be converted; and those who still will not believe,
and remain stubborn, might at least be left confused and might
pale at the reasons we will bring forth.

In every creature there is a limit to its creation, its being, and its
powers. Eternity has no limit and no end whatsoever, *for eternity
is the possession of unending eternal life.*[4] Time is not unified,
eternity is, because time is in part past, in part present, in part
future. But God, most able to do anything, is eternal and embraces
all time. Because for Him everything is present, and what was, is,
and will be is for Him always present, and he always understands
and sees everything. And as we have said God is most capable of
doing everything and He understands everything, so the more a
creature is higher than matter, the more it is able to do more things
and to understand more things. And so mankind is more capable
and understands more than any other animal. And so also angels,
which are higher from matter than mankind, understand and know
more than mankind, and are capable of doing more things. And so
angels know the order of the entire universe. But future events,
that are contingent, that may and may not be, and that depend on
the free will of man, neither angels nor any other creature can
know them, for God has retained this knowledge of the future for
Himself alone and He communicates it to whomever He likes as
much and whenever He wants. It is certainly true that angels know
those future events that derive from a necessary cause, just as the

---

domenicane n.s. 18 (1987): 381–99; Gian Carlo Garfagnini, 'Ser Lorenzo Violi
e le prediche del Savonarola' *Medioevo e Rinascimento* 3 (1988): 261–85.

[3]This exact passage is not in the Bible, though it echoes a number of
passages such as Isaiah 34:5 or Ezekiel 21:7.

[4]St Thomas Aquinas, *Summa theologiae*, 1.10.1. See also Boethius, *De
consolatione philosophiae*, V.6.

astrologer knows when he determines a future eclipse from the necessary movement of the heavens. Angels also determine and see on the basis of *how those things happen in the majority of cases*, as one, for example, determines that an olive tree will produce olives and that a stalk of grain will produce grain, because this nearly always happens *and happens as it does in the majority of cases*, although at times the opposite might happen *and this might happen, but in rare cases*. Because of this, one can manifestly conclude that soothsaying and astrology, which seek to guess *future contingents*, are *completely* false things; because future events and those that depend on free will, that might and might not be, only God knows them and that creature to whom God chooses to reveal them, as we have said. And so I tell you that because astrology seeks to guess, it is the source of many superstitions and heresies.

Why such astronomy is *completely* false can be proven like this. Philosophy is either true or false: if it is true, astrology is false, for philosophy says that *there is no determined truth for future contingencies*;[5] if philosophy is false, astrology is also false because in philosophy one proves those things an astrologer presupposes *as principles*. If, therefore, philosophy is false and proves the principles of astrology, then these principles will be false; if the principles of an astrologer are false, what follows from them will also be false.

A second proof: either our faith is true, or it is false. If it is true, astrology is false because the canons of the faith reproach it; if the faith is false, astrology is also false because, according to astrologers, the faith of Christ—which began *from the beginning of the world*, because at that time they believed Christ would come and we believe Christ has come—, comes, according to astrologers, from the inclination of a fixed star that inclines mankind to this faith, and this faith is false: therefore, astrology is false, for these

---

[5]In other words, it is impossible to determine the truth of predictions or of future events. Some thirty years after Savonarola, the notion was cited *verbatim* by Francesco Guicciardini in his *Ricordi*; see Series C, ricordo 58: 'How well did that philosopher say it: *de futuris contingentibus non est determinata veritas!* Go anywhere, the more you turn around the more you find this saying to be quite true.'

stars that incline towards falsehood and on whom astrology is founded, are a false thing: therefore astrology is false.

Similarly, if the faith of Christ, in which there is more good, justice, and decency than in any other faith, is false, then every other faith is false; therefore astrology, which tends to believe this, is false. On the basis of what has been said, you can therefore conclude that soothsaying and such similar astrology is false, and that future events that depend on free will are uncertain for every creature, but for God they are certain and for those to whom He reveals them.

Moreover, first principles are more certain than the conclusions we infer from them using our intellects. But that is not how it happens in God, because He does not know the causes on account of the effects, but rather He knows, without reasoning [*discorso*], the conclusions [already present] in the principles and the effects [already present] in the causes. Angels, as well, participate in this light, because they understand without reasoning. The prophets also had this light of God, and thus David said in his psalm: *Their music goes out through all the earth* [Ps 18(19):5], meaning [the voice] of the apostles, which happened many years after David, and *yet* he, with that light, saw their work like something already done. By this light the holy prophets as well understand from external signs what they mean intrinsically, as Daniel did when, in the time of King Belshazzar when that hand wrote those signs on the wall, that is, *Mene Tekel Parsin*, and he understood the sense and the intrinsic meaning of those *extrinsic* signs and letters [Dan 5:1–30].[6] And so this light is a part of that eternity which God communicates to whomever He wishes.

'Well, then, what do you mean, friar, by all this? The events you have predicted in the last four years, where did you get them from?' I do not need to tell you this, for the mind is not disposed to understand it. I have, in fact, told it to some confidants of mine, one or two at most; but I really want to tell you that you must believe it, for I am not crazy and I do not act without reason. In the past I, too, mocked such things, but God allowed me to do so

---

[6]Belshazzar is often modernized to Balthasar. The story of Daniel at Balthasar's banquet became a fruitful subject for dramatic representations, the most famous of which may well be the thirteenth-century liturgical drama *Ludus Danielis* (*The Play of Daniel*) performed in the cathedral of Beauvais. The manuscript for this play is French and dates from about 1230.

in order that I might have compassion for you when you would not readily believe. But you must truly believe, because you can already see that by now a great part of what I preached to you has already come true, and I tell you that the rest will also come true and not one shred will be missing; and I am more certain of this than you are that two and two makes four, and more certain than of the fact that I am touching the wood of this pulpit, because this light is more certain than the sense of touch. But I want you to know very well that this light does not, however, make me saved: Balaam prophesied, but was nonetheless a sinner and a wicked man, even though he had this light of prophecy in him [Num 22–25]. But I tell you, Florence, that this light was given to me for you and not for me, because this light does not make man welcomed to God. And I want you to know that I began to see these things more than fifteen years ago, perhaps twenty, but in the last ten years I have begun to say them: and first in Brescia, when I preached there, I said some things; then God allowed me to come to Florence, which is the heart of Italy,[7] so that you might spread the news to all the other cities of Italy.

But your ears, Florence, did not hear me, but God. But the other people of Italy have always heard through the voice of others, so you will have no excuse, Florence, if you do not mend your ways; and believe me, Florence, that it is not I, but God who says these things. You can understand this because you have seen these people who were on the road of wickedness and have returned to penance; and believe that this result could not have been achieved by a poor little friar had God not worked through him. Believe, therefore, Florence, and convert and do not think that your scourge has passed, for I see the sword coming back.

Because of its nature a stone will go towards the bottom and does not know why, the swallow makes its nest out of earth and does not know why, but they do this out of natural instinct and they do not know the reason why they function like this. But mankind is led by free will. Along the same line there have been some who, in their simplicity, have predicted many things and did not know the reason why. And there have been others who have predicted many things not out of their simplicity, but they have known the cause and the reason why. So, in whichever of these

---

[7]Savonarola actually says *l'ombilico de Italia* ('the navel of Italy').

two ways you want to say one can predict something, I have predicted it to you: that all of Italy will be turned upside down, and Rome as well, and then the Church must be renewed. But you do not believe it; and yet you should believe, because it is sooner God that tells you this than me.

Now let us begin with the reasons that I have brought to you in the past several years that show and prove the renewal of the Church. Some reasons are probable and can be contradicted. Other are demonstrative and cannot be contradicted because they are based on holy Scripture. And the ones I will give you are all demonstrative, all based on holy Scripture.

The first reason is *because of the moral corruption of the prelates.* When you see a good head, you say that the body is well; when the head is bad, woe to that body. So, when God allows there to be ambition in the head of a government, lust, and other vices, know that the scourge of God is near. I will prove it to you. Go, read in the [twenty-]fourth chapter of Kings, near the end [where it speaks] of Zedekiah, where it says: *The Lord was angered against Jerusalem* [2 Kings 24:20]. *Also in First Kings*, where it says that God allowed David to sin in order to punish the people.[8] The same can be read in [the story of] Manasseh [2 Kings 21]. So, when you see that God allows the leaders of the Church to exceed in iniquities and simonies, say that the scourge of the people is near. I am not saying that it is in the leaders of the Church, but I am saying 'when you see it.'

The second reason is *because of the disappearance* of righteous and just people. Every time God removes the saints and the righteous, say that the scourge is near. Here is the proof of this: when God wanted to send the flood, he removed Noah and his family. *Similarly* He removed Lot from Sodom when he wanted to burn it. See how many men one can find today that one might call just and righteous; and so say that the scourge is near and that the wrath, with the sword of God, is roused.

---

[8]Savonarola is probably referring to 2 Sam 24 (the chapter immediately preceding 1 Kings), which tells the story of how God, in his anger against the Israelites, incited King David to 'number', that is, to take a census of the population of Israel and Judah. Eventually David saw this 'numbering' as a sin and begged God's forgiveness for it (v. 10); God, in turn, sent a pestilence on Israel to punish it for this sin (v. 15).

The third reason is *because of the exclusion of the just*. When you see that some lord or head of government does not want the righteous and just near him, but chases them off because he does not want the truth told to him, say that the scourge of God is near.

The fourth reason is *because of the wish of the just*. When you see that men of good life wish for and call for the scourge, believe that it will arrive shortly. See whether it seems that today everyone is calling for the scourge; and believe me, Florence, that your punishment would already have come were it not for the prayers and orations of the righteous, believe me that today you would be a garden.

The fifth reason is *because of the stubbornness of sinners*. When sinners are stubborn and do not want to convert to God and do not respect nor appreciate those who call them to the right path, but always go from bad to worse and are stubborn in their vices, say that God is angry. This reason and the two previous are proven by what God did in Jerusalem when He sent there many prophets and holy men in order to convert those people, but they were always stubborn and they chased away the prophets and stoned them, and all righteous people at that time seemed to be calling for a scourge. Similarly, many miracles were shown to Pharaoh, but he always remained stubborn. And so, Florence, await the scourge, for you know how long you have been told to convert and you have always remained stubborn. And you, Rome, Rome! This has been said to you, as well, and still you remain stubborn, and so await the wrath of God.

The sixth reason is *because of the multitude of sinners*. Because of David's pride the plague was sent. See whether Rome is full of pride, lust, avarice, and simony! See whether sins always multiply in her, and so say that the scourge is near and that the renewal of the Church is near.

The seventh reason is *because of the exclusion of the primary virtues, that is, charity and faith*. At the time of the early Church one lived with complete faith and complete charity. See how much of it there is in the world today. You, Florence, you wish to tend only to your ambition and for everyone to praise himself. Know that you have no other remedy but penance, because the scourge of God is near.

The eighth reason is *because of the denial of the believers*. See how today it seems no-one believes nor has faith any longer, and everyone seems to say: 'What does it matter?' When you see this, say that the scourge is near.

The ninth is *because of the decline in divine worship.* Go, see what is done in the churches of God and with how much devotion one lingers there. And so divine worship has declined! You will say: 'Oh, there are more clergy and prelates than ever! If only there were fewer!' Oh, tonsure, tonsure, *this storm has risen because of you!* You are the cause of all this evil! And today anyone with a priest in the house thinks he is blessed. And I tell you the time will come and soon when one will say: blessed be the house with no shaved tonsure in it.

The tenth reason is *because of universal opinion.* See, everyone seems to be preaching and waiting for the scourge and tribulations, and everyone thinks it is right that the punishment of so many iniquities should come. The abbot Giovacchino and many other preach and announce that this scourge will come in our time.[9] These are the reasons why I preached to you the renewal of the Church. Now let us speak about the images [figure] that point to it.

In order to explain the images in Holy Scripture, one must know that Scripture has two meanings: one literal, which is the meaning intended by the person who wrote and composed that letter; the other mystical, and this is intended in three ways: allegorical, tropological, and anagogical.

Let us take the allegorical. Know that in order for a piece of writing to have an allegorical meaning, it must have three things: first, it must have a literal meaning; second, it must be history and not a story [*fabula*]—and therefore poems do not have an allegorical meaning—; third, that it be Holy Scripture: and so, allegorically speaking, we say that the Old Testament meant and represented the New Testament.[10]

9Joachim of Fiore (ca. 1135–1202), biblical exegete, mystic, and seer. Elected abbot of his monastery in Corazzo (1177), Joachim resigned this office in order to lead a more contemplative life. Although his doctrine and prophetic visions were condemned in 1255, Joachim's visions continued to capture the imagination throughout the late Middle Ages and Renaissance. In the early 1300s Dante placed him in Paradise and describes him as 'gifted with the prophetic spirit' (*di spirito profetico dotato; Par.* 12, v. 141).

10With this definition of allegory Savonarola is discounting completely the possibility of an allegorical meaning for non-Scriptural texts, and in particular for the stories of classical mythology.

Also, a cherub was on the ark of the covenant and looked at another cherub: and they represented the Old and the New Testament [Ex 25:19, 37:8; 1 Kings 6:23–26].

Also, a wheel was in a wheel: the two wheels meant the same thing [Ez 1:15–16, 10:10].

Elsewhere it says: *And the word of the Lord came and I saw*.[11] This prayer begins at '*and*' (and this is a habit of prophets, in whom first the Spirit of God begins to speak and then they utter the words, and they join the external words with the internal ones), and then follows and says: *and I saw a man come with a short rope and measure Jerusalem, and then he fell silent* [Ez 40:3, Rev 21:15]. The prophet saw a man, and this prefigures Christ who came to measure Jerusalem, *that is*, the Church and to see how much was the Church's charity, and he measured it with a short rope, *that is*, with the wisdom of God, which measures everything. And after he had measured the width, he remained silent, that is, from the width he could tell the length as well, which must be proportionate to the width. And so he knew how much the charity of the Church was. This charity must be large and long so that it might reach out and extend to its neighbour, as far as its enemy.

And so, when I revealed this prophecy to you, I told you that the Church had two walls: one is the prelates of the Church, the other the secular princes, who also must support the Church. But when God comes to measure the Church, He will not find either of these two walls because one of these two walls has fallen on top of the other so that both of them are in ruins and all the square stones of these walls have broken and are no longer square, that is, they do not have the width of charity and have become rounded, turned to their own interests and gathered unto themselves; and with these stones they have bombarded the city, that is, with their bad example they have also corrupted and ruined the city and the citizens. And so the scourge is near, as it was and as it happened with Jerusalem.

---

[11] *Et factum est verbum Domini et vidi*. This exact passage (which is, in fact, an incomplete sentence that will be completed in the next Latin citation, which picks up and repeats the phrase *et vidi* 'and I saw') is not in the Vulgate. The expression *factum est verbum Domini*, however, appears often in the prophetic books and elsewhere to indicate that God spoke to the prophet. Savonarola is thus claiming a prophetic voice.

The second image I presented to you was the one when it was forbidden in Jerusalem to keep weapons of any type and no smith could fashion any weapon; even the prod to spur the bulls had to be blunted. The smith who is always at the fire represented the fire of charity, which must always burn within us. The beating hammer is continual prayer, which must always beat for God: *Knock and it will be opened to you* [Mt 7:7]. The blunted prod is philosophy, which does not prick as sharply as the study of sacred Scripture. And so King Nabuchadnezzar came and cruelly scourged that people that had no weapons, that is, no charity. This same thing will soon happen to the Church, where no shred of charity is left today.

The third image I presented to you was that of the Apocalypse, where it says that he saw four horses: one white, the other red, the third black, the fourth pale [Rev 6:2–8]. And I told you that the white one meant the time of the apostles; the red the time of the martyrs, which was the second age of the Church, the black one meant the time of the heretics, which was the third age of the Church; the pale one meant the time of the lukewarm, which is today. So I told you that the renewal of the Church had to happen and quickly. And so God will give his vineyard, that is, Rome and the Church, over to be tended by others, because in Rome there is no charity left at all, but only the devil. And let this suffice with respect to images. Now I will tell you about the parables that represent the renewal of the Church.

The first parable is: a citizen has a farm with two fields next to each other, one full of stones and thorns and weeds and of every other unfruitful thing; and that citizen does not plough this field and does not cultivate it. Every year he ploughs and cultivates the other field and looks after it with great care because it looks like fruitful land; nonetheless, the citizen has never gathered any fruit from it. Tell me, what do you think that citizen will do with these two fields? Certainly, if he a prudent, he will take all the stones and thorns in that first field and throw them onto the other field and he will begin to plough and cultivate this field. That citizen is Christ, who has become citizen, that is, a man like you, and He has a field full of stones and thorns, that is, the land of the infidels, full of hardness like stones and heresies like thorns; and He has the land of the Christians, which till now He has cultivated and which has not *yet* produced any fruit at all for him; so He will have the infidels convert and He will sow His law in that land, and this one, which He has cultivated so much, He will abandon and it will remain full of heresies. Therefore, the renewal of the Church will happen and many, who are here at this sermon, will see it.

The second parable: a fig tree was planted and the first year it bore many figs and no leaves; the second year it still bore many figs and some leaves, but very few; the third year it bore as many figs as leaves; the fourth year it bore more leaves than figs; the fifth year it bore very few figs and very many leaves; and, carrying on like this, it came that it produced nothing but leaves so much so that, not only it did not bear fruits, but its leaves hindered the other plants and did not let them grow. What do you think the gardener should do with this fig tree? He will certainly cut it down and throw it on the fire.

This fig tree is the tree of the Church which, although at its beginning bore many fruits and no leaves, has reached the point today of not bearing any fruits at all, but only leaves, that is, ceremonies and display and superfluous things that wear down the other plants in the land, that is, with their bad example the prelates of the Church lead other people into very many sins. The gardener will come, that is, Christ and He will cut this unfruitful tree down: thus the Church will renew itself.

The third parable: a king had an only begotten son; he found a poor woman, torn, muddy; the king, moved to compassion, took her and led her into his house and took her as his legitimate spouse; he had two daughters from her, whom he gave as wives to his only begotten son. After some time, the king's wife began to fall in love and do many wicked things with her courtiers and servants. The king found out; he took her and got rid of her, and sent her back into poverty and into the dirt where she had been before. Then one of his daughters began to sin as her mother had done and much worse; for this reason the king, irate, sent her away and removed her from himself and from his son and commanded that no bread be given to her. The other daughter, not cautioned by the sins and sufferings of her mother and sister, began to sin the same and do much worse than her mother and sister, and much more wickedly than them. Tell me, wise man, what would this woman deserve? She certainly deserves a much greater punishment than her mother and sister.

Now I will explain this parable to you. The king is God, who took that poor woman as his spouse, that is, the synagogue of the Jews as His Church, and it sinned, and you know how God sent her away from Him and back to the mud where she first lay, that is, He put her back into her earlier servitude and misery and blindness. The two daughters are the Eastern Church of the Greeks and the Roman Church, given by God as brides to his Only Begotten Son, Christ Jesus crucified, in which we must soldier under the faith of His Son, Jesus Christ.[12] The Eastern one sinned in its heresies, and so God sent her away from Himself and from His son Jesus Christ, and has commanded that she not be given bread, so no preacher nor anyone else goes there any longer to give it the food of the soul, spiritual food, nor to enlighten it. This other one is the Roman Church, full of simony and iniquity, that has sinned much more than the first and the second. What do you think she deserves, do you not believe that God would want to punish her? You certainly think so, and much more severely than her mother and sister, for they would rightly complain to God saying: 'If we sinned, you had us bear the punishment, but this other one, who has sinned more than us, why do you not punish her?' And so firmly believe that the Church will be renewed and soon.

Having discussed the parables, we will speak of the renewal of the Church as much as we have seen, as much as we know and have predicted it you. And so that you might understand better, you must know that there are two ways of knowing. The first is when, through some external sign, we know what that sign means internally. The second way of knowing is through the imagination.

About the first: when Pope Innocent died,[13] something happened that made you laugh at me, for I had said that the Church had to be renewed; and because of that sign you thought I had made a great mistake and what I had predicted could not come to pass; and I, through that external sign, saw that the Church was going to be *completely* renewed and I was counting on what you were saying against me.

About the second, which is through the imagination, I could see in my imagination a black cross above that Babylon Rome, and on this cross was written '*The Wrath of the Lord,*' and the weather here was calm, tranquil, and clear; therefore, because of this vision, I tell

---

[12]In the original, the phrase "given as brides" is in the feminine plural and clearly refers to both the Eastern and the Roman, that is, Western Church, whereas the phrase "in which we must soldier" is in the feminine singular and clearly refers only to the Roman Church.

[13]Pope Innocent VIII (Giovanni Battista Cybo), b. 1432 in Genoa, elected 29 August 1484, d. 25 July 1492.

you that the church of God is to be renewed and soon, because God is irate: and then the infidels will convert and this will happen soon.

Another vision: I saw a sword above all of Italy and it was quivering, and I saw Angels coming and they had a red cross on one side and a lot of white stoles on the other. And these Angels gave the cross to anyone who wanted to kiss it and so they handed out the white stoles. And there were some who took these white stoles; there were some who did not want them, some others not only did not want them, but they also advised others not to take them and they were able, through their persuasive powers, to see that many did not take them. After this, when these Angels had left, many Angels returned with chalices in their hands, filled to the brim with good sweet wine, but at the bottom there were most bitter dregs. And these Angels offered the chalice to everyone; and those who had gladly taken the stoles gladly drank the wine that was sweet on top, and they savoured it; to the others they gave the most bitter dregs, because they did not have stoles, and these would rather not have them and they twisted and turned, but they had to drink them. I immediately saw that sword that quivered above Italy turn to point down and strike these people with great storm and ruin, and it struck everyone. But those who had taken the white stoles felt this scourge less and drank the sweet wine that was in the chalice. The others were forced to drink the most bitter dregs and, in that scourge, begged the others who had the white stoles and said: 'Give me a little of your stole, so that I might not have to drink these most bitter dregs,' and they were told: 'There is no time for this.' For this reason, I tell you that the renewal will take place and soon.

I will explain it to you. The quivering sword—I do want to tell you, Florence—is that of the king of France, that is showing itself to all of Italy. The Angels with the red cross and the white stoles and the chalice are the preachers that are announcing this scourge to you—and they give you the red cross to kiss, that is, the passion of martyrdom—and are telling you to bear this scourge that has to be for the renewal of the Church. The stole means purifying one's conscience and cleaning it of all vices, so that it be white with purity. The chalice, filled to the brim with good wine means the chalice, the passion, which everyone must drink from; but those who have taken the stoles and cleansed their conscience, they will drink the sweet wine, that is, they will feel little of this scourge, as is represented by the sweet wine at the top of the chalice, that is, they will be the first to be scourged; but it will be sweet, because they will bear it patiently and, if they die, they will go to eternal life. The other will be forced to drink the most bitter dregs, which will seem bitter to them, as they certainly will be. And this sword has not yet turned to point down, but it has shown itself throughout Italy, for God waits for you to do penance. Mend your ways, Florence, for there is no other remedy but penance. Put on the white stole while you still have time and do not wait any longer, for later you will not have time for penance.

Now we will speak about this renewal from the perspective of the intellect, and this is of two types. Earlier I spoke to you about renewal using formal and non-formal words.[14] You must know that I did not dig the formal words out of Scripture nor find them anywhere else, nor have I composed them out of my imagination, nor received them from anyone in heaven or on earth, but from God. I cannot tell you more clearly: hear me, Florence, God says these words. Now then, I tell you that I have said them to you, Florence, hear me well, these are the words: *'Rejoice and be glad, you who are just, nonetheless prepare your hearts against temptation by reading, meditating, and praying, and you will be freed from a second death. You, worthless servants, who lie in filth, lie in it until now: your bellies are full of wine, your loins are dissolved by lust, and your hands are dripping with the blood of the poor; this, then, is your part. But know that your bodies and your souls are in my hands, and in a short time your bodies will be struck by scourges, and I will consign your souls to the eternal fire.'*[15] The other formal words are these: *'Hear, all you who dwell on the earth, the Lord says this: I, the Lord, speak in my holy zeal. Behold the days are coming when I will unsheathe my sword above you. Turn, therefore, towards me before my anger brims over. For then, when the tribulations have come, you will seek peace and you will not find it.*[16]

---

[14]It seems that by formal words Savonarola means 'in Latin' and by non-formal words 'in Italian.' In fact, in the Middle Ages and early Renaissance, Latin was regularly called 'grammar', so by 'formal' Savonarola may well mean 'grammatically' (that is, in Latin) and by 'non-formal' he may mean 'colloquially' (that is, in the vernacular).

[15]As Savonarola says, this passage is not in the Vulgate nor in Patristic literature. Savonarola clearly intends his listeners to believe that these are original words that God is saying directly to him and in Latin.

[16]As was the case with the previous citation, this passage also is not to be

As for the words that are not formal, remember what I said to you three years ago, that a wind will come similar to the one in Elijah's story and that this wind will beat against the mountains. This wind has come and this has been the rumour that has spread this year all over Italy; and it spoke of this king of France, and this rumour flew everywhere like the wind and beat against the mountains, that is, against the princes of Italy, and it has kept them confused about whether to believe or not that this king would come. And, look, he has come. And you used to say: 'He will not come, he has no horses, it is winter' and I used to laugh at you, for I knew what would come to pass. Look, he has come, and God has turned winter into summer, as I told you then. Remember as well that I told you that God would go beyond the mountains and would take him by the bridle and would lead him here, in spite of and contrary to everyone's opinion; and, look, he has come. Remember also that I told you that great fortresses and great walls would be worth nothing; see whether it has all come to pass. Tell me, Florence: where are your fortresses and your strongholds? What good were they to you? Remember also that I told you that your wisdom or your prudence would be worth nothing to you, and that you would understand everything backwards, and that you would not know what to do, or what to take, like a drunken man or someone out of his wits. And now it has come and it has proven to be true and *nonetheless* you never wanted to believe me, and still you do not believe. I speak to you, you stubborn man: you will also not believe the rest, for God will not want to give you so much grace that you might believe, because your stubbornness does not deserve it. Remember those other times, three or four years ago, when I used to preach to you? I had so much strength in my voice, so much passion, so much fury in my speech that people feared a vein would burst in my chest. You did not know why, my son, nothing else could be done.

Remember three years ago, on Lazarus' Sunday,[17] when a lightening bolt fell on the dome, what I told you that morning? That that

___

found in the Bible, though it echoes passages such as Exodus 15:9, Deuteronomy 32:41, and especially Ezekiel 21:3–5.

[17]Lazarus Saturday (not Sunday, as Savonarola says) falls on the Saturday before Palm Sunday and commemorates the raising of Lazarus from the dead (Jh 11:11–44). Savonarola may have said 'Sunday' because his public response

night I could not rest at all and wanted to take that Gospel passage about Lazarus to preach on it, but could never work with it in my mind. And you know that these words came out of my mouth at that time: *Behold the sword of the Lord falling on the earth quickly and swiftly*. And I preached to you that morning and told you that the wrath of God was rising and that the sword was ready and soon; and now I repeat this to you: you really should believe.

Remember how three years ago I began to preach on Genesis and did not know, then, the reason why, but I did all I could in order to renew old things? And when we came to the Flood it was not possible for me to go any further, so abundant was the subject matter. And then I had to go preach away from here. Then, last Lent, I began again with the Flood where I had left it off and I began to do the Ark, thinking to finish it, when suddenly the subject matter became so abundant that I could not finish it that Lent. Having picked it up once again, before I could finish it I was again interrupted because I had to go on your behalf to the king of France; and there were still two sermons left before I could finish it and bring it to a close, and no sooner was it finished, remember, the flood came and that day things here were about to be thrown upside down by the French. I will infer this, that this was the work and a mystery of God and not something ordained or arranged by me; and you certainly should believe it, Florence, and not remain so adamant in your incredulity.

Remember also that I told you that in the past I had been a father to you and that God had been the mother, for I had reproved you sharply and bitterly and shouted at you in a loud voice that you should mend your ways, as a father does who diligently reproves his children; and that now I wanted to be a mother to you and God wants to be the father: just like a mother, when she sees her child err, will threaten him and shout at him and say that she will tell the father as soon as he arrives, and have him punish him; but then, when the father arrives, she does not accuse the child, but says: 'If you should ever again make this mistake I will have your father punish you,' so, too, although I now reprimand you, I do not reprimand you with that force and sharpness as I used to, for I see that the father, that is God, has come to punish you. And so I say

---

to the the bolt of lightning that had fallen that Saturday night would have been made on the following morning (Sunday).

to you and beg you, in a low and humble voice: my children, do penance, do penance.

Remember, as well, Florence, that I told you that I gave you an apple, as a mother does when she gives an apple to her child when he cries in order to calm him down and then, when he still cries and she cannot calm him down, she takes that apple away from him and gives it to another child. I say this to you, Florence: God has given you an apple, that is, He has chosen you for himself; if you do not do penance and convert yourself to God, He will take that apple away from you and give it to someone else; this is as true as I am standing up here. And so, Florence, do these four things I have told you and I promise you that you will be richer than ever, more glorious than ever, more powerful than ever. But today nobody believes that the Angels participate with mankind and converse with them, nor that God speaks to any man. I tell you, *quod similitudo est causa amoris*, that is to say, similarity is the root of friendship. And so, when someone draws near to God and to the Angels through faith and charity, the more he becomes a friend of God and of His Angels: and they speak and converse with him.

I do not mean to say, nor have I ever said it, that this is the reason why God speaks with me; I say neither yes nor no; you are so far from the faith that you do not believe; you would much sooner believe in some demon who would speak with men and predict the future. You are witless and out of the faith. Tell me, if you believe that Christ was incarnated in the Virgin and that He let himself be crucified—what could be more difficult to believe than this—, you should nonetheless believe this, too, which is easier to believe, that is, that Christ speaks with men. *Moreover*, if you are a Christian, you must believe that the Church must be renewed. Daniel says that the Antichrist must come and that he must persecute Christians there, in Jerusalem; therefore, it is necessary that Christians be there, therefore it is necessary that those who are there be baptized. But, in order to do this, there is need for men other than those the Church has today. *Therefore*, the Church must be renewed so that men should become good and should go there to convert the infidels to Christianity. Go, read the Doctors on the Gospel of Matthew, where it says: *This Gospel will be preached in the entire world [Mt 26:13] and then the end will come.*[18] Believe me, Florence! You really ought

---

[18]Savonarola is most probably thinking of Thomas Aquinas; see, for example, Aquinas' *Summa theologiae*, I.ii.106.

to believe me because, until now, I have not seen a single shred of what I told you fail to come to pass, and in the future you will also not see any fail.

Many years ago I predicted to you the death of Lorenzo de' Medici and the death of Pope Innocent. *Also* what has happened now in Florence, the change in government. *Also* I said to you that on the day when the king of France would be in Pisa there would be a renewal of the State here. I did not say these things *in public* from up here, but I said them to those who are here at this sermon, and I have witnesses here in Florence.

I know that this morning I am crazy *and that I speak all these foolish things* [2 Cor 11:21], but I want you to know that this light does not justify me; but, if I am humble and have charity, then I will be justified. And this light has not been given to me for myself, nor because of my merits, but for you, Florence. And so, Florence, this morning I told you these things, so openly, inspired by God to say them to you like this, so that you might know the entire thing, so that you might not have any excuse afterwards when the scourge comes, and so that you might not say: 'I did not know.' I cannot say it more clearly to you and I know that this morning I will be called crazy, for many have come to take notes. If you say I am crazy, I will be patient. I have spoken to you like this because God has wanted me to speak to you thus. From the time I began to preach to you on this Apocalypse we have been greatly opposed; you know some of them, God knows some, and His Angels some.

One must fight *against two-fold wisdom*, that is, against those who have the Old and the New Testament, *against two-fold science, that is*, against philosophy and against astrology and the study of sacred Scripture and *against two-fold malice, that is*, against the evil the lukewarm are doing today, who know that they are doing evil and they want to do it. This was not so at the time of Christ because there was only the Old Testament and, if they went wrong, they thought they were doing good. And so I tell you that, if Christ were to return down here today, He would be crucified once again. I tell you, I have revealed nearly nothing to you because, I tell you, if I were to reveal everything to you I would be here for at least six days. Believe me, I have already been in danger of death many times.

I told you: *Behold the sword of the Lord falling on the earth quickly and swiftly*. Believe me, God's knife will come, and soon. Do not mock this *'quickly,'* and do not say this is a *'quickly'* of the

Apocalypse that takes hundreds of years to arrive.[19] Believe me that it will be soon: to believe does not hurt you at all, in fact it helps you, for it makes you return to penance and makes you walk along the path to God; not to believe can harm you and does not help you; so believe that the time is soon; the moment cannot be told, for God does not want it told, so that His chosen people will always fear and have faith and charity, and will always walk along the path to God. And so I have not told you the predetermined time so that you might always do penance and that you might always be pleasing to God; because, for example, if one told the people: 'The tribulations will arrive ten days from now,' everyone would say: 'I can wait a while longer before I mend my ways,' and it would be like giving them a licence to do wicked things in the meantime, and this would not be helpful. And so God does not want the predetermined time to be preached. But I can very well tell you this, that the time for penance is now; do not mock this *quickly*, for I tell you: if you do not do what I tell you, woe to you, Florence, woe to the people, woe to the simple citizen, woe to the great man!

Lastly, I conclude: I have been crazy this morning, and you will say so, and I knew you would say so even before I climbed up here. God has wanted it this way, and so I tell you, and keep this as the final conclusion, that God has prepared a great banquet for all of Italy; but all the food is bitter, and he has offered only salad, a little bitter lettuce. Understand well, Florence: all the other food has still to come and it is all bitter and a lot, for this is a great banquet; so I conclude for you, and keep it in mind, that Italy is now only at the beginning of its tribulations.

Oh, Italy and princes of Italy and prelates of the Church, the wrath of God is upon you, and you have no remedy whatsoever, expect to mend your ways! *And I will begin at my sanctuary* [Ez 9:6]. Oh, Italy, oh, Florence, *the tribulations are coming upon you because of your sins! Oh, nobles, oh, powerful persons, oh, plebeians, the hand of the Lord is upon you, and power cannot resist it, nor knowledge, nor flight!*[20] And that will not be all, for you do not know how things have been ordained. Oh, princes of Italy, flee

---

[19]Early Christians expected Christ to return very soon, almost immediately (see Rev. 22:20).

[20]The passage is not in the Bible; Savonarola has compiled it by drawing upon phrases from a variety of passages from, among others, Leviticus, 1 Kings, Isaiah, Judges, 1 Samuel, etc.

the land of the North Wind,[21] do penance while the sword is not out of the sheath, and flee from Rome while it is not bloody! Oh, Florentines, flee from Florence, that is, flee for your penance from sin and flee from wicked people.

This is the conclusion. I have told you all these things drawing on human and divine reasons, in modesty, holding back my tongue. I have begged you; I cannot command you because I am not your lord, but your father; it is up to you, Florence; I pray God for you, that He might enlighten you, *to whom be the glory and the power for ever and ever* [Rev 1:6]. *Amen.*

---

[21] Savonarola is alluding to Ezekiel 1:4: 'I saw a storm wind coming from the north'.

On Ruth and Micah

On the Books of Ruth and Micah
Sermon No. 28
2 Nov. 1496

Sermons of the Reverend Father Friar Girolamo from Ferrara delivered on feast days in the year 1496 after Lent was finished and after he had rested for about a month. He began on the day of St Michael, 8 May 1496.

'On the Art of Dying Well'

A sermon on the art of dying well delivered by the Reverend Father Fra Girolamo from Ferrara on 2 November 1496 and recorded by Ser Lorenzo Violi from the spoken words of the aforementioned Father while he was preaching.[1]

In all you do, remember the end of your life and then you will never sin [Ecclesiasticus 7:40(36)]

It is not difficult, my most beloved in Christ Jesus, to prove to someone that he has to die because, with no need for any other proof, daily experience demonstrates it. But it is definitely difficult to lead someone to the realization of death and to induce him always to think about death. And the reason for this is that every desire follows a cognition, but not always its own cognition, for natural desire follows the extrinsic cognition of He that rules Nature; as is the case with the natural desire of stones, which seek to go to the centre [of the earth] following not their own cognition, because they have no cognition, but the cognition of the One who

---

[1] I take this paragraph from the 1496 edition; the National Edition does not have it.

has given them that desire.[2] And so it is with all other things in Nature, but we will not speak now about this type of cognition and this type of desire because it is not our intention. Animal, or rational desire, instead, follows sensory or intellectual cognition, intrinsic to animals or to men.

It therefore happens, sometimes, that the cognitive power presents something to the desire under the guise of so much pleasure that the desire follows it with great passion; and, at times, it is so attracted by it that it becomes fixated on it and does not know, *so to speak*, how to draw back. For example, someone sees a woman over there, and beginning to think about her his desire draws him so strongly that it makes him, *so to speak*, fixated on that thing, so that all his thoughts and all his thinking are then aimed to that end. It happens in the same way when one becomes enamoured of God because of the cognition one has of Him, that love so binds him that it draws him completely to God; and all his thinking is directed to Him and his thoughts are firmly set in pleasing only his Creator. By the way, I say that even though animal and rational desire follows its own cognition, nonetheless, once it has experienced its passion, it holds firmly to that first consideration that was the cause of his love and then it draws along all the other cognitions and considerations and makes one nearly unable to think about anything else but the thing he loves. Therefore, since the desire for existence is most natural, and because man loves existence more than anything else, so this desire for existence has such a pull on man that it fixates him in this thought, to the point that he arranges all his thoughts and nearly all his works towards this desire for existence and does everything in order to sustain it. And so, just as a lover does not think of separating himself from his beloved and even if he had to think of it he would have great difficulty in doing so, so it is very difficult for men to separate themselves from thinking about and looking after life's needs, and to think [instead]

---

[2]Savonarola follows contemporary science that believes all matter in the sublunar world to be constituted of four basic elements: fire, air, water, and earth. Each element naturally seeks or gravitates to its own place, or 'sphere' within a universe made up of concentric spheres: fire to the highest sublunar sphere and earth to the lowest. Stones, therefore, naturally gravitate (fall) towards the centre of the earth. From the sphere of the moon up, matter is made up of the 'quintessential element' (from *quinta essentia*, or fifth essence), unknown in the sublunar world.

about death. And as these Logicians say, *Sicut se habet oppositum in opposito, ita se habet propositum in proposito*, that is, just as man loves life passionately, so he passionately hates death and flees as much as he can anything that might be contrary to his existence or to his life. And so he flees thinking about death as if it were something inimical which he dislikes very much, and even the thought of it is hateful to him. Therefore it is very difficult to draw man back and make him think of death and to deter him from that most natural thinking about life and from his desire for existence, which is very pleasing to him, while the thought of death is detestable to him. And so, as easily as man gives himself over to thinking about life, it is just as difficult to draw him back to thinking about death; because, as we said, *sicut se habet oppositum in opposito, ita se habet propositum in proposito.* This difficulty is also caused by the senses, to whose pleasures we are very much given, and sensual cognition leads man to think of nothing else but current and pleasurable things. It is also caused by concern and care for human matters so that men, being quite occupied in them, are unable to think of death.

This morning, therefore, since we wish to speak of the art of dying well and, as I told you yesterday morning, to give you a little dried meat,[3] we do not want to wear ourselves out trying to prove that man must die, for this would be superfluous and you would say: 'Father, this is a waste of time; we know we must die,' and so I want to leave this aside and to try to convince you to have always this knowledge fixed in your mind, that one must die; and we will demonstrate that, in thinking about his death, one reaps great fruit and that certainly, if one constantly thought about this, one would be blessed. All saintly men of the past have thought about their death, and this has allowed them to live in this world with great righteousness, so much so that now they are in Paradise and in bliss. So, it is very useful for man to think of death, for in the Christian religion the beginning and the middle are of no use

---

[3]In Sermon 27, delivered the previous day (1 Nov. 1496), Savonarola had used a recurring image of a bowl of salad filled with a variety of greens; near the end of the sermon he had promised his audience that the following day (2 Nov.) he would provide them with some 'dried meat,' that is, with a sermon on the art of dying. See Savonarola, *Prediche sopra Ruth e Michea*, vol. 2, p. 351.

without the end. So one must always think about making a good end, and this is done by thinking always about death. And that is why the Sage in the book of Ecclesiastes makes the statement we have taken as our theme: *In omnibus operibus tuis memorare novissima tua, et in aeternum non peccabis* [Ecclesiasticus 7:40(36)] that is, 'in all your works, man, remember your last days, *that is,* your last things. Remember, man, that you must die; and, when you always remember this, *in aeternum non peccabis, that is,* 'you will not commit any sin.'[4] Well then, my beloved, we will speak of death and we will give everyone the remedy for dying well. And first we will talk of those who are healthy, who must always think that at any time they can fall ill and die. Then we will speak of those who have already begun to fall ill, how they must think of their death. Third, we will speak of those who are burdened by illness and confined to their beds, nearly at their end, what *also* they must do. Well then, may God grant us the grace to speak of this death in such a way that it might stick well in your mind and that you might reap the fruit of this preaching.

If I were to say, people, that I want to prove to you through reason, authority, and example that one must die, you would say that this is a foolish thing. So, it also seems a foolish thing to me that one, knowing he must die, should not want to think of his death but should seem to devote all his efforts in trying to stay on this earth and in building beautiful palaces and in gathering a lot of stuff and growing rich. It seems man has placed all his thoughts in this, and is not thinking of his death and the other life, as if there were nothing on the other side. Oh, what foolishness this is, not to think of anything but of the here and now. You do not foresee that you have to die no matter what and that you must leave everything on this side: I say, whether you want to or not, you do not know the time nor the way you must die. In *Proverbs*, chapter thirty, Solomon says that some animals are wiser than man: *Quattuor, inquit, sunt minima terrae, et ipsa sunt sapientiora sapientibus: formica, populus infirmus, quae praeparat in messe cibum suum; lepusculus, plebs invalida, qui collocat in petra cubile suum; regem locusta non habet, et egreditur universa per turmas suas; stellio nititur manibus et moratur in aedibus regum* [Prov 30:24–28], 'four animals are wiser than wise men, and first the ant,

---

[4]Savonarola does not render the *in aeternum* into Italian.

a race with no strength, which gathers in the summer for winter; the second is the rock rabbit, which makes its nest on stone so that it be more secure; the third is the locust, that is the cricket, which has no king whatsoever, but always hops around here and there in order squadron by squadron; the fourth is the lizard, that is the gecko, which walks on its hands and always resides in the houses of kings.' These four things, Solomon says, are wiser than wise men.

We deem that person who arranges all his things well towards his goal to be wise, *for the wise man directs.*[5] But note that there are several goals. Some are specific. That is, the goal of a builder is the shape of the house, and so he arranges all the aspects of the building to that end. Similarly the goal of the captain of an army is victory and he arranges his entire army to that end: and so are the goals of other specific things. But philosophers say that people who arrange their things to these purposes are deemed wise *according to something, and not naturally,*[6] that is, they are deemed wise in that one thing and not in the absolute. But we deem wise in the absolute that person who thinks about the final goal of man and of human life and arranges everything well and all his life towards it. The final goal of man is God and that person who considers this goal carefully is truly wise. But these wise men of the world who do not consider carefully this final goal cannot be called truly wise. But you will sooner find that the ant, which Solomon says is a race with no strength, is wiser than they are. For me the ant represents good little women who belong to the weak and fragile sex, but are devout and have arranged their life all towards God, and, with their good works, are always gathering merit with God to enjoy in the next life. These little women, then, represented by the ants, are wiser than wise merchants who travel throughout the land and all over the seas in order to gather wealth, which they know they will nevertheless lose, that is, they will leave it behind here on earth. But the simple little woman who has turned all her mind to God gathers treasure here on earth that she will then enjoy in Heaven where it will never dissipate. The rock rabbit

---

[5]'for the wise man directs, and is not directed' is a statement repeated several times by Thomas Aquinas; see his *Summa*, I^a, Q. 1, art. 6; II, Q. 2, art. 2. Aquinas draws the idea from Aristotle, *Metaphysics* 1.

[6]Savonarola is using two technical philosophical terms, *secundum quid* ('according to something') and *simpliciter* ('naturally, simply').

is also wiser than the wise. For me the hare represents certain good men, quite simple, completely dedicated to God, who always think about their death and make their bed on stone, that is, they have set their goal and their peace in Christ: *and the Rock was Christ* [1 Cor 10:4]. These men always think about their death and so they stand firm in Christ so that He might save them after their death. These rock rabbits are wiser than princes and great teachers and great prelates who have not built their nest on stone, but struggle to maintain their position, which in any case they will lose. The locust, that is, the cricket is also wiser than the wise. For me crickets represent certain good farmers, like those one often finds, who are like a cricket which has no king; these good farmers also have no-one to govern them or to teach them; they do not have many sermons, nor many laws, nor much learning, as we have, but once they have set their life and arranged it towards God, they keep God's commandments simply and without so much learning and they go about hopping and rising from the ground as much as they can in an ordered way, and they remain united in charity, always thinking about their death. These men are wiser than wise theologians, philosophers, law makers, orators and poets who spend their time thinking up arguments and subtleties and sophistries and do not think of God or of their death. The lizard, that is, the gecko, is also, as Solomon says, wiser than the wise; he says she walks on her hands and dwells in the houses of kings. For me this lizard represents certain thick-headed men who have no wits, but have good works; they do not know how to inquire into things, but they know how to do good works; and so he says that they walk on their hands, as if to say: 'It does not fly, but goes on and nonetheless it rises high'; thus these people do so many good deeds that they often rise to high contemplation, for they are of a certain simple goodness that is worth more than the learning of these wise men. These people, I say, live in the houses of kings, *that is*, because of their simplicity they live with the blessed, all of whom are kings and dwell with the first King, *that is*, with God. So, if you want to live righteously, note this: learn to be wise from the ant, from the rock rabbit, from the cricket, and from the gecko and think about your death and what will happen after your death. And if you learn from them, you will live righteously and you will be wiser than these wise men. But let me rest a while and I will show you how true wisdom is to think about death.

St. Jerome says that Plato used to say: *Vera philosophia est meditatio mortis,* that is, 'true philosophy is to think about death.'[7] Philosophy means love of wisdom. True wisdom, therefore, is to think about death; and that person who always thinks that he must die and that the purpose of human life is not in the here and now is considered truly wise. And so he arranges his affairs in such a way that, should death arrive any time, he is always ready to die well, so as to arrive at that final end ordained by God. Therefore, this statement of Plato's, that is, that true philosophy and true wisdom is to think about death, was well said. But we Christians understand it better than he did.

Come a little forward. Sometimes you have doubts about the faith. If you were to think and meditate often within yourself about your death, you would have no doubts about the faith, but would confirm yourself in it. Set, therefore, this first rule for yourself. Think, sometimes, within yourself about your death and say: 'No matter what, I will die.' And look, sometimes, at your flesh and at your hands and say: 'These hands and this flesh will become dust and ashes; soon they will all rot away; so-and-so died: that great teacher, that youth, that rich man, that handsome man, that strong man. A short time ago they were alive, now they are dead: they have all rotted away to ashes. Perhaps I, too, will soon die and in a breath all things of this life will be gone.'

Then think more profoundly and enter a little more deeply into this thinking about death and say: 'What happens after this death of ours? Where does one go after death? One cannot see him. What can we say happens to him? Man is, nonetheless, the noblest creature on earth. What is the purpose of mankind? 'The contemplation of God,' said the philosophers.' Yet, think about this and say: 'If the purpose of mankind is to contemplate God, the purpose of all things is where each thing is happy and at peace. We see that in this world mankind is not at peace, but is always tormented by various passions. So, it appears that the purpose of mankind is not to be found on this side [of life].' This is what Aristotle thought and he strove hard to prove his point, for he could not understand whether the contemplation of God was the purpose of mankind in

---

[7]Jerome, Letter 60, 'To Heliodorus,' par. 14. See also Isidore of Seville, *Etymologiarum,* Bk. 2, chapt. 24; Hugh of St Victor, *Didascalion,* Bk. 23, chapt. 1 (752A); etc.

this life or in the next. But you, Christians, if you want to prove this point, you will say this: 'God rules the world and looks after each and every thing, no matter how small, so he takes a more special care of mankind than of any other thing in the world because mankind is a noble creature; and if this is so, since God is just, he must reward good people well. But we see that in this world good people are always tormented and always have problems: so, the purpose of mankind is not in this world.' And so you will admit that God, who is a just and wise provider, has prepared another life on the other side. To whom, then, will that peace on the other side be given? You will surely say: to good people. But, there is no better person in the world than a true Christian, because a Christian life is the best life imaginable. So you will say that a true Christian who follows our faith will have that blessed life that God has prepared for his beloved on the other side; and in so thinking you will reconfirm that our Faith is true because, if our faith were not true, it follows that no other faith could be true and that man is the most unhappy creature in the world; but since our Faith is true, you will consider that Hell and Paradise are also true; and that if you go to Hell you will not stay there a hundred years, or a thousand, not a hundred thousand, not a hundred million, but for ever and in eternity.

The Philosopher was not certain of this, that Hell existed and that evil people went to it, yet he said: *Terribilissimum autem mors, terminus enim est, et post mortem nescit homo utrum bene vel male habeat,*[8] 'death, he said, is by its nature a most terrible thing because it is the end of life, which we love so much, but worse still if we add that we do not know what we will receive after death, good or bad.' But we, with the light of our Faith, know and are certain of this, that if one dies without the grace of God, one will go immediately to Hell. You could die today and not know whether or not you are in the grace of God, *for no-one knows whether he is worthy of love or of hatred*; and so, man, think of your death and order your life well and seek always to be in God's grace so that you should not fail at that moment. Oh, you, the devil plays chess with you and seeks to catch you and checkmate you at that moment, so be prepared, think hard about that moment because, if you win then, you win everything, but if you lose then, you have

---

[8]Aristotle, *Nicomachean Ethics*, III, 9 (115a 24–27).

gained nothing. Keep your eyes, then, on this checkmate, always think of your death because, if you should not find yourself ready at that moment, you will lose everything you gained in this life. And so, see how much care you must take at that moment. Now let me rest.

Oh, this is great madness, not to think of one's death and not to say: 'If I do not win at this point, I have gained nothing, I have lost everything.' Oh merchant, if you were expecting a verdict that could, in one moment, make you lose everything you own, you would have no peace, day or night, you would turn the world upside down in order to take care of that moment. And so, man, think of your death, of where your soul, which is worth more than anything else in the world, will go.

Now then, I remember that on another occasion when I was giving you a similar sermon, I told you that, if you wanted to prepare yourself well for your death you should have three pictures painted for yourself. In the first you should have Heaven painted above and Hell below, and you should keep it in your bedroom in a place where it would often be in front of your eyes, but not so often that you would become so accustomed to seeing it that it would no longer affect you. And I told you that you should always think and say: 'Perhaps today I will die,' and that you should look carefully at this image, and [consider] that death is always in front of you ready to take you from this life and is saying: 'You will die regardless and you cannot escape from my grip; look, where do you want to go, up here to Heaven or down here to Hell?' [fig. 7] All saintly men and women have thought like this about death and, whatever they do, in all their thoughts they always come back to their death. Therefore, have this first picture painted for yourself, for it will help you greatly to think of your death. Now hear some remedies and rules I wish to give you before we move on to the second picture.

In omnibus operibus tuis memorare novissima tua, et in aeternum non peccabis, 'always remember that you will die and you will not sin.' Every sin of mankind comes either from ignorance or from carelessness, for there is no sin that is not committed willingly, and the will does not err unless the intellect errs. The intellect errs either from ignorance or from carelessness. The error of will occurs, therefore, because the intellect has also been deceived because either it does not know or it does not think about what it does. You will say that there are also certain sins committed either because of

Figure 7. 'Death flying over the corpses of men and women.' Woodcut from G. Savonarola, *Predica dell'arte del ben morire*. Florence: Bartolomeo de' Libri, after 2 Nov. 1496, title page; rpt Berlin, 1926.

malice or because of weakness that do not derive from ignorance or carelessness. I answer you that, although it is true that some sins might be committed because of malice or weakness, *nonetheless*, know that they can all be attributed to ignorance or to carelessness, for malice and weakness make one either not understand what one does or not think about it. Take, for example, women who swear on their Faith something that is not true. In his *Secunda Secundae*, St. Thomas says that such swearing is a mortal sin if the woman knows that she is swearing and she swears to a lie.[9] 'Oh,' that woman will say, 'I did not know.' You see, therefore, this sin comes

---

[9] I have been unable to locate the reference.

from ignorance. The man who commits fornication knowing that it is a sin sins not from ignorance, but from carelessness, for pleasure makes him not think about it while he is committing that act; for, if he were to think hard that that was evil, he would not commit that sin; for, as St. Dionysius says, *Nemo respiciens ad malum operatur*, that is, 'no-one who looks upon evil as evil, can do it.'[10] And so, when you are tempted by sin, if you were to think hard that it is a sin and that what you are doing is contrary to God's commandment, you would certainly not sin. This would also happen if you were always to think of your death; you would refrain greatly from sins because there are two things that lead one to carry out every good deed: love and fear, and these two spurs are the masters that teach every skill.

Look at the woman who learns how to tend her child as soon as she has borne him, [she is] taught by nothing else but by love. The swallow learns to build its nest and tend to its young spurred only by love of its young. Love, therefore, is the master who teaches how to do things. Therefore, if you were to love eternal life, you would force yourself to find a way to acquire it, and you would not sin.[11]

The second thing is fear. Look at the little rabbit: when a dog chases it, it flees and in fleeing it makes sudden turns in order to break its enemy's stride so as not to be caught. It learns this from nothing else but its fear and its fear of the dog. So, if you were to think of Hell as your enemy, you would not sin as you do, but you would endeavour to flee it, and when tempted to do evil, you would say: 'Do I want, for the sake of a little pleasure, for a little honour, for a little wealth, which are all transitory things, to lose Heaven where there is eternal joy, and go to Hell, where there is constant pain?' Therefore, whoever were to think hard about his death would also think hard of Heaven and Hell and of the love of God and fear would enter into your heart and these [thoughts] would lead you to do good and flee evil.[12] This, therefore, is the reasoning behind that saying of the Sage: *In all your works, remember that you will die, and you will never sin.* And, on the other hand, carelessness about

---

[10]I have been unable to locate the reference.

[11]In order to make sense of this passage, I have corrected *tenere vita* (have/lead a life) into *tenere via* (keep a path/stay on a road).

[12]The change in the subject, from the impersonal 'whoever' to the personal 'you' is in the original; Savonarola is clearly moving his discourse from the generic to the specific and engaging his audience directly.

your death is the reason why you commit many sins. So, thinking about it makes one not sin either from ignorance or from carelessness because, as we have said, it generates fear and love in the heart, and these are teachers of everything. So, when one loves God and fears, one quickly learns one's way so as not to sin from ignorance. It also makes one think constantly about the other life, for which one refrains from sinning. And so, my son, when you are tempted, think then and say: 'If I were now at the point of death, would I not want to have done all the good deeds the saints did? Surely I would, and so I do not want to commit this sin, but think that I must die; and that, if I have done good, I will go to Heaven, where the saints have gone, and if I have done evil, I will go to Hell, where all evil people are punished.' Do this, then, my son, and think of your death, and you will send every temptation away. Now then, let me rest a little, for I will teach you how, little by little, you can enter into this thinking about death and so flee all sins.

Do you wish to learn, my son, this true wisdom that the wise men of the world do not wish to know? Ask God often to enlighten you, and pray that He might imbue your mind with His light, and that He might keep you firm in thinking of the other life. Mark this, I have told you that sin derives from ignorance and from carelessness. Therefore, the person in whom there is no ignorance or carelessness cannot err; this quality pertains only to the divine intellect in which, by its very nature, there is no ignorance nor any carelessness whatsoever, for God is infinite and highest wisdom; and when an intellect draws closer to, and resembles God more closely, it becomes that much more perfect, and fewer errors can be in it, for when an effect draws closer to its cause, it becomes that much more perfect. Therefore, since God is the first cause of all things, the closer one draws to God, the more one becomes better and more perfect. The blessed, therefore, and the angels can no longer sin either from ignorance or from carelessness because they are very close to God and confirmed in His grace by the light of glory, and they are very similar to God. The soul of Christ, *also*, before it suffered on the Cross, could not sin from ignorance or from carelessness because it was united with the divine essence, which it always saw. Similarly, the Virgin could not sin, not because she saw the divine essence in this life, as the soul of Christ saw it, or how the blessed see it now in the heavenly homeland, but because of the great abundance of the Holy Spirit that filled her, and thus she was confirmed so that she could not sin. The Apostles, however, could very well sin venially, for they did not have as much fullness of grace and of the Holy Spirit, and they were not as confirmed as the Virgin. See that St. Paul reprimanded St. Peter when living and eating with the Gentiles *even* the food forbidden to the Jews, *though* in front of the Jews he acted as a Jew. Therefore Saint Paul said to him: *If you, though a Jew, live like a Gentile, how can you compel the Gentiles to live like Jews?* [Gal 2:14] And then he added: *Reprehendi eum, quia reprehensibilis erat*, that is, 'I reprimanded him because he deserved to be reprimanded.' [Gal 2:11] Thus the Apostles, even though they had great abundance of grace of the Holy Spirit, they could *nonetheless* err and sin venially from carelessness; and so other people, who are inferior to the Apostles, can sin that much more.

Now, therefore, think how someone who is without the light of the grace of God can be if he is left in the state of nature. Think, how do you think he might be and how might he live without sin. I tell you that in order to refrain from sin one must have the grace of God, and one cannot refrain from it without it and without the light of faith; and so those who want to live righteously and refrain from sinning must first ask God for enlightenment. Follow, then, this first rule: pray every day and ask God for His light, and that He enlighten you to do His will, and that with this light He keep the thought of your death and of the other life, that is, of Heaven and of Hell, fixed in your mind because, I tell you, one cannot live righteously without this light. And it would be very appropriate for you to recite that Psalm: *Usquequo, Domine, oblivisceris mei?* [Ps 12(13):1] That is, turn to the Lord and say to Him: 'Oh Lord, how long until you will remember me?' For that is when we say that God has forgotten us, when He does not grant us His light. Recite this psalm, then, and at the end conclude with David: *Illumina oculos meos, ne unquam obdormiam in mortem; nequando dicat inimicus meus: Praevalui adversus eum*, 'Oh Lord, grant me your light so that I might not sin.' [Ps 12(13):4] Surely it would be very appropriate for you to recite this psalm often and to pray God to shed His light on you, and this is a gift that God bestows on His beloved; ask Him to keep with this light your intellect firmly fixed when thinking about death. This is the first rule and the first remedy I wish to give you; let us now go to the second.

The second remedy is to want to abstain from sin; have a pair of eyeglasses made for you called the eyeglasses of death; I spoke about them to you on other occasions, and I will say something about them again this morning. These philosophers say: *Oportet intelligentem phantasmata speculari*, that is, 'anyone who wants to understand something must create figments in his imagination,' and these figments are the eyeglasses of the intellect. Someone who uses eyeglasses to read keeps his book open in front of him and his eyeglasses between his eyes and his book, and a light by whose power the species, that is the appearance of the letters, come to the eyeglasses and from the eyeglasses to the eyes. Our intellect understands in the same way. First, the intellect that understands, which philosophers call the 'potential intellect,' is like the eyes; and the intellect which they call 'agent' is like the light; the things we can perceive with our senses are like letters in a book; the figments that are between these things and the potential intellect are like the eyeglasses. So, then, if you were to put on red eyeglasses the entire book would appear red to you, and if they were green the book would appear green, and so with other colours. *Similarly*, our intellect is often deceived by our imagination and moved in an amazing way because our understanding must inquire into the figments. That is to say, you have a pair of eyeglasses here and you want to read, so you fix your eyes on the letters and not on the eyeglasses, *even though* you need to look into the eyeglasses if you want to see the letters and understand them. So, if you have good eyeglasses your intellect will always see well and, *on the other hand*, if you have bad ones [you will see badly]. Take a pair of yellow eyeglasses, everything will seem yellow to you, if you have red eyeglasses, everything will seem red to you. The yellow eyeglasses are the figments of envy, or possibly of avarice; the red ones of wrath, because the passions of our spirit form figments inside according to those passions, because *qualis unusquisque est, talia et sibi videntur, that is,* 'whatever disposition one has, so *also* things will appear to him.' Red eyeglasses, therefore, mean wrath and vengeance. Take for example someone who is mad, full of wrath and hatred, his eyeglasses and figments will resemble wrath and hatred, and it will seem right to him to seek vengeance because he sees everything full of wrath and hatred; but take away that wrath and hatred, and you will immediately say:[13] 'I no longer want vengeance,' because the evil eyeglasses will have been removed. Note, therefore, that the imagination, firmly fixed, moves a person powerfully wherever it

---

[13]The switch from 'he' to 'you' is in the original.

wants; and if the imagination is full of good, it draws a person towards the good; if it is full of evil, it draws him towards evil: because the imagination moves a person *even* against reason. That is to say, if you go stand on a wooden beam placed high up and imagine that you will fall, you will immediately fall; if you fantasize about sensual things, you will immediately burn with evil [intentions]. So, if you want to do good and avoid sin, imagine firmly your death. These are the eyeglasses I tell you about: see to it that death is ever imprinted on your imagination and remember your death in everything you do; and in the morning when you get up, first of all make the sign of the cross; then put on the eyeglasses of death, that is, say: *Memento homo quia cinis es et in cinerem reverteris*, 'remember, man, that you are dust and ashes and unto ashes you must return.' Then turn yourself to the Lord and say 'Oh Lord, I have offended you and I have committed many sins, forgive me, I am perhaps near my death, grant me the grace not to offend you again.'

Put on, my son, these eyeglasses of your death and you will see that they will help you greatly in your life. You need to go to the council, when you are there see that you advise rightly and put on the eyeglasses of your death and say: 'I must say what is true because I will die and I will have to account for this and suffer punishment for what I have not advised rightly.' You who want to hoard possessions and become wealthy and draw up bad contracts, remember that you will die, put on these eyeglasses and say: 'I will render account for this later in Hell, and all the possessions of the world will not release me then from it.' You who chase ambition and honours, remember that you must die, put on the eyeglasses of your death and consider how, if you go to Hell, all the honours of the world will not release you from it. Woman, if you should take a fancy to go about finely dressed and to follow fashion, put on these eyeglasses of your death and do not seek, for the sake of your fashions, to fall into eternal damnation. Young boy, when you are spurred towards sin, put on the eyeglasses of your death, remember that you must die, and give yourself wholly to the service of Christ with a pure heart and a pure body. Priest and religious,[14]

---

[14]Savonarola is distinguishing between secular and religious clergy. Religious or 'regular' clergy are those who are members of an order (such as Dominicans, Franciscans, Benedictines, etc.) and therefore follow a rule (Lat., *regula*);

when you are tempted in any way, put on these eyeglasses of your death and you will find them very useful against every temptation. This is the second remedy and the second rule I give you this morning: that you always wear these eyeglasses of your death, that is, that you have this constant thought in your mind that you may, at any moment, die. These eyeglasses, my son, will let you see how short life is and how much care you must take in order to be always ready for death. Fashion for yourself, then, these eyeglasses with which, if you are always ready with them and you consider how at any moment you may die, you will order your life well and you will escape many sins. Now listen, for I will give you yet another rule to keep you better in this thinking about your death.

You have understood this role of the eyeglasses of your death; but since eyeglasses often fall off, one must give them a cap or a hook to attach them so that they do not fall off. The hook for attaching these eyeglasses, then, is something tangible that reminds you of your death because imagination comes from the senses and they are stimulated by things that are perceptible. Because of this, philosophers say: *Imagination is a movement resulting from the senses.*[15] Therefore, because one must make a firm habit of thinking about death, if you develop this habit in yourself, it will keep you firmly in this thought. All holy men and holy women had this habit and custom of thinking about their death and in everything they did they always had recourse to it. When holy men see themselves being honoured, they have recourse to the eyeglasses of their death and say: 'I am dust and ashes, I will die'[16] and they do not want to linger on any thoughts of this world. Similarly, when they are persecuted and suffer tribulations, they have recourse to the eyeglasses of their death and they say: 'We have to die, these ordeals will soon pass and we will go to Heaven' and in this way they never let the eyeglasses of their death slip off. Therefore, to develop this habit whereby you do not let these eyeglasses slip off,

---

secular clergy, instead, are not members of an order but are attached to a diocese and live 'in the world' (Lat., *saeculum*).

[15]Aristotle, *On the Soul*, III, 3 'Imagination is a movement resulting from an actual exercise of a power of sense.' See also: Boethius, *On the Highest Good*; Thomas Aquinas, *Summa Theologica*, Pars 1, Q. XII; etc.

[16]The phrase recalls the Ash Wednesday admonition to the faithful as ashes are smeared on their forehead: 'Remember that you are dust and unto dust you will return.'

you must help them with something tangible. So, follow this rule: go often to see the burial of the deceased, go often to interments, watch often those who are dying; if you know that some relative or friend of yours or some other person is dying, take pleasure in watching him die and then in going to see him interred, and linger on the thought of what man is, and consider what a transitory thing man is: and you will greatly keep yourself from sin.

And if you are also very weak, you should have a figure of death painted in your house, [fig. 8] and *also* carry a small figure of death made of bone in your hand and you should look at it often; and when you feel yourself tempted by ambition, you should have recourse to [this] death and say: 'How crazy can I be? Where are so many lords and so many great men who chose to give themselves over to ambition and sought honour and position? They are all dead, they are dust and ashes, they are all rot,' and so leave ambition aside, focus on living righteously, return your evil gains. And the same is true for temptations of greed and of the flesh and of other iniquities. And if you do this, you will certainly begin to think that you want to die well and you will seek the advice of someone who knows; and he will immediately say this to you: 'Since you do not know when you will die, do not spend any more time doing penance, but go quickly and confess and say: I want to confess today and not tomorrow, because tomorrow I may die.' Follow the example of the saint whose mind would say to him 'Tomorrow, then, you will do good deeds,' or 'Tomorrow you will start' and he would answer 'Let's do them today, not tomorrow, for tomorrow we may not be alive.' *In the same way*, make your will, put your affairs in order and arrange everything as if you were to die tomorrow, so that, any time the Lord might call you you may say: *Ecce me, Domine*, 'Here I am, Lord,' I am ready for death.

My son, do like the courier who arrives at the inn and, without taking off his spurs or anything else, eats a bite and thinks it has been a thousand years since he was on his horse and says, 'Come on, come on, quickly, let's go.' In the same way, set your mind on the thought that you must not linger here, but pass on and go to the other side and that every hour might be your last. And if there should come a war, a plague, or a famine, do not be afraid, but say: 'No matter what, I must die.' And if your imagination tells you that it is a hard thing to die by the sword, or from the plague, or of hunger, answer: 'I must die once of the sickness of death, let it be whichever death it wants.' Certainly, to die of side pains or of

Figure 8. 'O qua su, o qua giu.' Death shows heaven and hell to a young man. Woodcut from G. Savonarola, *Predica dell'e te del ben morire*. Florence: Bartolomeo de' Libri, after 2 Nov. 14 6, sig. a6v; rpt Berlin, 1926.

other ills is *also* to die of the sickness of death: we must pass once though this sickness. Note that the psalm reads: *Pretiosa in conspectu Domini mors sanctorum eius* [Ps 115(116):15] and in another place *Mors peccatorum pessima*, the death of saints is precious, and that of sinners is very bad [Ps 33:22].[17] Do not, therefore, fear the manner of your death, but what follows after the death of evil persons. Consider how the saints have been sawn [in two], shot with arrows, stoned: they have been killed in various ways and with great suffering. But many sinners have died in their beds and have gone to the house of the devil, while the saints have gone to Heaven. And so prepare yourself for death and do not fear the manner of your death for, as Saint Augustine says, *Mala mors putanda non est, quam bona vita praecesserit: Non enim facit malam mortem nisi quod sequitur mortem*,[18] 'one should not think death is bad when it is preceded by a good life, because death is rendered bad only by that which follows death,' that is, by the torment of Hell. And so, if war should come, do not be afraid, but say: 'Let whatever death come, I am ready; for the death that is preceded by a good life is not a bad death.' And this thought is good medicine against the tribulations of war. But if you want a good remedy against the plague, make some saint, or actually your angel, your familiar, and pray to him daily; for I promise you that if you make some saint or your angel your familiar, if in time of plague you are abandoned by people, you will not be abandoned by them; but they will come *even* visibly, if it is necessary, to govern you and to look after you. In time of famine, *as well*, you poor little wretch, with nothing to live on, do as I tell you: help yourself, first, with whatever you can, and confess, and take communion and live righteously; and if you have any surplus, sell it in order to buy foodstuff and help yourself in this way as much as you can; and then, also, even when you are reduced to dire need, do not be ashamed to go to your friend, to your neighbour, to your relative, and say: 'I need such and such; help me,' because if you should not want to do it, this would be an act of pride and you would not deserve God's help. But if you do this and you are also in extreme

---

[17]The RSV translates these words quite differently from their literal meaning and from Savonarola's rendition, saying instead 'Evil shall slay the wicked' Ps 34:21.

[18]St Augustine, *The City of God*, Bk. 1, ch. xi.

need, do as I say, have recourse to God, and say to him: 'My Lord, you have said: *Seek first the kingdom of God and his righteousness, and all things shall be yours as well* [Mt 6:33]. I have done all I should have done, I can do nothing else, I have nothing left to live on, help me, Lord.' If you do this, do not doubt, have faith in God's help and He will provide for you in every way; I say in every way, because He has said it, and He cannot contradict himself. These are the remedies I wanted to give you this morning in order to teach you how to die well. They all pertain to you who are healthy, but you must consider that at any moment you might get sick and die, for this thinking about your death is a very useful rule for the life of the spirit. Now then, this is enough for the first page in the book I told you to have painted.[19] Let us now come to the second one.

The second page which I already told you about another time is this: that you have a picture done of a man who has fallen ill, with Death at the door knocking to be let in. [fig. 9] Know that the devil is very quick at this time of death, as is written: *He lies in wait at his heels.*[20] So, as soon as the devil sees that you have fallen ill, but does not know whether you are to die of that illness or not, so as not to be caught [empty handed], he quickly says: 'Perhaps his time has come' and he gets ready all the wiles he knows and can do in order to catch you unprepared at this moment, and he tries with all his abilities to make you fail because of carelessness, just as he failed himself in Heaven.[21]

When the devil was created and saw himself to be so beautiful in Heaven, he began to delight in his self-love and said: 'It would be a wonderful thing if I could do without acknowledging any favour from anyone, but have this excellence by virtue of my own natural abilities: I would not care for any sight of God,' and he did as some crazy people do, who say 'I do not care for all that Paradise, I would be satisfied if God were to let me stay in this world forever.' and in this way the devil, forgetting the good thoughts he should have been thinking, deceived himself. In the same way, carelessness led Lady Eve to sin, for she did not fully

---

[19]The mixed metaphor is in the original.

[20]Savonarola is drawing on Gen. 3:15 *et tu insidiaberis calcaneo eius* ('and you shall lie in wait at his heel' my trans.), making up his own *Insidiatur calcaneo eius.*

[21]That is, he was evicted from Heaven and damned to Hell.

Figure 9. 'Death at a sick man's door.' Woodcut from G.
Savonarola, *Predica dell'arte del ben morire*. Florence: Bartolomeo
de' Libri, after 2 Nov. 1496, sig. b4r; rpt Berlin, 1926.

consider what she had been told. She did not sin from ignorance
because she had been created naturally knowledgeable. But the
devil caught her carelessness and began to say to her: 'Why did
God command you not to eat from this tree?'[22] As if to say 'Given
that you are such noble beings and superior to all other physical
beings, it certainly seems an unworthy thing that you may not eat
from whatever tree you like.' And so he tempted her with pride,
not with gluttony. And so, little by little, he got her thinking that
it seemed an indignity that she could not eat from that tree, and
little by little she became full of pride; as soon as pride took her

[22]Savonarola is paraphrasing liberally from Gen 3:1.

over, it weakened her flesh and she fell into sin from carelessness and she ate the apple that had been prohibited to her by God.

The devil, therefore, who knows that one falls into error and into sin from carelessness as soon as he sees someone fall ill, says to himself: 'Just as we sinned from carelessness in Heaven, even though we enjoyed great knowledge, and just as Adam and Eve also fell into sin from carelessness even though they had much wisdom and original justice, so much more easily will man fall, for he is a lot more careless.' And so the first thing the devil does when he sees you sick is to catch you in carelessness and he strives to find all the ways he knows to lead you not to think of your death. And he starts to get you to think about everything else but your death; and he gets you to think of your house, of your shop, of your land holdings, of the state, and to say: 'When this bit of fever is gone I will do this and that.' My son, be wise and have recourse then to the Crucifix and start to think that you could die of this little illness. And that first penitential psalm would then be very appropriate: *Oh Lord, rebuke me not in your anger,* [Ps 6:2] so that the Lord not allow you to be conquered by the demon's temptation. When the demon sees that he was not able to conquer you through your carelessness he tries to conquer you through your confidence in a recovery and makes you imagine that you are only slightly ill. So, my son, help yourself then and do not say 'I am just slightly ill,' but think that you could die from that slight illness; for slight illnesses sometime become great illnesses, and the sickness of death does not always come all at once, but begins weak and then grows strong. When the devil realizes that you want to think about your death, he instigates others to dissuade you from this thought and makes your wife and your relatives, as well as your doctor, tell you that you will soon be well, that you should not worry, that you should not think you could die from this. Be firm, then, and do not let yourself be convinced, but think that if this is the sickness of death no doctor will heal you; and always remember this, that these are all the devil's enticements to draw you away from the thought of your death. But then, when the devil sees that you are, nonetheless, firm in your thoughts of your death and that you are not certain you will recover, but sees you thinking about making your confession, he begins to make you delay your confession and says: 'You are not ready to confess today, you have not examined your conscience well, you will confess tomorrow.' And if you decide to confess the next day, the devil goes all day to seek out farmers, shop stewards, and a thousand tasks and a thousand impediments to interrupt your confession. Remember your death, then, my son, and let other tasks be, and say: 'This is the biggest task I have and my soul depends on it,' and do not let yourself be interrupted, but confess. After the devil sees that you still confess, he endeavours to draw devotion from your mind and he begins to persuade your wife, your children, and your relatives to bother you about your wealth: and one wants you to leave him one thing, and one another thing; and one tells you a story to keep you cheerful, and one another story: these are all enticements the devil uses to draw you away from your commitment to confess and to leave you utterly confused. Therefore, my son, remember this: as soon as you fall ill, appoint a good man, or a spiritual woman, whether a priest or a member of the secular clergy, a man or a woman in religious orders, to take care of you and of your health, to be always beside you, to remind you always that you must die, and that you confess and make your peace with God; for sometimes relatives and *even* one's own children, fearing that you might leave your wealth to someone else or that you might revoke some part of your will, when the confessor arrives they say: 'He is asleep, this is not the time to bother him.' So, you see how much the devil works at this time. Therefore, always think of your death; and when you feel ill, always consider this to be your last moment. This is the second picture; let us now go to the third.

If you do what I have told you, not only will you save yourself from Hell, but you might also save yourself from the pains of Purgatory, where there are very great pains and whoever is in it thinks every hour is a thousand hours till he gets free of those pains. And so today everyone should do something good for the dead, for they wait for our prayers, because they can no longer merit anything on their own if they are not helped by the prayers of the Church. Oh, if only you knew how harsh the pains of Purgatory are, you would sooner have all wars, all famines, and all plagues of this life fall upon you than to be in those pains of Purgatory. Now, then, let us go to the last picture and come to the end.

The last picture I said you should have painted for yourself is of a sick man in bed brought to make his confession at that final moment where few save themselves. [fig. 10] It is very well possible that a man reduced to that point might save himself, but know that it is very difficult. But in order to explain this point well for you, let us start here.

God stirs our free will and has given man time till death to repent and to turn to God, and until that time He helps him and lends him a hand. But once this time has passed, God no longer relieves him and does not help him any more. And thus, when one dies in mortal sin one remains obstinate in that sin and can no longer turn back because he is devoid of divine assistance, without which one cannot release himself: thus, on his own, one can no longer release himself from sin. And so, when people arrive at that final moment without repenting and without confessing themselves, it is difficult for them to run back because they are near the time of obstinacy that follows death.[23] One must not, therefore, bring oneself to this extreme because few, I tell you, reform themselves at this time. See, therefore, my son, what a dangerous thing it is to bring oneself to such an extreme without first repenting. What, then, are you doing with yourself now while you are healthy? Do penance now, my son, I tell you, and do not let yourself come to such an end, because often God does not convert those who do evil all their life and plan to repent at their deathbed; and this is quite right because, since they were often called to return to God and refused to do so, it stands to reason that at the final moment, as well, they should fail to convert. For it is written: *Because I have called and you refused to listen, I have stretched out my hand and no one has heeded me, and because you have ignored all my counsel and would have none of my reproof, I also will laugh at your calamity; I will mock when panic strikes you.* [Prov 1:24–26] The Lord God says: 'You did not want to return to me and many times when I had you called you laughed at this, so, too, will I laugh about your matters when you are at the point of death.' For this reason, since man procrastinated to the end and was ungrateful of God's calling, he deserves that God, too, at that moment should withdraw His grace; and thus it is difficult to save oneself at that point.

Another reason is that the pain of death is extremely intense and the soul suffers greatly when it separates from the body; and since the soul is one, it is all taken by that pain and it can think little

---

[23]That is, they are nearing Hell.

Figure 10. 'A deathbed confession.' Woodcut from G. Savonarola, *Predica dell'arte del ben morire.* Florence: Bartolomeo de' Libri, after 2 Nov. 1496, sig. b6r; rpt Berlin, 1926.

about its sins and seek God's help. Another reason is that when a man is burdened by the pain of death he has such a great desire to escape from it that he thinks of little else. Another is that even if one were, at that point, to think of death, one does it *at most* out of his fear of Hell, which is not enough, unless he converts out of love, as Saint Augustine says.[24] Another reason is because his wife and relatives come around him and convince him he is not going to die and they say to everyone: 'Do not frighten him, tell him he will get well, one must not upset the sick.' And in this manner they feed him with empty air without reminding him of his

---

[24]St Augustine, *In epistolam Joannis ad Parthos tractatus decem,* PL 35:2049.

obligations. And people come to gesture to him, and they call him, and they ask him: 'Do you recognize me?' and they squeeze his hand and say: 'He recognized me' and they have nothing else to say and have no idea what might be good for the salvation of that soul; and thus it is difficult to save oneself in those last moments. Another is that at that point the devil places Desperation in front of him,[25] and shows him that he has committed many sins and that it does not seem reasonable that God might want to save him and says to him: 'Your tongue has always been ready to speak evil, your eyes have always taken delight in looking at dishonest things, your ears in hearing rumours and evil things, your sense of taste has always sought exquisite things, your sense of smell the same.' And so the devil talks to him about all the iniquities he committed with all his senses and with every part of his soul. And so one can apply to him those words our Saviour Jesus Christ spoke about the Final Judgement, *that is, Erunt signa in sole, et luna et stellis, et in terris pressura gentium prae confusione sonitus maris et fluctuum, arescentibus hominibus prae timore et expectatione, quae superven- ient universo orbi,* [Lk 21:25] 'There will be signs of damnation in the sun,' *that is,* in the intellect that has never thought of anything else but the things of this earth, and 'in the moon,' that is in the will that has loved the creature more than the Creator, and *in the stars,* that is, in the external and internal senses all wrapped up in perceptible things, and 'in the earth,' *that is,* in the body's heart, 'pressure of people,' that is of the various thoughts that at that time confront and afflict the sick person with the pains of his infirmity: and that man fails because of his fear and because of what he expects from the Final Judgement. Moving to the other side, so as not to let him relax in any way, the devil begins to tempt him even in his faith and says: 'If I cannot have you one way, I will have you another way,' and gets him to think that the Faith is not true, and says: 'What do you think the Faith is? Once the body is dead, the soul is dead.' At last, for all these reasons and for many other it is difficult for one who has reached this point to save himself. And so, in order to overcome these temptations of the devil, one

---

[25]Savonarola is drawing upon the tradition of morality plays in which allegorical figures, such as Desperation, would walk on stage and recite their lines. As an oratorical technique, this is a gripping way for Savonarola to get his audience to visualize the drama of conflicting emotions as the moment of death approaches.

would need someone there to recite the Creed continually, as our friars do when one of their brothers dies: they are all called by a friar who goes through the house knocking on a wooden board and, as soon as they hear the signal, they immediately rise up and begin to say *I believe in God the Father* and, walking to the sick man's cell, they always recite the Creed. At last, it is difficult to have been brought to this point and not to have prepared the road ahead. 'Well, then, Father when one has been brought to this point, what should one do, then?' Listen, for I will tell you right now.

My son, do not let yourself be brought to this point. I say this to you, Soul, if you let yourself be brought to that point I fear one will have to weep for you, as Jesus wept for the city of Jerusalem when he said *Si cognovisses et tu, scilecet fleres*,[26] that is, 'if you knew the evils and pains that are to come upon you, you, too, would weep, you would.' *Et quidem in hac die quae ad pacem tibi est*, [Lk 19:42] that is, 'and certainly you would weep on this day that seems peaceful to you.' *Nunc autem abscondita sunt ab oculis tuis*, that is, 'you are not weeping now because your tribulations are hidden from your eyes.' *Quia venient dies in te, et circumdabunt te inimici tui vallo, et circumdabunt te undique, et ad terram prosternent te, et filios tuos in te sunt, et non relinquent in te lapidem super lapidem, eo quod non cognoveris tempus visitationes tuae*, that is, 'the days will move against you, and your enemies will surround you,' *that is*, the devils will form a circle around you and will lead you into Hell, and they will bring you to great affliction and distress and they will throw you on the ground in the pit of Hell with all your works. 'And they will not leave in you a stone upon a stone,' *that is*, no good work of yours will help you. *Eo quod non cognoveris tempus visitationes tuae, that is*, 'because you did not recognize the time of your visitation,' when you were called by the Lord you did not want to hear.

Do not let yourself be brought to this point, Soul, but if you should be so brought, do not despair: follow these remedies. First, seek the crucified Lord, look upon His goodness, for He chose to be crucified and to die in order to save you. Trust in Him greatly, for, if you seek Him with a contrite heart He will help you, even

---

[26]Here and in the exposition that follows to the end of this paragraph Savonarola is drawing from Lk 19:41–44, Jesus' lament over the city of Jerusalem.

if you should have committed thousands of sins. Look at how benevolently He forgave the thief and so do not despair, but have faith that He will forgive you, as well, if you seek Him humbly, for He shed his blood for you. Second, be sorry with all your heart for your sins and propose not to commit them again; and if He wishes you should live longer, commit yourself always to do good and never again to offend your Lord. Third, call for a good confessor and confess thoroughly with every care, and take communion. Fourth, see to it that there is always someone there, next to you, in prayer. And you who are around the sick person, when he dies do not chatter there, but pray for him, all of you, because at that time, more than anything else, he needs prayers because on his own he can say very few. And in order to offer hope to the person who has been brought to this final moment, and in order to show how useful other people's prayers are to him, hear what Saint Gregory writes in his *Dialogues*.

He says that there was a brother of one of his monks, a man named Theodore, who was very much fit for the gallows and was kept at the monastery out of compassion and out of love for his brother the monk. When the other monks would often reprimand him, he would never accept any correction, but would, instead, get angry and be greatly offended, and he would mock the monks and say he would never be a friar.[27] And since there was a plague at that time, God sent him one; being greatly oppressed by that illness and nearly on the point of death, the friars drew all around him and there, all on their knees, they fervently prayed God for him. All of a sudden he began to scream out: 'Get away from here, all of you, get away from here.' When the friars asked why he wanted them to leave and why he was screaming, he answered: 'Don't you see a snake here that has nearly devoured my whole body? And there's a part left that it cannot devour because of your prayers; and this pains me more than if it had devoured me completely.' The friars realized then that it was the demon and they said to him: 'Make the sign of the cross' and he answered 'I can't because this

---

[27]At this point the text switches from *monaco* ('monk') to *frate* ('friar'). This change in terminology may be a momentary lapse either on the part of Savonarola or of Lorenzo Violi, the notary who jotted down the text of the sermon as Savonarola was delivering it; this may also be a subtle rhetorical technique on Savonarola's part to draw the lesson closer to his fellow friars.

snake is holding my arms as if they were tied.' Because of this, all the friars then fell to the ground on their knees and resumed their prayers much more fervently begging God to free him. And all of a sudden this man began to say: 'God be thanked, God be thanked: I've been freed by your prayers; now I want to be a friar' and he lived righteously and a short time thereafter he died.[28]

Then Saint Gregory immediately offers another example, of a man called Crisaurus who was rich and as full of vices as he was of money: proud, avaricious, and lustful; and in his life he tended to nothing else but to worldly things. At the end, when he was laid out sick and at his final moments, many demons appeared to him and they seemed to want to draw his soul out of his body; and he became completely pale and began to tremble and sweat and call for his son Maximus and scream: 'Maximus, help me, receive me into your faith.' When they heard these screams, Maximus and everyone else in the house rushed there; and when they were there in front of the bed and asked him what he wanted, he kept turning his face away so as not to see those demons, but they kept going in front of him and he kept turning away; and they would go to one side, and he would run away to the other side. And after he had done this many many times, finally he began to scream several times in this manner: *Inducias vel usque mane, inducias vel usque mane*, 'Oh Lord, give me time till tomorrow morning.' And in the end he did not get his request and he died like that.[29]

Saint Gregory places these two examples, which he says are examples for us, one after to the other in order to show us that we must not allow ourselves to be brought to such an extreme so as not to end up like this last man; but yet, if we are brought to it, to hope in God, as that first man did. Therefore, no-one should ever delay his penance till the very end of his life, but he should always be ready and confess often, and take communion, and be thoroughly cleansed and ready, as if he expected death at any hour. For the person who is always ready like this and always thinks that he must die stays away from very many sins. Just as the wise man says: *In omnibus operibus tuis memorare novissima tua, et in aeternum non peccabis*, that is, 'if you want to live righteously,

---

[28]St Gregory the Great, *Dialogues*, trans. Odo John Zimmerman (New York: Fathers of the Church, Inc, 1959), p. 245.

[29]St Gregory the Great, *Dialogues*, p. 246.

always remember your death in everything you do, and you will not sin,' and this knowledge of your death will be very useful for you and will bear very great fruit. So, my beloved, let everyone seek to live righteously and if he wants to die well let him always remember that final moment of his death so that, if we do this,[30] we will have grace in this life and in the next the glory of our Saviour Jesus Christ, crucified and killed for us, *to whom be the honour, the glory, and the power for ever and ever. Amen.*

---

[30]The switch from 'he' to 'we' is in the original.

On Exodus

Sermons on the Book of Exodus
Sermon No. 1
11 Feb. 1497

'Renovation Sermon'

A sermon gathered by Ser Lorenzo Violi[1] from the spoken voice of the Reverend Father Frair Girolamo from Ferrara on 11 February 1497 [i.e., 1498] when he began to preach once again.[2] And as soon as the Father entered the pulpit the people, in happiness for having received the word once again, began to sing the *Te Deum laudamus*, and so it finished with great jubilation, and then the Father began as follows:

Lord, why have those who trouble me increased? Many are rising against me; many say about my soul: there is no salvation for him with his God. But you, Lord, are my shield around me, my glory, and you raise my head high. I have called out with my voice to the Lord, and he answered me from His high mountain. I slept and slumbered, and I woke up, for the Lord preserves me. I will not fear a thousand people surrounding me. Rise, Lord, save me, my God. For you struck down all my enemies, you broke the teeth of sinners

---

[1]On Lorenzo Violi see p. 99, n. 2. Ser was an honorific title usually given to notaries.

[2]In May 1497 Pope Alexander VI Borgia prohibited Savonarola from preaching and excommunicated not only the friar but also anyone who supported him or listened to him preach. Savonarola observed this prohibition against preaching in public until 11 February 1498 when, with this first sermon on Exodus, he returned to the pulpit and openly challenged the validity of the excommunication. Needless to say, the tensions already present in Florence were greatly aggravated by this open challenge and contributed significantly to Savonarola's downfall just short of two months later on 8 April 1498.

without cause. Salvation belongs to the Lord, and He is your blessing upon your people. [Ps 3]

My Lord, this morning I, who am dust and ashes, wish first to speak about your majesty; but, if it is not presumptuous of me, I would like to speak with you face to face; but this is not possible, for my eyes cannot withstand your light [Ex 33:20]. You, my Lord, have set limits on every creature, and my physical eyes cannot go past the limits you have placed on them because they are finite, they have their limits, and these are to see colours and physical light, but they cannot peer inside your infinite light.[3] My intellect and natural light, while in this body, cannot penetrate your light and cannot see you, for it has many impediments and many things in my fantasy prevent it. Not even when it will be separated from this body will it be able to see you and understand you on its own, for you are infinite, and you have placed limits on every intellect. Therefore, it will not, even then, understand you, nor see you, except through your creatures and within its own finite limits.

Yet, Lord, because I still want to speak a little with you this morning and because I do not want it to seem that I am speaking to several gods, I direct myself and speak to you, my Lord, who are, according to the philosophers, the first cause, to you, the first principle, the first motor, pure act, immutable God, ruler of the universe. *Also*, according to the faith, I speak to you Triune God in one, to you Holy Trinity, to you Jesus Christ, son of the eternal God, born of the Virgin into this world, and killed for our love. I speak to you, therefore, my Lord, and say that you have placed me upon a great sea. I no longer see the port, and cannot go back, and do not want to go back even if I could. I cannot and do not want to. I cannot because you do not want it; I do not want to because you do not want it; for I neither can nor want to resist your will. I am happy to stay here where you have put me, but I do pray you, my Lord, that you stay with me. These enemies of ours say that you are not with me: *non est salus illi in Deo eius* [Ps 3:3], that is, that there is no salvation for me with my God. Are you,

---

[3]The same concept of mankind's inability to peer inside the light emanating from God and to see Him is found in Dante's Paradiso, when the pilgrim must, ever so slowly, accustom his eyes to the growing brightness of the heavens and, ultimately, to the undescribable brightness of the beatific vision.

therefore, not with me, oh my Lord, where I find myself? I pray you, my Lord, that you be with me. I do not ask you for gold nor for silver, not for peace, nor for tranquillity, nor that you take me from this sea in which I find myself, but I ask you only to give me light. Give me, Lord, the grace to see.

I ask you what the blind man asked you: *Domine, fac ut videam* [Lk 18:41]: Lord, make me see, open the light of my intellect, enlighten me, let the light of natural reason comfort me, let me not be deceived by our enemies. Let me also be comforted by the super-natural light of the faith, that I might never hear anything said against Holy Scripture and the doctrine of the Church. Let me also be comforted by the super-natural light of knowledge of future and hidden things, that I might see everything well, that I not be deceived, and that I might not then deceive the people, as I have not deceived them till now. And, yes, I also pray you to begin a new time, and that it be the start of great things. Answer our prayers, Lord, answer your servants, set your hands to new tasks, and to things greater than what you have done till now: *rise, Lord, and come.*

Oh Mother of God, what are you doing? Oh saints, oh blessed of Heaven, what are you doing? Oh angels, oh archangels, oh virtues, oh thrones, oh powers, oh dominations, what are you doing? Assist the work of the Lord, pray, all of you, to the Lord that His work might proceed and that a new time might begin, that He finally set His hands to new tasks.

What do you say, Lord? What is your answer? This is the answer: *nolite timere, pusillanimes, Dominus enim vobiscum est* [Is 35:4]. That is, 'do not fear, you faint-hearted, for the Lord is with you.' This was the answer, these are the words we received from heaven this morning. Now wait and see if this is good news.

Good news has come from heaven: *nolite timere, pusillanimes, Dominus vobiscum est.* These, in fact, are the words: I alter none of them; that is, 'do not fear, you faint-hearted people, for the Lord is with you.' Do you want to see Him yourselves? Where the Lord is, there is peace: behold, He has given you peace and He gives it to you constantly in everything. I say to you, who are righteous: you who are united and have a single heart. Do you remember the heart that was above the Virgin's little crown?[4] [fig. 11] That heart

---

[4]In his *Compendio di revelatione* (Florence: Piero Pacini da Pescia, 23 April

represented all our hearts united together in peace. You, righteous, have peace in times of trouble because, although there are troubles around us, we *still* are always happy and at peace. Righteous people are at peace in death *as well*, and many righteous people have died and have gone to rest in peace. We are also at peace in our wealth, because we do not seek the wealth of the world, but on the contrary we disdain it: this is a sign that we have greater wealth than there is in this world. *Therefore*, do not fear times of trouble: all we need is internal peace.

Do you not remember how many times in the past I told you that we will always have to struggle? And although sometimes we rest a little, we must then return to war. When soldiers have finished a skirmish they return; one has a damaged shin-guard, and another a weapon, and another a helmet, and they fix all these arms, and then they get ready for a new war, and they teach one another; one says: 'Hold your lance like this, and you hold your sword like this, and you do this, and you do that.' Then the drummers come forth and our soldiers begin to yell out: 'Marzocco! Marzocco!'[5] And so they parade around and they are all ready and set for a new war. We, too, have done the same; having gone through some skirmishes, we have fixed the damaged weapons; some, who were not very knowledgeable in this art, have remedied their situation and learned things; others, who did not have so much humility, have acquired it; others still, who did not have perfect obedience, have become more obedient; and so some people have acquired one thing, others another thing. Then we paraded, we went on processions, said many prayers, sang many

1496), Savonarola described in detail a complex, three-tier crown for the Virgin Mary. Above the crown, which itself contained many hearts made from various precious and semiprecious metals and stones, there was a single heart composed of many small hearts of various colours. [fig. 11]

[5]The battle cry of the Florentine republic. Marzocco was the name of the Florentine heraldic lion represented sitting on its hind quarters and holding a crest with the Florentine lily under one of its front paws (see Donatello's famous rendition of the Marzocco currently in the Bargello; it originally stood on the *tribuna* in front of the Palazzo della Signoria, where it is now replaced by a copy). The name Marzocco may derive from *Martocus*, that is, 'little Mars,' a nickname it received when, sometime in the fourteenth century, the sitting lion replaced the statue of Mars, the Roman god of war, that used to stand at the Ponte Vecchio.

songs, we were jubilant and fervent, and sang: *Behold, how good and how joyful it is for brothers to live as one* [Ps 132:19(133:1)].[6] And after this we came back another time and here we are again on the field. *Do not fear, you faint-hearted.*

Moreover, have I not told you many times that we must fight and win? I tell you that it is inevitable that we must win, and when this thing seems all but extinguished, it will rise up once again more glorious than ever. Remember how everyone said: 'He is done for. This thing has been struck down.' Yet we are still here and we want to fight and win more than ever. And I tell you, there never was a more glorious time, nor a happier time than this one, and we want to do glorious and great things, and God will be the one to do them, much to the consolation of the righteous.

'Oh Friar, even some of the righteous have died, that is is true, but many of the wicked have also died.'

Do you not remember how I told you that some more of the righteous would die? But wait a little while yet; this means: prepare yourself, wait, for if these things seemed great to you, those that are to come will seem even greater to you. And many of those who have died, have died two deaths: one in this life, the other in Hell. I could even name you a few, but the righteous who seem dead to you are not dead, for they are in the other life and they pray and help us in our task.

'So, Friar, what are you trying to say?'

We conclude that we need to fight and win, and that we must set our hands to new tasks—not this morning, for I did not come to preach to you, but rather to talk with you, for we still do not know what book we must pick up and explicate to you this Lent. Pray the Lord to make us pick up something that will be useful to you. And, as I told you, we did our parade, and we came onto the field, and we want to fight and win more than ever. The Devil as well has done his parade and is rousing his soldiers who, sometimes with excommunications, sometimes with rumours, seek only

---

[6]The lauda *Ecce quam bonum et quam iocundum habitare fratres in unum* was one of the rallying songs of the Savonarolan movement. For its role, and the role of music in general in Savonarola's mission, see the work of Patrick Macey, and especially his prize-winning book *Bonfire Songs. Savonarola's Musical Legacy*. For the musical setting of the lauda and of motets derived from the biblical verse, see Macey's *Savonarolan Laude, Motets, and Anthems*.

to do evil, and they will fill this Carnival season with vices, and we want to make it an Easter full of praise of God and prayers, and then we will see who will win. Now, then, let us conclude: that the Lord God is with us and gives us great consolation, and we will inevitably win.

Nolite timere, pusillanimes, Dominus enim vobiscum est. Do not fear, you faint-hearted, for the Lord is with you, and also with me, because I want to be with you and you with me. As I said these words, that human wisdom we sent away several times came back towards me: she came back this morning, that wisdom, she, I say, who does not believe these things, who does not believe that God is with us, she who does not believe that God speaks to mankind. She came back and raised many points against me and many strong arguments, telling me I was crazy, so much so that I agreed with her and I confessed *quod stultissimus sum virorum et quod sapientia hominum non est mecum* [Prov 30:2]. That is: that I am the craziest of men and that the wisdom of mankind is not with me. But I told her that, because of this, I have a much better time than anyone else because, since I am crazy and crazy people do not know their own craziness and they think they are the wisest of all men, they have a much better time than anyone else.

Yet, she raised many points against me and said: 'Come here, Friar, I want to convince you. Either the faith is true or the faith is false. If the faith is not true, given you have put yourself into so many troubles and entered the clergy with all its bothers, and that you have missed out on all good times, there you have it, you are crazy and done for. If the faith is true and God is not with you (she always assumed that God was not with me), there you have it, said she, you are done for and you are an enormous fool for having picked so many quarrels and for not having God with you, for you will lose this life and the next. *Moreover*, those who have peace of heart are blessed, and so those who seek strife are crazy, for they do not seek their ultimate goal. And if the faith is not true, and you seek strife, once you have entered into such an open sea, you cannot enjoy bliss in this world; *ergo* you are crazy. And if the faith is true and you do not have God with you, then you are crazy (she always supposed this, that God was not with me). *Moreover*, she said that those who contradict all men are crazier than everyone else: 'You contradict the entire world and you think no-one has spirit except you, and that no-one is perfect except you, and so you are absolutely crazy: this is the highest craziness of all.'

I can tell you, she had me in a corner with these arguments of hers and with her reasons. *Then* she added: 'Those who put their soul and body in danger are crazy. With these things of yours, you have put yourself in danger, so you are truly crazy, because, if the faith is not true, you are in constant physical danger, and if the faith is true, you lose your soul, for you do not have God with you. *Ergo*, you are crazy whatever the case.' See now how this human wisdom thought she had wrapped me up and convinced me.

Not long ago, one of these sages of human wisdom came to see me and said to me: 'Friar, tell me the truth. I know it, anyway, I know you do these things in order to gain earthly glory, and you know that ultimately earthly glory is nothing, *ergo* you are crazy. *Moreover*, Friar, do you want to see what your craziness consists in? Look at what you based yourself on: you have based yourself on the people, and you know there is nothing more false or more changeable than the people.[7] Look at the Hebrew people, how on Palm Sunday[8] they welcomed Christ into Jerusalem with so much festivity and with so much joy, and a few days later how they crucified him. So, you can now see what your craziness is. *'Moreover*, Friar,' this human wisdom said, 'see whether this other reason proves that you are truly crazy. Those who see obvious dangers and spend the entire day laughing and singing, are truly crazy. You do this and spend the entire day with your friars singing *Behold, how good and how joyful it is for brothers to live as one*. *Ergo* you can know your craziness. *Also*, those who reprimand everyone and make themselves hateful to everybody are crazy. You reprimand everyone and have made yourself hateful to everybody. Therefore, you are crazy.' I confessed to this human sage *quod sum stultissimum omnium virorum et quod sapientia hominum non est mecum*. That is, that I am crazier than anyone else and that the

---

[7]The notion that the people were fickle has both Christian and pagan origins and was standard currency at the time (as it is now). In this sermon Savonarola refers to the standard Christian example drawn from the Passion story. His contemporary, Niccolò Machiavelli, would draw on Titus Livy's *History of Rome* (Bk 6, ch. 7), to expand on this notion in his *Discourses on the First Ten Books of Titus Livy* (see Bk 1, ch. 58), or in his *The Prince* (see chs. 6, 9, 17). Ironically, Machiavelli uses Savonarola himself as an example of a leader who fell as soon as the people, in their fickleness, stopped believing in him (*Prince*, ch. 6).

[8]The original says 'Olive Sunday' because current practice used to bless and wave olive rather than palm branches.

wisdom of mankind is not with me, and because of this that sage thought he had convinced me. Now, for your consolation, listen to how I answered him.

She rejoiced and said: 'He did, in fact, admit it and he did say these words: *I am the craziest of all men*, etc.'. O, human wisdom, you did nothing to get me to confess and just say those words. You left out the rest, you left out half the text you should have cited completely. You did like those who dispute, who bring up only the parts that suit their arguments and leave the rest aside. And you also did like the Scribes and the Pharisees who said of our Lord: *non est hic homo a Deo qui sabbatum non custodit* [Jh 9:16], 'this man who does not observe the Sabbath cannot have been sent by God'; but they did not mention the miracle he performed on the Sabbath. The words I confessed to you belong to someone enlightened by God, but you said only the words that follow, and not those that come before, that is, *visio quam locutus est vir cum quo est Deus, et qui, Deo secum morante, confortatus ait* [Prov 30:1], this is the vision spoken by the man with whom God is and who, comforted by God, said: '*I am the craziest of men and the wisdom of men is not with me.*' And then he added: *non didici sapientiam et novi scientiam sanctorum* [Prov 30:3]. 'I have not learnt wisdom from men nor have I understood the knowledge of the saints.' And so, human knowledge, you did not convince me as you thought.

But come here, you that contradict me and say this is not the work of God. If I show it to you and you then see that this is the work of God, where will you be? What do you think will be of you, when you have opposed God? And so you will see that, if you do not change, you will be scourged in this world and the next. And to your reasons, oh human wisdom, I first respond that the faith, in any case, is true, and that to suffer many troubles and tribulations in this world for the faith of Christ is absolute peace; and because of this we remain happy and joyful in tribulation. Look there at my brothers, at the good women, at the good youths who are on their way to God and live righteously, who are always happy and joyful; and nothing can upset us, and so we will have bliss in this world, if the faith is true, and then in the other world *if for these reasons* it is true, for you know I have proven this to you many times and with many reasons.

Second, I granted you that the wisdom of mankind is not with us, and because of this you say that we are not with the wise but with the crazy. And I answer you that I and my followers are with

the sages of heaven and with the saints, and we do not care at all
for the wisdom of the world. And my sages say that you are all
crazy, that you do not know how to find your true ultimate goal,
nor do you know that the true ultimate goal is in the other life and
it is Christ.

Moreover, when you say that I seek earthly glory, I answer that
the infamy that is done to us is much greater than the glory we
acquire in the world. And when you say that our foundation is in
the people, I answer you that this is not true: this is not our
foundation, but it is God alone. *Also*, if I am always happy in
tribulations, this is a sign that there is something else here and
some hidden treasure that you do not see that keeps our heart
always joyful. You can see that our defence is prayer, and singing,
and rejoicing with psalms and hymns, [Col. 3:16–18] so you can
understand that God alone is our foundation. Let as many tribulations come as you want, we all remain happy and slumber
peacefully in our sleep, and this is not natural in tribulations and
in great troubles; and so you can understand that there is some
other power [*virtù*], that you do not see, that does this. And when
you say that I oppose the entire world, I answer that one must tell
the truth for love of Christ and fear nothing. And so I do not want
your human wisdom; I believe in divine wisdom and in that
wisdom I have learned from the saints. Now then, now that we
have answered your charges, let us see whether we can answer
the point about the excommunication that, you say, gives you
scruples. Now then, let us resolve these doubts.

Do you have scruples? I was looking to see if there was anyone
with scruples here. I want to resolve this question without canons
and without so many chapters.[9] But first I wanto comfort you. Take
comfort, you faint-hearted, *et nolite timere, quia Dominus vobiscum
est*. The Lord is with you: if you live righteously you do not need
to fear the spiritual sword, nor the corporal one. This place is now
filled with angels and there was never a more glorious nor happier
time than this one, when new and great things are to be done, so
rejoice, for joyous times are coming.

Now then, let us resolve the question, but first I want to tell you
one thing, why God has allowed the excommunication to come.

---

[9]That is, without having recourse to the Canons of the Church or written
books.

You must remember that already seven years ago, and many times since then, I told you we have to fight against a double power, a double wisdom, and a double malice. What was this power, if not the spiritual and temporal power? And so, in order for what we said to come true, it was necessary to unsheathe the spiritual sword and to fight with it.

Now note, therefore, that manual works attain their goal according to the hand of the agent that moves them, and if the hand of the agent does not move them, they would not attain their goal. God has made mankind and wants it to attain perfection and its goal. The goal of mankind is bliss, and Christ wants to introduce righteous living into the world in order to lead mankind, by means of it, to living a blessed life. And so God introduces good works into the world, so that those works might lead mankind towards righteous and blessed living.

But the devil, who is the enemy of righteousness and would not want mankind to be brought to bliss, hates righteous living and does not care for fasts, Our Fathers, or alms per se, but hates them because they lead to righteous living; and so he seeks to ruin these good works. If they did not lead mankind to righteousness, however, he would not care about them. Similarly, the devil does not care about prophecies per se, because he too has already given out a few, but he does care about those that lead to righteous living. If the teaching of the apostles had not led mankind to righteous living, the devil would not have persecuted it so much. Similarly, at the time of the martyrs, he would not have incited tyrants against them, had their teaching not led mankind to righteous living. Similarly, at the time of the heretics the devil would not have spurred Arius and the other heretics against the preaching of the holy doctors, had not that teaching led mankind to righteous living.[10] The same is happening today, because this teaching has led and is leading souls to righteous living, so the devil incites many persecutions against us.

Tell me, have other prophecies not been uttered in previous times? And did they not suffer such opposition? This is because they did not lead to righteous living. See how strong righteous living is, for it has been able to do so much that, in spite of all

---

[10]Arius (d. 336), one of the early heretics, was excommunicated more than once and condemned by the Council of Nicaea (325 A.D.) for his views that the Son was subordinate to the Father.

opposition, it has always triumphed. Look at the time of the apostles, who had the law of Moses before them, kept and approved for so many years, and *still* they, men without refinement, were able to do so much with their righteous living that they brought this law into disuse. Oh, if today someone should come along to ruin and remove the law of Christ, you would think it strange. But righteous living directed everything there, in Judaea. The same happened here, among the Gentiles. When they adored idols, the Gentiles would say: 'We adore idols of gold, of silver, of stone, you adore one who is crucified,' and so they could find excuses not to enter into this faith. But righteous living clarified everything and made them rush into this faith. So I tell you that in our times God has wanted to bring men together on one side by way of righteous living, and leave the wicked on the other side, for they do not go well together.

It has been necessary, I tell you, to separate the wheat from the straw. Christ has taken the winnowing-fan, that is, the shovel, and has thrown the grain over there and separated it from the straw. The first winnowing-fan the Lord took was preaching, which revealed in part the imperfections of the lukewarm. But because some of the lukewarm covered themselves and made themselves appear righteous in the presence of others, feigning to walk on the path of righteousness, not revealing themselves unless they could profit from it, so God sent the other winnowing-fan, that is, excommunication, which led to the discovery of many who were not walking in truth. Did I not tell you that many would be exposed whom you never would have imagined? And this was the reason why God allowed the excommunication to be issued, in order to separate the lukewarm from the righteous. Now let us see if this reason is valid or not.

Take comfort, you faint-hearted, *do not fear, you faint-hearted: the Lord is with you.* Do you think, perhaps, that I want to bring forth canons and laws and this chapter and that chapter? I do no want to bring forth lots of chapters. I want everyone to understand me. Youths and women, listen to me, for I want everyone to understand this: I will put in your hands some arguments to use to defend yourselves. First, according to natural reason, then according to the light of faith, third according to the super-natural light of prophecy. And for each of these three lights I will give you some arguments so that you will understand.

First, according to the light of nature. Come here, philosopher, and see whether I, too, can philosophize. Tell me: is it true that one must find a first cause? 'Yes.' And this, too, is true: *that in all things the first cause has more influence than the second?*[11] 'Yes.' Now note that the first cause always moves before the second because, if the first did not move first, none of the others would move. The first is, as if to say, a hand that takes the power [*virtù*] of the sky and pulls it, and comes to the elements and pulls the power [*virtù*] of the elements, it then comes to the seed and takes and pulls the power [*virtù*] of the seed and makes the fruit. And so this first cause, that is, God, produces things in this universe by way of second causes. If He wanted, He could very well do without the second causes. If the Lord wanted He could generate here, right away, an apple without second causes because He made heaven and earth out of nothing. However, down here He produces the effects and natural causes through second causes so as to communicate better His goodness to them, and He wants them to participate, themselves, in such works. If you were to see a painter take the hand of a child and paint a figure there, you would say that the painter had done it, not the child. You can conclude, then, that God makes everything and He does not make what is nothing, that is, sin, because to sin is to be lacking and not to be doing, and God is never lacking in divine Wisdom. So you can conclude that second causes are instruments of God, and He is the one who primarily does everything.

Now hold firm to this basis and note this other point: that God governs lower natural things by way of higher ones, and the lower angels by way of the higher ones, but mankind is all equal in nature. It is true that one has a greater intellect than another, and so men with greater intellect are naturally lords over other men, lords, I say, not for the sake of power, but in order to show the way to others and to teach them. But because mankind is by nature a social animal and lives in society, it was necessary to make someone governor of the common good, and such governors are instruments of God, moved, as I told you, as second causes by the first cause. And so a prince, ordained by men so that they might live better in community, is an instrument of God, just like the

---

[11]Thomas Aquinas, *Super librum De causis expositio*, 1.1.

angels are, created to govern mankind and to lead it to righteousness.

Now hold on firmly to this other point and note that every
instrument has three characteristics. The first is matter, the second
is form, the third is power [*virtù*], which proceeds from the hand
of the agent, that is from the one who guides the instrument. Take,
for example, a saw. Its matter is iron; second, it has form, that is,
teeth and other parts, because it is a saw; third, in order for it to
work it needs the hand of the craftsman, because without it the
saw, by itself, can do nothing. And so, note that, as far as matter
is concerned, the saw is the same as all other pieces of iron.
Similarly, all men are naturally equal. However, if a saw is brought
to a smith and he buys it and throws it among his broken tools,
this instrument is then the same as all other tools, for it has no
higher agent to move it. The same is true of a prince: if he is not
moved as an instrument by a higher agent, that is, by God, whose
instrument he is, since he is equal to you and has no-one to move
him, he is a broken tool like all the others, and then you can say
to him: 'You do not work well because you are not led by the
principal agent.' And if he says: 'I have power,' you can say to him:
'That is not true, because there is no hand to guide you. You are
a broken tool.'

But if you said to me: 'When will I know that the principal higher
agent is not moving him?' I will answer: See whether he is behaving
against the wisdom of that principal agent who should be moving
him. And because the wisdom of that principal agent leads to and
loves righteous living and the common good, see whether the
orders issued by that instrument are contrary to righteous living or
to the common good, and if you see that they are, then say: 'You
are not moved by the higher agent, and therefore you are a broken
tool.' Therefore, Saint Thomas says that if a prince issues a law
against righteous living or the common good, the people are not
held to obey it.[12] Therefore, every time you see the prince act
against righteous living or the common good, you can say to him:
'You are not a saw moved by the hand of the higher agent, but a
broken tool.'

And note that this error in the prince can derive from two
sources. First, from the prince's depravity. Look, when emperors

---

[12]See Thomas Aquinas, *Vindiciae contra tyrannos.*

ordered their subjects: 'Go to war for the freedom of the homeland' the subjects were obliged to obey and at that point emperors were good saws; but when they ordered: 'Adore idols' the subjects were not obliged to obey. In fact, they should not have done it, because at that point the order did not come from the saw, but from the broken tool. The second source can be the bad advice given to a prince, and then the saw is not moved by the hand of the higher agent, but by the bad advice, and so it should not be obeyed.

Now, along these lines, tell me: what did these people want to achieve by this excommunication? I can tell you, this time they will not saw well and will not make a fine stall.[13] What did they want to achieve? Everyone knows it, even children, that they wanted nothing else but to get rid of righteous living and the common good because they wanted to ruin every good government and they did not care that they were opening the way to all vices. So when the excommunication came, on with taverns, lewdness, and every evil; and righteous living was thrown to the ground. And so you can see that the saw is not moved by its principal agent. I am amazed at you, that you doubted this. What is the need for so many laws and so many canons? The thing is clear on its own: you can see it too well. There is no need for other arguments because one can see why this was done. And I tell you, if we have been cursed from below, we have been blessed from above, I tell you.

Do not fear, you faint-hearted, the Lord is with you. See how God has comforted our natural light, as we had asked. And for this reason, with regards to natural light, we understand clearly that this excommunication does not hold. Now, with regards to super-natural light. Behold: *Dei perfecta sunt opera* [Deut 32:4], the works of God are all perfect. We say something is perfect that touches and has attained its goal. The angels who see God are perfect and are called perfect in their own kind because they have attained their perfection and the end to which they were ordained. Our perfection, therefore, is not just our faith, because it is an imperfect knowledge of God; instead, the perfection of our faith and of our law is charity, which lets us understand divine things clearly. Therefore, those who have charity understand those things that belong to salvation.

---

[13]By using the image of a *scanno*, Savonarola is alluding to choir stalls (and, by extension, the heavenly stalls of the blessed in paradise). This is clearly is a sarcastic barb against the pope who excommunicated him.

And so you see that today, when there is no charity, everything is understood badly and every day there are new laws and more new laws. So many laws are confusing, and every law established today is a money net. I think that by now we have become worse than Jews.[14] Court cases go on for ten or twenty years when they could be brought to conclusion in an hour. And one should burn all these writings, all these laws, and spare the good ones.

Now, this certainly happens because there is no charity. The apostles did not have many laws because they all burned with love of charity: *charity is the fullness of the law*.[15] What the law of God says is not said except for charity. All theology is ordered towards charity, all the canon laws, the civil laws, all the ceremonies of the Church are ordered towards charity, and the entire world has been created by God towards charity, because the heavens and the entire world are ordered towards mankind in order to feed and keep its body alive. The body is ordered towards the soul, and the soul towards charity and superior grace, and so the entire world is ordered towards charity.

So, those who issue commands against charity, which is the fullness of our law, *let them be anathema*, let them be excommunicated, and those who issue commands against charity are excommunicated by God.[16] If an angel were to do it, *let him be anathema*. I say 'if he were to say it' because he would not do it, and it cannot be that he would; that is why I say 'if he were to say it'—*because the conditional does not bring something into being*—,[17] *let him be anathema*, let him be excommunicated. And if all the saints, and

---

[14]The antisemitism evident in this statement should not be imputed only to Savonarola, but to all early modern European preachers and society. The critical literature on European Jewry and its situation in the Renaissance is quite extensive; among its many texts, the interested reader might consult Heiko Oberman, *The Roots of Antisemitism in the Age of the Renaissance and Reformation*, trans. J.I. Porter (Philadelphia: Fortress Press, 1984) or R. Po-Chia Hsia, *Trent 1475: Stories of a Ritual Murder Trial* (New Haven: Yale University Press, 1992).

[15]The phrase is not in the Bible, but alludes to 1 Tim 1:5.

[16]The sentence is repetitive even in the original. Savonarola is saying 'let them be excommunicated' (understood: by the Church) and then underlining that they already 'are excommunicated' by God.

[17]*quia conditionalis non ponit inesse.* Savonarola is dealing with the standard 'if clause contrary to fact' that any student of grammar will recognize.

even the Virgin, were to do it—which they cannot do, as I told you, and they will never do it—, *let them be anathema*. One cannot, I tell you, issue commands against charity because all creatures are subject to this law, and so everyone must first want to die than undermine charity. Tell me, therefore: if anyone were to see a wolf coming to devour the sheep, and see the destruction of souls, and see people acting against charity, should he not lay his life down for his sheep? *Maiorem caritatem nemo habet quam ponere animam pro ovibus suis*, 'no-one has greater charity than that man who lays down his life for his sheep.'[18] Will this person, therefore, be excommunicated? Do not believe it. Those who act against charity are excommunicated.

Do you think, then, that I should flee? I have been strong up to now and so I tell you that I will remain strong. Would you want me to abandon my children, who are also your children, who have been led here by God to righteous living under my shadow? The good shepherd does not abandon his sheep, *but lays his life down for his sheep*. I tell you, you will first have to cut me in a thousand pieces. You might say: 'Agree with the union, enter into this congregation here.'[19] I tell you I will never do it, and I do not want my children to slacken their rule, for this is contrary to righteous living and contrary to charity. I would sooner die a thousand deaths. I will boldly say this because you, Lord, want me to say it. These citizens bent on living righteously, these women and children living righteously, are they not my spiritual children? Do you still say that I should go to Rome and do you still want me to leave them in the hands of gamblers and sodomites, in wantonness and

---

[18]The phrase is not in the Bible, but echoes John 15:13 and clearly alludes to the parables of the lost sheep (Matthew 18 and Luke 15) and the concept of the Good Shepherd (John 10).

[19]On 17 November 1496, in response to Savonarola's continued intransigence and recalcitrance against him, Pope Alexander VI dissolved the Dominican Congregation of St Mark (which he had established in May 1493) and placed Savonarola's Tuscan convents under a newly formed Tusco-Roman Congregation headed by a new vicar (not Savonarola) chosen by the General of the Dominicans. Savonarola strongly objected to this fusion and restructuring saying that his convents had been transferred from his strict rule to a very lax observance of the Dominican rule, thereby endangering the spiritual health of his fellow friars and nuns.

in every vice, [do you want them] to draw back from the righteous path they have taken?

Moreover, you say I have preached heretical things. Look a while at what I have written to you and what I have published, see whether these seem like heresies to you. I have tossed you a bone to chew on, as people say. You also say I should stop preaching. I will never do this because it is contrary to all charity. Did you not see that when I stopped preaching there was a drop in righteous living and vices grew and gained courage and everything began to fall into confusion? And so the faith of Christ was laid to the ground and the sheep were left in the hands of the wolves. Look carefully whether you can find any law or any canon or any council that says something contrary to what I have said, and if it does, let it be excommunicated *and let it be anathema.*[20] If any doctor [of the Church] or bishop says anything contrary to this, let him be called anathema and told 'You have not studied well.' And if there were any pope or anyone else who would speak against what I have said, let him be excommunicated. I am not saying there is any pope who has done so, but if there were any that would do so or say so, I tell you that then this man would not have been the craftsman or the principal agent who moved the saw, but that saw would have been moved by someone else, that is, by the bad influence of other people. I want to assume that his intention was good; if it was bad, let God be the judge of that.

You also say I should comply with this excommunication. I will not comply with it because I do not want to act against charity.

So, this is the reason, according to the super-natural light, as I told you, whereby you can see that an order that goes against charity is not valid. Now to a more obvious reason.

We are still at the beginning and find it difficult to preach. Pray for us that we might regain our strength so that once we have delivered a few sermons we will be able to proceed better.

'Now then,' you will say, 'come here, Friar: do you think this excommunication is valid? Explain this to us a little bit.'

'No, it is not valid.'

---

[20]Savonarola is using the third person, thus clearly saying that the law, canon, or council should be declared anathema (*anathema sit*), and not he. Had Savonarola wanted to suggest that he should be excommunicated, he would have said *anathema sim* (using the first person singular).

'Oh, who told you so?'

'God told me so. I say, it is God who told me this, pay attention to how I speak to you.'

'Oh Friar, if your God told you it is not valid, our God told us that it is valid, and we say that Christ is on our side.'

'Well, then, let us look at this for a moment. I tell you that Christ is with us and I will show you that He would sooner stay with excommunicated people like these than with you who call yourselves blessed. At the time of Christ, an edict was issued saying that those who acknowledged Christ's name would be excommunicated and ejected from the synagogue.[21] I, for one, prefer to be with Christ, and to acknowledge him, and to stand with these excommunicated people.'

'But, Friar, note that many righteous persons are against you.'

And I answer you that not all those who seem righteous are righteous. I remember telling you once before that there were three types of persons. One type is like the devil, for they appear not to have any vices and not to be sullied by carnal sins, however, they suffer only the spiritual sin of pride, like the devil, because the devil does not gamble, he is not a glutton, he does not keep a concubine, he is not a usurer, but sins only in envy and pride and hate. Some people are like this, stuck in these spiritual sins, just like devils. Others give themselves over to vice, to lusts, to concubines, to usury, and to all carnal vices, and these people are animals. Others give themselves over to these vices and then to spiritual vices as well; and these are half human and half devil. Now go, then, and look at those who oppose us: you will see that they are all full of vices and bent on sin, some are entirely devils, some half devils, and some animals. Start, by all means, from Rome to here and you will see the type of people they are. You will certainly see that nearly all wicked and vile people are contrary to our work. Then turn around and look at those who believe in our work: you will see that they live righteously, they go to confession, they take communion often, they live in purity.

So, if you are a righteous person, which group will you draw near to? If you want to live righteously, you will surely draw near to the righteous ones and to those who live righteously: *with the righteous you will be righteous, with the wicked you will grow wicked*

---

[21]There was no such edict. Savonarola is fabricating evidence.

[2 Sam 22:26–27]. I see you drawing near to the opposition, therefore you must be wicked like them. As for me, I want to dwell with the righteous, and if I need to be excommunicated in order to live righteously, I will be with the excommunicated.

You know very well what this excommunication seeks to do and with what intentions it was devised, and to what purpose, and what a ruin for the righteous life and for the common good it would be to obey it. And so, if you are righteous, you will see very well what you must do and you will not fear any excommunication because every righteous person must help and favour righteousness.

'O, Father, there are also some righteous people who have scruples and do not see the situation as clearly as you do.'

I answer you that they probably are not praying enough to be enlightened by the light of truth, or perhaps they have a slight vein of pride in them that hinders or obstructs divine light from entering. But if they were to pray with correct intention they would be enlightened, *because the light rises in the darkness for those with an upright heart* [Ps 111(112):4].

'O, Father, if I continue to have scruples and remain so, what evil have I done?'

Listen here: you want me to tell you the truth? You have acted against God, because if everyone remained as you are the city and righteous living would fall into ruin. Draw near the righteous, therefore, if you want to be righteous and resolve not to remain among the wicked whom I see opposing us.

I want to tell you a story that was relayed to me by a respectable person whom one can trust. There was a man in Rome who was talking with a great teacher there, perhaps the greatest there is. Speaking of these things about the friar,[22] that great teacher said: 'I will tell you the truth. I have determined that all those who have spoken to me against this thing and against the friar, be they Florentines or something else, they all seem to me to be men who lead wicked lives, and those who have spoken with me on his behalf seem to me to be good people.' Now see how things stand! I tell you, anyone who opposes these things opposes Christ. I will tell you again: those who oppose our work oppose Christ. Hear me well, oh Rome, those who oppose our work oppose Christ. Oh

---

[22]That is, speaking about Savonarola.

Christian people, if you oppose it you are fighting with Christ, not with the friar.

'Oh, now you will say the priests of the Church are also gathered together against our work.'

I will answer you. When St Peter pulled out the knife, our Saviour said to him: *quomodo implebuntur scripturae?* [Mt 26:54] That is, how will the Scriptures and the prophecies be fulfilled if this thing were not to go like this? I say the same to you: if this opposition had not risen, how could the prophecy and what I have foretold to you be fulfilled? In the end, you force me to be a prophet. You know all I have foretold to you a long time ago and many times since about the opposition from the priests and from the lukewarm. They have now all gathered together in opposition, and the reason for this is that some are goaded by their concubines, some by their ambition, and each one is led by his passion. When the tax on priests was imposed, they wanted me to speak out against it and defend them.[23] I did not want to do so nor speak about it because, if I had said that the tax should not have been imposed, one would have said that I opposed the public good, and if I had said that the tax was necessary, I would have been told: 'You speak against the canons of the Church' and so they would have liked to catch me [in a trap]. So, you can see how things are, then. But let Christ direct his work. I do not care about opposition because, as I told you, we will always win and in the end we will triumph.

A new time, I tell you, is beginning and great wars are coming towards us, and even greater things are to be revealed, and much greater wars than these ones will come. I do not ask for peace, my Lord, but I call out 'War! War!' War, I say, against the devil. The peace of Christ is enough for us.

Moreover, look at what this thing is. Everyone admits that this excommunication is not valid in God's sight, but they have scruples in the sight of the Church. I am satisfied not to be removed from Christ and to be blessed by him.[24] Oh my Lord, I turn to you and

---

[23]In 1497, facing a severe financial crisis, the Piagnoni government of Florence sought to tax the clergy, willingly risking papal censure for, s they put it, the greater good of the city. See Lorenzo Polizzotto, *The Elect Nation*, pp. 46–47, 50, 64, and 365.

[24]At this point the original Italian text in the National Edition reads *non essere legato da Cristo* ('not to be tied up by Christ'). Such a reading, however, makes

tell you this, that if I should ever have myself absolved from this excommunication, you must send me to Hell. I would fear I had committed mortal sin, should I have myself absolved of this excommunication. These priests go seek counsel on whether anyone who associates with someone who is excommunicated participates with him *in the condemned crime*, and they forget the fundamental point, that is, whether the excommunication is valid or void. On the other hand, because of their ignorance, they pose the question badly because they want to know whether, by coming to the sermon, they are excommunicated. Tell me: is it a sin to preach? Is the preacher damned? If the person who imposed the excommunication were to say so, he would certainly be speaking against the Gospel. This is not, then, a *condemned crime*.

'Oh, I meant disobedience.'

And I tell you, if they observed that rule that says that no-one should receive a doctorate nor become a canon who was not sufficiently learned, there would not be so much ignorance and you would not have such a doubt—though there are a few learned men, but I do not speak of them. But in order to dispel all your scruples, I tell you, my priests (I call 'my' only those who want to live righteously; there are many, even among my own, who are sons of Christ): *confortamini et nolite timere, pusillanimes, Dominus vobiscum est*. 'Take comfort and do not fear, you faint-hearted, for the Lord is with you.' And I invite you all for this coming Thursday (I speak to my priests who want to live righteously): come Thursday, after Vespers, to San Marco, for we will deliver a beautiful lesson and I will expound for you what you have to do and how you must live righteously without scruples.[25]

'What more do you want to say now, Friar?'

---

absolutely no sense in this context. I have therefore hazarded a correction, changing *legato* to *levato*, thus changing the passage to read *non essere levato da Cristo* ('not to be removed from Christ'). The idea of being 'removed' (*levato*) does fit very nicely into the entire discussion of excommunication, which is the act of removing someone from a community (*ex communionem*). In making this correction, I have assumed either that the original word *legato* is a typographical error for *levato*, or that the scribe taking down the sermon as it was being delivered misheard *levato* as *legato* (an easy mis-hearing).

[25]That Thursday sermon is not part of the series on Exodus and appears not to have been recorded. The second sermon on Exodus was delivered on 18 February, an entire week after the first.

'Listen: I will tell you.'

'O, Father, there are others, too, who talk about this excommunication, and they are the friars who do not give absolution.'

Do you want me to teach you how to get them to give you absolution? Well, I should keep silent on this topic. But I will tell you this: do this ... (*Note, you who are reading this, that at this point the preacher said nothing, but he clinked his keys together; with this sound everyone understood that he meant to say that if you give them money they will absolve you. And then he continued and said*)[26] Would you like me to give you a good piece of advice, as well, one that will heal your entire country? Get rid of them.

'O, Friar, you go too much to the quick.'

One has to say the truth, here. I speak of the bad ones and say nothing of the good ones. But do not fear, we will certainly have confessors who will satisfy you, so go, finally, to confession and you will thank God that He has given you the grace to remove you from tepidness. I mean from the hands of wicked confessors, understand me well. *Moreover*, tell me, you priests and clerics: in 1478 did you hear confessions? Did you say Mass and the Office?[27] Why do you behave worse now than back then? I did not hang any archbishop nor any priest, nor kill anyone.

'Oh, they were defending the state.'

---

[26]This phrase is not in Latin, but in Italian; the National Edition gives it in italics, so I have kept them. It is, clearly, an intertextual note added by Lorenzo Violi, the transcriber.

[27]In the wake of the Pazzi conspiracy of 26 April 1478, when an attempted assassination of Lorenzo and Giuliano de' Medici (at elevation during the Easter Sunday High Mass in the cathedral) killed Giuliano but failed to kill Lorenzo, the city turned against the conspirators. Before the day was over, many of the conspirators, including the leaders of the Pazzi family, were caught and massacred, many by being unceremoniously hung to death from the windows of the Palazzo della Signoria. Several of these unfortunates were clergymen, including Francesco Salviati, archbishop of Pisa (see the famous sketch the young Leonardo da Vinci did of him hanging dead). Because of this mob violence against clergymen and the murder of an archbishop, Pope Sixtus IV Della Rovere excommunicated Lorenzo and placed Florence under an interdict. The city and its clergy, however, sided with Lorenzo and generally ignored the interdict. The pope's official indignation at the violence committed against the clergy may well have been re-enforced by private indignation at the failure of the Pazzi plot; apparently Sixtus IV had been fully aware of the conspirators' plans and had even supported them.

And I defend the state of Christ, and the faith, and good Christian living.

'O, Friar, was one to fear that excommunication, back then, or to observe it?'

I do not want to discuss this now, but I believe the answer is no, and let that be enough.

Do you think God wants these evils to exist or excommunications to be declared in order to be able to do all sorts of wickedness? You would be wrong. Come now, I speak to you, priests and friars, and I include myself when I speak to the friars. I am a bad friar,[28] and it is not me who speaks to you, understand me well; what I say to you, it is not me that says it to you, but Christ who says it to you in me.[29] Listen to what I tell you. Open your ears wide. You are looking for what is hidden under lock and key; but if this is opened up, you will find many of your secrets inside, and they will all become known. So, be careful what you are looking for.

I want to reveal to you a good point to use against me.

'O, Friar, will this be against Christ?'

No, it will not be against Christ, because Christ's honour comes first. I do want to tell them, but they will not do it.[30] Do you not want Christ's work to grow? Wage no war against Him, for Christ's work prospers when it is opposed. By waging war against this work, you give it more prestige than it otherwise would have had. See how it grows under this excommunication. And you thought you could lay it low, but it will grow the more you oppose it.

On now, to the third reason: whether the excommunication is valid or not. I have already given you two reasons why it is not valid. Now for the third one, according to the super-natural light of prophecy. This light first says these words: that is, that this excommunication is worth nothing and is not to be observed and, moreover, that we are obliged not to obey it because, if we were to obey it, many evil things would follow.

---

[28]Savonarola uses the depreciatory variant *frataccio*, which could mean anything from 'nasty friar' to 'bad friar' to 'dirty friar' etc.

[29]The original Italian says *in me* ('in me') rather than *per me* ('through me'). By this simple choice in adverbs Savonarola is clearly suggesting that Christ is *in* him and that he is not just an instrument *through which* Christ is speaking.

[30]This sentence is uttered as an aside to himself.

'O, Friar, I do not believe you in this. You have not performed any miracles, so why should I believe you and not the Church?'

Do as you wish. For the moment the Lord does not wish to do otherwise.

'O, Friar, you had also said that we should let the excommunication come and that we should parade it around on a spear. I thought you would reveal everything at that time.'

I answer you that the excommunication has not all come, for if it had all come, you would have seen everything. But if you have eyes, you must surely have seen many signs and their results: you saw Rome, how someone lost his son,[31] and someone one thing, someone another, and you have also seen who has died here; and I could also tell you who is in Hell. You will see their court trials, too. In fact, you would have seen everything had everything come. You have seen half, because half has come.

'O, Friar, I thought you would reveal what is hidden under lock and key.'

That time has not yet come: a great treasure is not revealed all at once. When a war is waged against a prince, if he has a treasure in a fortress, he keeps it as long as he can till the very end, and does not spend it quickly right away. Before he has to draw upon it, he first spends from the public purse and from other sources. For our part, we have taken out only one of David's five stones, that is, the light of this doctrine [1 Sam 17:40].[32] But I warn you, we are closer than ever to taking out these stones. You have not yet forced Him to perform a miracle: when He will be forced to do

---

[31]Savonarola is referring to the assassination of Juan Borgia, Duke of Gandia, son of the reigning Pope Alexander VI Borgia. The murder was committed on the night of 14–15 June 1497 and suspicion immediately fell upon Cardinal Cesare Borgia, the victim's brother, who soon thereafter renounced the cardinalate and assumed his deceased brother's political role in the family's dynastic strategy. Rome is clearly a metonymy for the Pope.

[32]Preparing to confront the giant Goliath, David bent over and picked up five smooth stones to use as weapons for his slingshot. The five stones eventually raised a lot of questions among medieval thinkers who posited that David, trusting God, needed only one stone and therefore, by picking up five, was revealing that he did not trust God; the standard response is that one should trust in God, but take the necessary precautions, nonetheless. Savonarola seems to adhere to the standard response and is preparing more than one argument to win sinners over to his cause.

it, God will stretch out His hand as His honour requires. But to tell the truth, you have seen so many signs that you do not need a miracle.

First, you have the sign that God is with you, for He has miraculously preserved you. The emperor and his adversary have come all the way to our gates, so much so that you thought you would be conquered, and *yet* all of a sudden he turned back.[33] There have been so many threats of war and destruction against you, and *yet* nothing has come of them. And although you have lost Pisa, nonetheless it was not through war. Florence, you greatly fear war. I tell you: do not fear it, let them wage war against you as much as they want, for the Lord is with you and will free you from everything. Italy, wage as much war as you know how to, come against Florence, all of you, for we do not fear anything. We will stay in our rooms and we will scatter our enemies, and the angels will fight on our behalf, so do not worry about it, Florence, for the Lord is with you; and you have seen so many signs that you should believe it.

Second, you have this sign that this doctrine is true: till now what was foretold has come to pass, though not all of it, but you can tell that the rest will come soon. Did I not predict the great famine? And there was one. Did I also not tell you that the wolves would be seized by the chickens? But this is not all. I told you that the lukewarm and those who seemed righteous would be exposed; and so it happened, and I say to you: *unless you mend your ways, he will draw his bow.*[34]

That is not all. Another *further* sign that this doctrine is true and comes from God: you have seen that it has led to righteous Christian living. So you must admit that it comes from God. *Also:* a doctrine that is loved by the righteous must be true. This one is

---

[33]The reference is to the 1494 descent into Italy of King Charles VIII of France, bent on claiming his rights to the throne of Naples, and the response this elicited from Emperor Maximilian I, who also had rights to Naples. While the emperor never actually came to Florence's gates (though there was fear of it), Charles did and walked away with several Florentine fortresses in Tuscany.

[34] *nisi conversi fueritis arcum suum vibravit.* The passage, as is, is not in the Vulgate; Savonarola makes it up himself by drawing from at least two different places in the Vulgate: 'unless you mend your ways' (*nisi conversi fueritis*) from Mt 18:3 and 'he will draw his bow' (*arcum suum vibravit*) from a variety of places such as Ps 7:13, Jer 51:3, Lam 2:4, etc.

loved and sought by the righteous, therefore it is true. *Also*: one has prayed a lot to God for this doctrine and one continues to do so, asking God to advance truth; and if God were to leave in the dark those who pray and who walk with an upright heart, He would show that He does not care for mankind; therefore, one must admit that in every way this doctrine, which is always advancing, is true and comes from God, and is not false and does not come from the devil. *Also*: a doctrine that grows all the more in times of trouble and always increases the fervour of those who believe in it comes from God. This doctrine has this effect (for I can tell you I have never seen so much fervour among the friars and the laity as there is now among our followers); therefore, we must say that it comes from God. *Also*: a doctrine that unites all hearts in charity and in one will comes from God. This doctrine has had this effect and has united priests, laity, and foreigners; therefore, one must admit that it comes from God. *Also*: a doctrine that lets all those who believe in it be joyful and happy in Christ comes from God. This doctrine I have preached to you lets all those who believe in it dwell happily in righteous living; therefore, one must, of necessity, confess that it comes from God. *Also*: a doctrine with which all other doctrines are in agreement, must be true. All the canons, all philosophy, all theology, divine light, and every other true doctrine agree with this one; therefore, we must say that this doctrine is also true. *Also*: a doctrine that has very powerful enemies and yet survives and grows must have some divine power [*virtù*] to support it. This doctrine I have preached to you is such that it has had, and still has, nearly the entire world against it, and has been and is being persecuted so much that, had it not been helped by God, it would inevitably have been destroyed; therefore, one must admit that it is God who upholds it and that it is true and that it comes from Him. You want to see a miracle? Everybody hinders and opposes this doctrine, yet it survives, and you *still* see that, although it does not fight and has no squadrons nor weapons nor money nor soldiers that might defend it with force, yet it continues to advance and to win, and always some of its enemies fall and one sometimes perishes here, another sometimes there. Does this not look like a miracle to you? And *yet*, those who have no eyes do not see it. *Also*: look at the doctrine of our enemies, you will find nothing in it but lies. How often have they said: 'He has fled, he is done for, he has fallen, he has stolen so many thousands of ducats' and yet we are still here. From this you can judge this doctrine of theirs, full of lies and falsehoods, to be false and not true. The ducats they say I have did not help me gain absolution, this time. Oh, how many lies have they told! And so you must realize that if their doctrine is full of lies, and wicked living, and rumours, defamations, and discords and hatred, ours is full of truth, and we have always held firm as with one will that our doctrine comes from God and that Christ is with us and not with them, as they say. Now, then, do you want me to draw my conclusions for you and show you that Christ is with us and not with them?

'Yes.'

Now, listen and I will show you.

Now then, Christ, what side do you want to be on? Ours or theirs? You can see that our side has always told the truth and that we have always been immovable and that this doctrine has brought in righteous living and so much fervour and so many prayers, and *yet* we have been excommunicated and they have been blessed. And yet one can see that their doctrine leads to evil deeds, and to giving oneself over to eating and drinking, to avarice, to concubines, to the sale of benefices, and to many lies, and to doing all sorts of wickedness. Which side, then, do you want to be on, Christ? Either on the side of truth or of lies, on the side of the excommunicated or of the blessed? Christ answers: *ego sum via, veritas et vita* [Jh 14:6]. Christ says: 'I am the truth, and I want to dwell with the side that has truth, and with those whom you say are excommunicated, because they pray and do good deeds, they are united in charity, but these other people are always spreading rumours, they speak all sorts of evil, they are disunited.' I say, which side do you want to dwell with, Christ? With the excommunicated or with the blessed? He answers: 'These people always sing *Behold, how good and how joyful it is for brothers to live as one*, and they are always joyful; but these other people are always unhappy, their hearts are angry, they have no truth whatsoever. Therefore, I want to dwell with the excommunicated.'

The Lord therefore notes that He wants to dwell with the excommunicated and the devil will dwell with the blessed. O, Lord, you have perverted your order; how is your wisdom? You used to want to dwell with the blessed and not with the excommunicated, because to be excommunicated means to be severed[35] and cut off

---

[35]The original says *preciso* ('precise'), but this must clearly be a mis-transcription for *reciso* ('cut, severed') and so I correct accordingly.

from Christ, and to be given into the hands of the devil, and to go every day from bad to worse. The excommunicated go every day from good to better and they constantly improve. Well, then, you see that the Lord is with us and that He sees that the excommunicated improve daily and become stronger in righteous living, and so He wants to dwell with us.

So, my citizens, you must lay down your life, your wealth, and everything else for the sake of this truth and be ready, like good Christians, to die for love of Christ. Women and children, you must be ready, when necessary, to die for the truth and for love of Christ. My brothers, I want us to lay down even our lives for this truth. My Lord, I turn to you: you died for the truth, and I am happy to die for truth: I offer myself in sacrifice to you: here I am; I am happy to die for you, and I pray you fervently that I might never die for any other reason but to defend your truth, so that it be the salvation of your chosen ones and of this people. I pray you, My Lord, my almighty God, *who are blessed for ever and ever. Amen.*

Ten Rules to Observe in Times of Great Tribulations [1494; 1497]

The first rule is to pray God devoutly and with steadfastness that He might send good captains and shepherds to console, cheer, and comfort the people of God, who in those times, because of the great tribulations and because of the weakness and scarcity of natural and supernatural light, easily slip from good and fall into sin: *especially*, in time of great tribulation, when the strength of the above-mentioned light is generally lost or diminished, and so one easily slips from true judgement, deceived by his own self-love and by the demon and by his own body. And so one's own light is not enough for the infirm, nor their having heard and understood many good things, but they must have outside help, that is, comforters and consolers.[1]

The second is to pray God to grant you the spirit of discretion, that is, liveliness and subtlety of judgement so that you might discern and know true good people from false and evil people, for at that time there will be an abundance of lukewarm people and hypocrites so much so that anyone who is not especially enlightened will not know what road to follow. And so our Saviour says this about the final temptations: *Surgent pseudochristi et pseudo-*

---

[1]Savonarola is making a subtle distinction between a comforter (*conforta-tore*) and a consoler (*consolatore*): a comforter gives comfort to the afflicted by inciting or exhorting them, by giving them courage and strength; a consoler, on the other hand, gives them comfort by consoling, that is, by seeking to reassure them and to re-establish internal peace. In pre-modern Italy the term *confortatore* often applied to the hooded figure who, under cover of anonymity, would assist the condemned on the night before and up to the moment of execution, exhorting him to make his peace with God and to accept the punishment about to be inflicted upon him by earthly law.

prophetae, et dabunt signa magna et prodigia, ita ut in errorem inducantur, si fieri potest, etiam electi [Mt 24:24]: that is, in those times false disciples of Christ will rise up and false prophets, and they will perform great signs and marvels, till even the elect—if it is possible—will be drawn into error.

The third rule is to pray God to grant you a true and living light to make you see that external ceremonies, although good in themselves, are worth nothing towards salvation if there is no spirit in them—because it is written that man is not justified by the works of the law, that is, by ceremonies and external works—; and that He bestow upon you the grace to purge yourself and to justify yourself and sanctify yourself on the inside, and not only on the outside.

The fourth is to pray God that He grant you a living and true spirit of divine love, which follows from true contrition, and from which then comes the true poverty and simplicity of Christ and disdain for earthly things, as we have seen and can see from experience is the case with holy men. And so, disdaining all earthly things and considering them to be like excrement, if in tribulations you were to lose your wealth, or your children, or your own life, you would not be troubled, but, on the contrary, you would bear everything patiently and with the joy of holy spirit.

The fifth rule is to pray God that this spirit and grace confirm in you the seven gifts of the Holy Spirit,[2] giving you, in time of tribulation, this special help as well; because *especially* in those times, the grace and the virtues [that come] with the general help of God are not enough, but, in many specific cases that happen suddenly and unexpectedly, it is necessary that at that time you be lead and ruled by a special succour; now by particular and specific wisdom, now by advice, now by a living light of the intellect, now by a clear scientific knowledge, now by fear, now by fortitude of spirit, now by meek piety. By these gifts the soul easily makes itself available and obedient to the particular inspiration of the Holy Spirit, and so in time of great tribulations it easily follows its lead.

These five rules must be observed with reverence before the tribulations come.

Five other rules to be observed when tribulation is present follow.

---

[2]Wisdom, understanding, counsel, fortitude, knowledge, piety, fear of the Lord (Isaiah 11:2).

The first is to take communion often, well disposed by true contrition and confession of one's sins, because the first effect of this sacrament is to convert one to Christ. And so, the more often one partakes in this sacrament worthily, the more he grows in his love for Christ, and the more he unites himself with God, and the more grace he acquires and the ability and the strength to withstand all tribulations. And so, in the primitive Church, because of the great tribulations that there were, Christians used to partake of communion every day so as to be strong and stalwart for any tribulation, keeping themselves always prepared and well disposed to partake of communion worthily.

The second rule is to pray assiduously, for frequent and attentive prayer confirms a person in all virtues and makes him strong and stalwart and incites fervour to the point that the demon cannot draw close to him. It also enlightens a person marvellously on everything he must do and makes him a servant of God. And so the Saviour says: *Oportet semper orare et nunquam deficere* [Lk 18:1]; that is, it is always necessary to pray and never to fail to do so.

The third rule is constantly to pray God to hold the enemy back, that is, the devil and his kin, removing from them the intelligence, the desire, and the power to do evil, and believe firmly that it is the hand of God that moves everything and brings all tribulations, and that prayer is the most effective way to implore anything from Him.

The fourth rule is to pray God to bring a quick end to all tribulations, removing their causes, such as bad leaders and the great power they have over their followers when they do not want to convert to penance and when they remain obstinate in their evil doing, as it is written: *Dissipa gentes quae bella volunt* [Ps 67:31 (68:30)]: scatter those who seek war.

The fifth and last rule is to pray God fervently that, by way of these tribulations, He might make good people perfect, purge the imperfect, and rouse many sinners to penance, because in tribulation many turn to penance, while in prosperity they do not convert but, on the contrary, become worse.

Figure 11. 'The little crown of the Virgin.' Woodcut
from G. Savonarola, *Compendio di Revelatione*.
Florence: ad istanza di Piero Pacini da Pescia, 23
aprile 1496, fol. 31r.

On the Prudent and Judicious Way of Living in the Order
[14 September 1496]

The great care friars have for the health of their own body and the care superiors have for their subjects is a temptation of the devil who seeks in this way to undo the Order little by little. The illness and weakness of our bodies derives, first, from distrust, that is, from not trusting God; second, it derives from eating too much. Therefore those who adhere to what our holy fathers ordained in the rule and constitution regarding abstinence, with the statement and the reservations we voiced, will be spiritually stronger against temptation, and stronger in good works, and stronger in body and healthier, and will have a longer life; but those who are sensual and do not observe this rule, will be weaker in spirit and in body, and will have a shorter life. And this is meant in a general way, because every rule has its exceptions. This does not mean, however, that among those who observe this rule someone might not get sick, or that someone might not die young, but that on the whole more will get sick from among those who do not observe it, and that they will die sooner than those who observe the rule of fasting.

And the rule is that all those who are older than twenty-one and have strong and healthy bodies must continue with their fasting. Those who are underage and weak must fast at least on Mondays, Wednesdays, and Fridays; and on the other days in the evening, eating nothing else but bread so as to put out their hunger and their temper, and some fruit may be added to this when the superior will see fit. Except for the young ones and the weaker ones, who, if they are healthy, must fast at least on Wednesdays and Fridays; or, in fact, on Mondays they may eat a little bread in the evenings, and nothing else, and the other days, that is on Tuesdays, Thursdays, and Saturdays, they will do like the others who are under twenty-one years of age or are older than twenty-one but are weak. Those who are sickly, not being able to fast, will do what they are told by those in charge of them. And they, together with the others, are promised every day the blessing of our Lord Jesus Christ and of his most sweet mother the ever-Virgin Mary, if they diligently observe these things, *namely*: first, great zeal for the Order, that is, a great desire to observe every rule—if they can—, and to see that others observe them; second, humility of heart; third, silence; fourth, frequent prayer; fifth, reverence for each other, both in your heart and with your body.

These things are confirmed by the authority of Scripture. Isaiah, 40th chapter: *The Lord is the everlasting God, the Creator of all the earth. He does not faint or grow weary, his understanding is unfathomable. He gives power to the faint, and to him who has no might he increases strength* [Is 40:28–29]; as if he were answering those who ask: 'What does it mean that our fathers were more abstinent than us and were healthier, and lived longer than us?' and he were saying: 'Because they trusted in the Lord.' And if we trusted in God as they did, we would be healthy in our abstinence as they were, because God has not changed, nor is he absent, nor is he weary; and, although some of those who practise abstinence get sick and die, this is not, however, because of their abstinence, but because of some other cause, because of some hidden judgement of God, whose wisdom is unfathomable.[1]

And so trust in God, who gives power[2] to those who are tired, and to those who are not *so strong*—as the Gloss says— he multiplies their spiritual and bodily strength, and preserves it for a long time. But those who are sensual and diffident fail in body and in spirit; and so he adds: *Even youths shall faint and be weary* [Is 40:30], *that is*, those who live sensually, as children do,[3] will grow

---

[1]The original Italian says *investigabile* (that can be investigated), but clearly the argument implies the opposite (that cannot be investigated); perhaps the negative particle *non* was inadvertently dropped by the editor or the typesetter. Later in this work Savonarola will, in fact, refer to Isaiah 40:28 *nec est investigatio sapientiae eius*, 'his understanding is unsearchable' (RSV).

[2]The original says *virtù*, meaning 'ability, talent, power,'; it does not mean, in this case, 'virtue' in the Christian sense. Savonarola is using the term much as Machiavelli would to indicate ability and talent to accomplish things.

[3]Savonarola uses the term *fanciulli* to indicate someone in his very early teens; for a good discussion of age categories in fifteenth-century Florence, see Taddei, '*Puerizia, Adolescenza* and *Giovinezza*: Images and Conceptions

weak and will struggle all day long to maintain their body; but because they do not place their trust in God, even though they are naturally strong in their body, they will catch many diseases, and so he says: *and young men shall fall into infirmity* [Is 40:30]. But those who will place their trust in God, observing what the holy fathers have ordained, will renew their strength, and so he continues: *they who wait for the Lord shall renew their strength, they shall mount up with wings like eagles* [Is 40:31]: they will change their feathers and will renew themselves like eagles do, and they will put on the new feathers of contemplation. *Current et non laborabunt*: they will run quickly and without tiring towards the perfection of spiritual life; *ambulabunt et non deficient*: they will walk from virtue to virtue without failing until they reach the harbour of the life of the blessed.

Saint Thomas also says (in his *quarto Sententiarum, dist.* 15, q. 3, art. 1, q. 2, ad 3) that the human body falls ill more frequently because of excess food than because of abstinence, and he cites Galen, who says: *the greatest medicine is abstinence*; and says: 'Experience clearly shows that those who are abstinent live longer than those who are not abstinent.' And so, we cannot say that the removal of food is a cause of death; but, on the contrary, one must say that it is the conservation and the prolongation of life.

And because every spiritual and bodily good comes from God, and so that we do not fail to do our part, it seems to me that we must pray every day: first, for spiritual goods; second, for bodily health, third, for temporal goods, that God protect us, as our poverty and need require, so that we need not distract our mind and our body with different things, but that we might peacefully dedicate ourselves to our prayers and our studies, for His honour and the salvation of our soul.

Therefore, we will first pray for the salvation of the Church universal, but especially for the Church and city of Florence, and we will say: *Shepherd of Israel, listen* etc. [Ps 79:2(80:1)]. *Then*, we will ask our Lord Jesus Christ for the strength of spirit that proceeds

---

of Youth in Florentine Society During the Renaissance' and also Sebregondi, 'Clothes and Teenagers: What Young Men Wore in Fifteenth-Century Florence' both in *The Premodern Teenager. Youth and Society 1150–1650*, ed. Konrad Eisenbichler (Toronto: Centre for Reformation and Renaissance Studies, 2002), pp. 14–26 27–50 respectively.

from the light of grace, and we will commit this care to him saying: *God, have mercy upon us*, etc. [Ps 66(67)]. *Then*, we will commit the care of our body to the Virgin Mary, and we will ask her for health saying: *We fly to your patronage* etc.[4] Then, the care of temporal things we will commit to our father Saint Dominic, and we will ask him for it saying: *Oh Loving Father Dominic* etc.[5] We will commit our defence against our adversaries to the angels who look after us, and we will ask them for it saying: *Angel and Archangels, Thrones and Dominations, Principalities and Powers, Virtues of heaven, defend us and guide us from heaven*. Then one says: *Lord have mercy, Christ have mercy*;[6] *Our Father* etc.; *And lead us not* etc.;[7] *Remember our congregation* etc.;[8] *Save your servants* etc.;[9] *After childbirth, Virgin* etc.;[10] *Pray for us, Blessed Dominic* etc.;[11] *Adore God* etc.;[12] *Oh Lord, hear my prayer* etc.;[13] *Let us pray, Oh God of all power and might, to whom belong* etc.;[14]

---

[4]We fly to your patronage, O holy Mother of God; despise not our petitions in our necessities, but deliver us from all danger, O glorious and blessed Virgin.'

[5]'O Lovig Father Dominic, remember your words; as you stand before the supreme Judge, intercede for your poor people.' (from the liturgy for the feast day of St Dominic, 8 August).

[6]This is the *Kyrie*, recited as part of the Mass.

[7]By dividing the *Our Father* in this manner, Savonarola seems to indicate that it should be recited according the the standard practice in the recitation of the Hours, that is, silently up to the verse 'Grant us this day our daily bread' and then aloud from the verse 'And lead us not into temptation' to the end.

[8]V. 'Remember our congregation.' R. 'Which you have possessed from the beginning' (from the Office). Also, Ps 73(74):2.

[9]V. 'Save your servants.' R. 'Who hope in you, O my God.' (from the Office).

[10]V. 'After childbirth you remained a Virgin. O mother of God, intercede for us. Alleluia' (from the Gradual for the Feasts of the Blessed Virgin Mary).

[11]V. 'Pray for us, Blessed Father Dominic.' R. 'That we may be worthy of the promises of Christ.'

[12]'Adore God, all you His Angels: Sion heard, and was glad: and the daughters of Juda rejoiced' [Ps 96(97):7–8].

[13]V. 'O Lord, hear my prayer.' R. 'And let my cry come unto Thee.' (from the introductory verses to the Mass and from the Office of the Hours)

[14]'O God of all power and might, to whom belongs every thing that is best: implant in our hearts the love of your Your name and increase within us true religion; that You may nourish in us those things that are good and by the zeal of our devotion may preserve what You have nourished' (from the Collect for the Sixth Sunday after Pentecost).

Keep us as your servants etc.;[15] *God, who your Church* etc.;[16] *Oh God, who in wondrous order do ordain* etc.[17]

---

[15]'O Lord God Almighty, we beseech you to keep us your servants both outwardly in our bodies and inwardly in our souls, that by the glorious intercession of blessed Mary Ever-Virgin we may be delivered from our present heaviness and attain in the end everlasting happiness.' (from the Collect for the Saturday Office of the Blessed Virgin Mary)

[16]It is unclear which prayer Savonarola is indicating; one possibility is the following: 'Deus, qui Ecclesiam tuam beati Dominici, Confessoris tui, Patris nostri, illuminare dignatus es meritis et doctrinis: concede ut eius intercessione temporalibus non destituatur auxiliis, et spiritualibus semper proficiat incrementis. Per Christum Dominum nostrum. Amen.' The contemporary English version reads: 'Lord, let the holiness and teaching of our Father Dominic come to the aid of your Church. May he help us now with his prayers as he once inspired people by his preaching. We ask this through our Lord Jesus Christ. Amen.' The prayer comes from the Litany of Saint Dominic.

[17]'O God, who in wondrous order do ordain and constitute the services of men and Angels, mercifully grant that our life may be defended on earth by them that stand near You, evermore ministering to You in heaven. Through Christ our Lord. Amen.' (from the Office for the feast day of the Archangel Michael and all the Angels)

Figure 12: 'Savonarola discussing the gift of prophecy with the
seven sages of Antiquity.' Woodcut from G. Savonarola,
Dialogo della verità profetica. Florence, ca. 1500.

A Guide to Righteous Living
[18 April – 22 May 1498]

All good Christian living proceeds from the grace of our Saviour Jesus Christ, without whose grace no-one can be saved; and therefore whoever wants to lead a righteous life must first strive to acquire this grace; secondly, when he has acquired it, he must seek to increase it; thirdly, he must endeavour day and night to persevere in it until his death.

As for the first: whoever feels that he is outside the grace of God because he is in mortal sin should think hard and very carefully about the fact that he must die and that he does not know either when, or where, or how; and that, if he were to die in mortal sin, he would go immediately to hell, where there is nothing other than pain and tears and great misery — and the greatest misery is to be deprived of the glory of heaven —, and there he must remain for ever, never to get out.

If he thinks about this with faith and considers it well, he will begin to fear, and from fear he will come to love God, and he will begin to regret his sin not only out of fear of hell, but also because he has offended God. And in this manner, regretting or being displeased with his past sins, he will firmly resolve to sin no more and, firmly resolved to this, he will arrive at true contrition, which is the first element of penance.

Then he must diligently consider all his sins, that is, those of his thoughts and of his evil desires, and those of his speech, and those of his evil deeds, and also those of omission, when he did not do what he was obliged to do.

And then he should pray God to help him find a good confessor, and in fact he should diligently search for him, making sure that he be a man of good life; and, if he should not know very well how to confess himself, he should have his confessor help him. And after the confession, he should humbly receive his penance from him and do it devoutly, adding something to it of his own, especially when the penance is light. And since Man is weak and falls easily into sin, whoever wants to live righteously must confess often because, in doing so, he will confess better, and will better refrain from sin, and, by virtue of the sacrament of confession he will acquire greater grace.

He must also take communion at least four times a year, that is, at Easter, Pentecost, on the Assumption of Our Lady, and at Christmas,[1] and more or less according to his confessor's advice. And he must do these things with great devotion in order to acquire the grace of Christ. And although no-one can know for sure whether he is in the grace of God if not by revelation, none the less a devout person can have some idea of this and some indication of it. And one sign of grace is when a person firmly resolves out of love of God never to offend Him, and regrets that he has offended Him in the past; another is when a person keeps God's commandments and delights himself in them; another is when he begins to be weary of the world and all its pleasures; another is when he delights in hearing the word of God and preaching, and finds pleasure in Masses devoutely said and in divine offices; another, when a person patiently bears his tribulations. Noticing, therefore, these signs in oneself, a person can suppose and believe that he is in the grace of God, and therefore he must try to increase it. And this is the second thing we must discuss.

As for the increase of grace, one should know that anyone who wants grace to increase within him must distance himself from its opposite and draw near to its root, as one does when one wants to heat cold water, one removes it from the cold and brings it close

---

[1] Easter and Pentecost are movable feasts. The first marks the resurrection of Jesus and is celebrated on the first Sunday following the full moon after the vernal equinox (which makes it fall sometime between 22 March and 25 April); the second marks the descent of the Holy Spirit upon the Apostles and is celebrated fifty days after Easter. Pentecost is considered the birthday of the Church because, with the descent of the Holy Spirit on them, the Apostles began to carry the message of Jesus into the world. The other two feasts are fixed. The Assumption of Mary is celebrated on 15 August and honours her bodily assumption into heaven at the end of her earthly life (although long part of popular belief and celebration, the dogma of the Assumption was not promulgated until 1950). Christmas, which celebrates the nativity of Jesus, falls traditionally on 25 December.

to the heat. Now, what cools charity and the grace of God in a person is one's affection for earthly things, and so one must withdraw one's affection from these transitory things as if they did not exist. However, since a person still needs to look after his corporal life, both his and that of his family, he must therefore desire earthly things only inasmuch as he requires them according to his social status; and, in order not to think a lot about such things, he should strive to live simply, be it in his food or in his dress or in other things, leaving aside all ostentation. And, if he should not be able to have all those things his social status requires, he should be happy with what God gives him, because what nature requires should be enough for a good Christian, since he does not have to remain in this world, but pass on to his celestial homeland. And he must not take care to enrich his sons, in fact, he must not enrich them, because, if they are good men, they will not care for or need wealth; and, if they are bad men, it will be good for them not to be wealthy, so that they may not be able to do all the evil they would like to do. So, if a person devotes himself to simplicity, desiring nothing more than what he needs, he will easily withdraw his affection from earthly things.

He must also withdraw his affection for the flesh and live chastely, fleeing women and other occasions for lust; and, even though he be married, he must keep himself chaste as best he can, as his spiritual father instructs him.

He must also flee the praises of men, and not care about their insults, but follow the proverb that says: do good and let people say what they want. And in this manner, abandoning all affection for earthly things, he must draw through prayer as near to God as he can. However, because a person cannot always be praying, he must set times for prayer and set times for work: for example, in the morning when he gets up from sleep, he must say his prayers and then go to Mass, where he must stay devoutly, and contemplate the passion of Christ, and confess his sins to God, and take communion spiritually with the priest, and pray God to keep him, that day, from sin and from all dangers. And then he must go to his honest work and earnings, where still he must often raise his mind to God, and often say that little verse: *Be pleased, Oh God, to deliver me! Oh Lord make haste to help me!* [Ps 69:2(70:1)]; or, if he does not know it, he should say: Lord, help me! and especially when he wants to start something. And, when he goes to eat, he should first say a prayer; similarly, when he returns to his work;

and in the evening when he goes to sleep, he should first say his prayers and devotions; and, on feastdays, he should devote himself completely to divine things. In doing these things, he will continually increase in himself his contempt for the things of this world and he will grow in grace, which is a splendour in the soul that joins it in love with Christ; and the more he advances the more he will fall in love with God and find joy and peace in his heart.

As for the third part, one must note that perseverance is what will be crowned; and so whoever has begun to live righteously must endeavour, day and night, to persevere in it. And the first thing he must do is separate himself from all those occasions that can make him fall into mortal sin, such as bad company, which he must flee as one flees from a snake, and he should not worry about their enmity, that is, if they wish us evil because of this, for it is better to lose the friendship of men than of God; instead, he must always converse with good men, or else be on his own. A person must also beware of going to places that are dangerous for the soul, such as dances or taverns; and, in fact, he must protect himself, as if from fire, from all those things that can easily lead him into sin. He must strive very hard to restrain his tongue and to say nothing but good things about his fellow man; and never praise himself, but rather lower and humble himself in front of all men; nor judge his fellow man badly, especially in doubtful matters. In tribulations he should be patient, and believe that God gives us tribulations for our good, as He did to all his saints. And he should never let himself be conquered by negligence or sloth so that he fails to do the good he started doing with a steadfast spirit. But since perseverance in grace is the greatest gift from God, one must always in one's prayers ask God for it, and constantly reaffirm one's good intentions in front of Him, and offer always to be willing with His help to serve Him. In so doing, one will have grace in this world, and in the other world glory, which God may grant to all of us, for He is blessed *for ever and ever. Amen.*

The Book on the Life of the Widow [1491]

Proem

Even though I feel inadequate to write about widowhood, my dearly beloved in Christ Jesus,[1] nonetheless, obliged by your prayers, I will delve into the treasury of Sacred Scripture in the hope that God, though your merit and prayer, will open my mind to that which, on my own, I would not have been able to think about, let alone write about and recommend to you. And I will do this that much more eagerly since I know widows are loved by God, for He takes very special care of them, as the psalmist of the Holy Spirit [2 Sam 23:1], the prophet David, says: 'God will receive the orphan and the widow into his arms.' [Ps 145(146):9] Therefore, when our Saviour saw that widow who had lost her son cry, He was immediately moved to compassion and said to her 'Do not cry, woman,' and raised her beloved son from the dead. [Lk 7:13] And He has so much compassion for widows and their orphans that He severely forbids, under the ancient Law, that any harm whatsoever be done to them, saying: 'I order you among other things that you do not wrong widows and orphans, for, if you wrong them, they will cry out to me and I will hear their voice and their tears, and my wrath will inveigh against you and I will strike you with my sword and I will make widows of your women and orphans of your children.' [Ex 22:22–24]

Do not, however, assume from this that it is right for you to ask for revenge against those who harm you, for, when He says 'they will cry out to me,' He means to say that their tears and tribulations are a crying out in God's sight asking for revenge for the oppressed, even though the holy widows should pray for them, as is written

---

[1]Savonarola uses the masculine form for the adjective, 'dilettissimi' even though the work is clearly addressed to women.

about Abel against Cain, where it says 'The voice of your brother Abel's blood cries to me from the earth.' [Gen 4:10] Because, even though Abel was not asking for vengeance, nonetheless his blood was crying out. So, since God protects widows so much, it seems to me that I would do something very pleasing to Him if, through his grace, I should bring to completion this little treatise of ours. And since examples move more than words, and also since I want always to keep Sacred Scripture as our base, I will, first of all, propose to you the life of that widow, the prophetess Saint Anna, and from this I will write about the life of widows.

Book One
On the nature of the true widow

'At the time Christ was born, there was a widow named Anna, a prophetess, daughter of Phanuel from the tribe of Asher, who was already very old and had spent many days of her life and of her maidenhood; she had lived with her husband for seven years and, after the death of her husband, she had persevered in widowhood until her eighty-fourth year; serving God with fasting and with prayers, she never left the temple day or night. And this woman, when Christ was presented at the temple, came forth praising the Lord and speaking of Him to all who were waiting for the redemption of Israel.' [Lk 2:36–38]

From these words we can divide our treatise into three parts. First, we will see what a widow should be; second, how she should live; third, how she should teach others, so that she may gain a precious crown in heaven.

And so that the soul of those women who have lost their husband should warm to this work, I will first explain how it is better to serve God as a widow than as a married woman.

Chapter 1
Exhortation to live as a widow

After a woman is freed from her husband by his death, although she could without sin remarry, nonetheless this return to the works of the flesh, if it is not excused by youth or by some other good reason, is reprehensible, even according to worldly values, for such a woman lets people think that she is not completely disinclined to the flesh. Therefore, our holy widow Anna, so as not to gain this reputation and because of her wish to lead a perfect spiritual life, once her husband had died, did not want to remarry again. In this manner she provides widows with this example, that they must hold fast to their desire for continence, for they will be more prompt to serve God; and there are many reasons why this is so.

First, because, as the Apostle says to the Romans,[2] 'a woman who is married, as long as her husband is alive, is bound under law to her husband;' [Rom 7:2] for thus was condemned the first woman, who was the cause of his sin, as God said to her: 'You will be under the power of your husband.' [Gen 3:16] This condemnation was understood to apply through her to all women who married. Therefore, it is necessary for a married woman to serve not only God, but also her husband, and in this manner she is torn between the two. Therefore, the Apostle says to the Corinthians: 'A married woman must think about the things of this world and how she can please her husband; but she who has no husband must think of nothing else but God.' [1 Cor 7:34] And because God wants all our heart, it follows that a widow can serve God better than a married woman, who also will be less able to give herself to prayer the more she might have a husband who is irksome or, worse, if he is wicked, without piety, lustful, or jealous, or otherwise evil, for he will not let his wife serve God, but he will prevent her in every way from doing so, always muttering against her and yelling at her, leading her to commit many sins, even, and especially, sins of lust, since the devil works hard to this end, so that she may do nothing good at all. Most of the time, those women who remarry find this kind of a husband, for God wants this to be a punishment for them for they chose not to recognize the grace of his liberation.

Second, it is better to remain a widow in order to be freer from the prickings of the flesh, for there is nothing that distances one from the spirit and that blinds one to divine things as letting oneself be conquered by concupiscence. Thus David, who was full of the Holy Spirit, because he did not hold back his depraved appetite when he saw Bathsheba, fell into the sin of adultery and then was so blinded by it that he did not hesitate to kill so cruelly and in

---

[2]Although not one of the twelve original apostles, Paul was nonetheless often referred to as an Apostle, and especially as 'the Apostle to the Gentiles' because of his work among non-Jews.

such a treacherous way her husband, Uriah, — who was so saintly and faithful to his state — for no other reason but only to satisfy his lust.[3] Therefore, whoever wants to live spiritually must distance oneself from the flesh, and a married woman cannot do this completely because, as the Apostle says to the Corinthians, 'a married woman does not have power over her body, but is in the power of her husband, and similarly a married man does not have power over his body, but is in the power of his wife' [1 Cor 7:4] and, therefore, she cannot completely abstain from the flesh. Even if she could in good conscience abstain, it would however be very difficult and nearly impossible for her to do so, for whoever stands near a fire must of necessity become warm, and this carnal deed is such that the more one does it, the more one's desire for it grows, and, consequently, the more one distances oneself from God. Therefore, the Apostle advises in that same place that at times a husband and wife must separate themselves in order better to give themselves over to prayer [1 Cor 7:5], as if to say: you cannot give yourselves to prayer if you do not separate yourselves, for the flesh is contrary to the spirit, and the spirit to the flesh.

Third, because a married woman must deal with children which, as daily experience shows, are a great burden to raise when they are small, and this is a great hindrance to the perfection of spiritual life. A widowed woman, however, is free from this and therefore can serve God better.

Fourth, because a widowed woman is not as tied to the management of the family as is a married woman. Now, it is not necessary for me to prove how much distraction the management of others engenders in the mind of those who want to serve God, for experience demonstrates it. Whence, even Saint Martha used to become upset during the feasts she organized for Christ, who said to her: 'Martha, Martha, you are prompt and anxious in this service of yours and you worry about a thousand things, but Mary has chosen the best part, which will last and will not be taken away from her.' [Lk 10:41–42]

Fifth, because a widow is freer not only from the vice of the flesh, but also from opportunities for avarice and pride, which three sins are at the root of all evil. For a married woman must go about

---

[3] The story of David's love for Bathsheba and his commissioned assassination of her husband Uriah is narrated in 2 Sam 11:2–27.

well dressed according to her position, and she must dress her daughters and sons similarly, and this dressing gives birth to much vainglory and pride and envy among women; and these are also the cause of other sins, and many times they spend on themselves what should be given to the poor. A widowed woman, however, has her black dress and must not go beyond that, and so she is not forced, as is a married woman, to gather money in order to dress herself, and it is not shameful for her, on the contrary it is honourable for her to go dressed humbly, and, therefore, she does not have the opportunity to go proudly among other women, nor to be an occasion for sin.

Sixth, because a married woman often cannot avoid going to dinners and marriages and feasts organized by her relatives or friends, at which events many sins are sometimes committed, especially nowadays. A widowed woman is free from this distraction and this occasion for sin, for she can always honestly excuse herself on the grounds that this is not appropriate to her state.

Seventh, because widowhood is in itself a rein to saintly living, for, being in such a state, she is no longer allowed to do what she may have been able to do as a married woman, such as talk with men, wander through the streets, sit at a window. In these things a married woman is freer because, in her case, there is not as much suspicion among men as there is for a widow, and you know that freedom is the cause for many sins. However, when a woman is constrained, assuming that she will not abstain because of virtue, nonetheless, she will look after herself because of shame, and this necessity often turns itself into a virtue, and, therefore, a widow, reined in by her state, does not commit as many sins as a married woman.

For these reasons, therefore, and for other similar reasons, a widow is much freer than a married woman to do what is good. Therefore, as Saint Jerome tells Saint Paula, when Saint Melania, who had an infirm husband and two little children, saw them all die on the same day, she ran to the feet of a crucifix and said: 'Lord, I thank you that you have freed me from such a burden and such servitude; now I will be able to serve you more expeditiously and with greater freedom.'[4] This saint, therefore, together with our

---

[4]Melania the Elder (342–c.409). At 16 she married Valerius Maximus, Prefect of Rome, but was widowed six years later. At about the same time she also

Saint Anna, illustrates for you how much better it is to serve God in widowhood than in marriage.

But since not all women who do not remarry after the death of their husbands are true widows, I now want to show you which ones are the true widows and which ones are in a better state than the others.

Chapter 2
On true widows

There are many different types of widows. Some, once their husbands die, think about remarrying, and these, though they be widows because they do not physically have the pleasure of a husband, are not, however, widows in their mind, for they desire a husband. This desire of theirs can be both good and bad. Good, when they cannot live in widowhood, or because they are in the flower of youth and have no vocation to enter the religious life, and to remain like this would be dangerous for them. It would then be better for them to remarry, and for this reason Saint Paul, writing to Timothy, says: 'I want young widows to remarry and to become mothers of a family, for I do not want to give the devil the opportunity to tempt them.' [1 Tim 5:14] It would also be good to remarry if the widow were to be in such a state that, because of material needs, or because she has no income whatsoever, or for various other circumstances, she cannot live otherwise; or truly if she were to recognize that she cannot live chastely, for chastity is a very rare gift from God and it is not given to everybody. Therefore, it would not be bad in this case to remarry, because, even though this proceeds from a bad root, nonetheless, the result would be good, and because of this the Apostle says to the Corinthians: 'It is better to marry than to burn in lust and not to resist sin.' [1 Cor 7:9] But if a widow should remarry or should want to remarry for lust or for avarice, or in order to go where she knows there is wealth, or for pride, or when she is sought after by a man of high degree, or because she has fallen in love, or for some other

---

lost two of her children, whereupon, at the age of 22, she consigned her surviving son to a tutor, gave away her all of her wealth, and went to Egypt to live as an ascetic. For Jerome's reference to her see, Jerome, Epistle 39.5 'Ad Paulam de morte Blesillae.'

depraved and perverse reason, without a doubt this desire of hers would be a sin.

These women, therefore, who want to remarry, are widows only physically, and to these we do not direct our words.

Some widows do not want to marry any more, and among them there are several different types. There are many who do not want a husband, either because they do not have a dowry, or because they fear a bad marriage, or because they do not see a way for them to remarry, or for other hidden or evident reasons, but nonetheless their conversation is not appropriate to their state, because they do not maintain chastity in their hearts and they also appear in public, and so reveal to dissolute youths what they desire. They dress neatly and in tight-fitting garments, with veils or kerchiefs drawn and creased, not very covered at the front, with their eyes shamelessly raised, and they eagerly linger in the company of youths, and they laugh with them, and jest, and even speak of matters that are not religious. One must flee from these women and one must not in any way talk with them. Therefore, the Apostle says to his disciple Timothy: 'My son, be careful of these young widows for, once they have satisfied their lust, they want to become brides of Christ, while they bear his damnation for having broken their first promise, which they had with their husbands. These are idle women who learn to go about from house to house, chatty and curious, and they speak of things they ought not.' [1 Tim 5:11–13] These women would do less ill to remarry than to live in this manner. Therefore, they are not the type of widow to whom we address our treatise.

Some other widows decide not to remarry and to live chastely both with respect to the spirit and to the body. However, they do not do this for love of God, but rather for some sort of social respectability, or for love of their children, or for love of material goods, or in order not to find themselves with a second husband who is worse than their first, or because their nature leads them to this. Therefore, although in the opinion of the world they live honestly and are considered to be venerable mothers, nonetheless they are still not the type of widow to whom we want to speak, for they are not like our widow Saint Anna, who had no other desire but to serve God day and night. And all these widows have dedicated themselves to serve the world and to lead a respectable and honest life according to worldly value, but they know little of divine matters: they rarely go to confession, pray and fast, they practise divine matters very little, and they rarely attend sermons. I pray for the sake of the depth of Jesus Christ's mercy that they should not spend the grace they have received from God in search of earthly honours, but so as to receive their reward in heaven and not on earth, for the Apostle tells Timothy: 'A true and destitute widow should hope in God and should persevere in prayer and supplication day and night.' [1 Tim 5:5]

There are some other widows who have firmly resolved to remain chaste and to serve God with all their heart, and these also are different: because some cannot separate themselves either from their sons or their daughters or from their relatives because of their youth, for it would not be right for such widows to be alone; or because they cannot separate themselves from the family because of some other necessity or charitable obligation, and they must absolutely live with someone and they must be like mothers to many. And these widows, although they may not be completely free to serve God, nonetheless, for every labour they do within the family, when they do it for the love of God and in the knowledge that they have been forced by God to do it, they will be rewarded in eternal life. Nor should they in any way remove themselves from these responsibilities of theirs, for the Apostle also says to Timothy: 'If there is any widow who has children or grandchildren, she must first learn to administer her house well and return to her relatives the service that was provided to her; because whoever despises the care and governance of his own, and especially of those of his own house, is unfaithful and worse than unfaithful.' [1 Tim 5:4, 8]

Some other widows, desirous of serving God, could easily remove themselves from their families and would be freer in their prayers and fasts, but they do not do it either because they are faint-hearted, or because of compassion, or because of some other reason, as is the case with some widows who are already quite old and could retire in the company of other honest women to a safe and secluded place and dedicate themselves to contemplation.[5] I

---

[5]For an excellent study of a Florentine hospice for widows (as opposed to a convent for women in general), see Richard C. Trexler, 'A Widows' Asylum of the Renaissance: The Orbatello of Florence" pp. 66–93 in Richard C. Trexler, *The Women of Renaissance Florence*. Power and Dependence in Renaissance Florence, 2 (Binghamton, NY: Medieval & Renaissance Texts & Studies, 1993). For a discussion of the social problem of widowhood and Savonarola's treatise,

advise these widows that, if they can seclude themselves without detriment to their love of neighbour and without scandal, they should do it for the better peace of their spirit and for their greater perfection, especially if they see that their remaining in the company of others is a great burden to their spirit. However, here one needs good counsel and must consider many things.

Finally, one finds other widows who, having withdrawn from every bother and disturbance of the world, serve God in contemplation day and night, and these are in a state that is more quiet and better able to earn them greater perfection. Our widow Saint Anna was in this state, for Scripture tells that she served God in fasts and prayers, never leaving the temple day or night: which she could not have done had she had to care for a family. And if all those widows who want to serve God do not have the ability to do so, like Anna, they should, nonetheless, strive to follow her as much as they can.

Therefore, we conclude that a true widow is someone who not only maintains her chastity and intends to maintain it, but someone who is also completely dedicated to the service of God, as was Anna. And since no-one can direct oneself to the service of God without knowing what the end is, and what are the means to attain this end, after having explained what a widow should be in her intentions we still need to explain how she must direct her intentions, and what she must understand first of all so that she may then know how to direct her works, because the end determines the means to achieve it.

Chapter 3
On the intentions of true widows

Once a widow has thought and decided that it is better to live continently, and she has firmly resolved to serve God, she must first understand what the aim of this life of hers might be, so that she might know how to direct her works and regulate her conduct appropriately. Now, the main reason why not only widows, but also every Christian must live uprightly, is God's honour, which

---

see Konrad Eisenbichler, 'At Marriage End. Savonarola and Widows in Late Fifteenth-Century Florence' in *The Medieval Marriage Scene: Prudence, Passion and Policy*, eds. Cristelle Baskins and Sherry Roush. New York: Boydell & Brewer, forthcoming.

one must love more than one's own health. For this reason our Saviour teaches us to pray in this manner: 'Our Father who are in heaven, sanctified and honoured be your name; your kingdom come.' [Mt 6:9–10] Here it is, He first wants us to wish and to ask for the sanctification of his name in the hearts and on the tongues of all creatures, which is his eternal kingdom; because we must love God above all things and all creatures, and we are creatures: therefore, we must love Him above ourselves. Thus we must strive [to see to it] that the name of God not be blasphemed, or that the faith and Christian religion not be disgraced by our evil works, so that God should not say to us what He says to the Jews when He says: 'Through you' — that is, through your evil works — 'the name of God is blasphemed among the infidels.'[6] [Rom 2:24]

Seeing Christians do so much evil, the infidels curse the faith saying it is not a true faith, for they say: 'If it were true, Christians would not sin so much, especially if they expect a great reward after doing good works, and a great punishment after evil works.' Even if they should not say this, nonetheless, every evil work of ours is to the dishonour to God, just as every good work is to his honour. And this applies to widows more than to many other persons because they should be humble and lead a very chaste life; for, having lost the companionship of their earthly husbands, they should seek no other groom but Jesus Christ. And when one sees that they do not lead a good life and that they do the contrary, they give occasion for gossip and for many other sins, all of which lead to the dishonour of God, to their own dishonour, and to scandal among one's neighbours.

---

[6]Savonarola has altered Paul's 'among the Gentiles' to 'among the Infidel,' perhaps subconsciously, but quite probably in response to the constant threat posed by Moslem advances and attacks against Christian Europe. Less than fifty years before, in 1453, Constantinople, the political and spiritual capital of Eastern Christianity, had been captured by the advancing Ottoman Empire. The Italian coast was constantly under threat from Moslem corsairs and navies; in 1480 the city of Otranto, in southern Puglia, had been captured and briefly held, and 800 of its men (including the bishop) were killed inside the cathedral—dire warning to the rest of Italy. The problem with Moslem navies threatening the coast would continue until the end of the sixteenth century when finally, with the battle of Lepanto, Moslem sea power in the western Mediterranean finally began to wane.

A true widow must then inflame her heart with zeal for the honour of God and commit herself to die rather than to dishonour her Creator. Secondly, she must seek her own salvation, aware of the fact that one cannot always remain in this world, for it is decreed that when one dies one must go to one of two extremes: either to eternal life or to eternal punishment. Therefore, having lost every consolation in this world, she must strive not to lose the consolation of the hereafter, but to acquire eternal joy among the blessed. However, because many, considering this, decide to do the right thing and then, not knowing how to do so, they start off along crooked paths because they do not understand what one seeks first and foremost in the spiritual life, therefore, it is still necessary to understand what one seeks above all in the spiritual life, and this is purity of heart, which consists first in the cleansing of one's conscience through a true confession that proceeds from a contrite heart, a confession of all mortal sins and, when it is also possible, of all venial sins.[7] Also, in order to have purity of heart, one must also withdraw one's affection from all earthly things and strive instead to value the glory of heaven so much that all the wealth and honours of the world will seem to us as base as mud. Therefore, the soul that wants to become perfect must every day subtly examine and pry into its wishes and desires, and when it recognizes itself to be fond of some earthly thing, regardless of how small, which it sees itself loving immoderately, this soul should remove its affection from it as much as it can, since to the extent that someone is fond of a created thing, to that extent one does not love God. For He should be loved with all one's heart, with all one's soul, and with all one's strength [Mk 12:30], that is, with all one's mind, with all one's will, with all one's memory, and with all the other powers who do not want the mind to contemplate or to dwell on anything else but on God and on what has been ordained to his glory. And let her love nothing else but God, and if she love anything else she should do it only inasmuch as it is an indication of Him — just as a bride loves the ring her husband gave her because of her love of her husband. And in her memory nothing

---

7A mortal sin is a grave transgression that breaks a person's relationship with God and thereby consigns the sinner to perdition; a venial sin, instead, is a minor transgression that does not rupture this connection and thereby does not exclude the sinner from salvation.

else should rest but He and his gifts. And all her works should be directed towards Him, as the Apostle says: 'If you eat or drink or do anything else, do all this for the glory of God.' [1 Cor 10:31]

Therefore, if we want to reach the perfect love of God and the perfect peace that comes from contemplating his glory, it is necessary to detach one's affection from all earthly things and in this manner to purify the heart, as our Saviour says: 'Blessed be the pure of heart, for they shall see God.' [Mt 5:8] Whoever does not keep one's eyes constantly on this purity cannot reap profit from the spiritual life, for that person does not know what to do, for all fasts, vigils, prayers, alms, lessons, and all preaching are aimed at this purification. And those who do not always aim for this purification, commit many sins, grievous many times over, and they think these are little sins, for they do not know nor do they see how contrary these sins are to the purity of heart which they do not keep in sight. However, those who always aim for it see all small sins and regret them, for they see that they pollute the mind, which they always seek to cleanse.

And because, even though a man may seem not to bear affection for any created thing, he still does not know for certain whether he is in the grace of God, for Solomon says that 'there are many just and wise men and their works are in the hands of God, and no-one knows whether he is worthy of love or hate,' [Ecclesiastes 9:1] but this is left to the judgement of God.[8] One acquires eternal life in the faith of our Lord Jesus Christ, so it is necessary to be extremely keen to receive this grace, for whoever dies without it is damned. For this reason a soul that seeks to reap spiritual profit, which cannot be done without grace, must often and keenly consider whether she has it and whether she displays the signs by which one can suppose that a soul is in the grace of God.[9] That is

---

[8]The sentence is badly constructed in the Italian version as well, thus indicating lack of revision on the part of the contemporary translator from the Latin original.

[9]Here and throughout this paragraph, the Italian version is written in the feminine singular form, clearly referring grammatically to the preceding feminine noun *anima* (soul), the subject of the discussion in this paragraph. However, it also seems that over the course of the paragraph the feminine singular form comes to refer not just to the *anima* (soul) in general, but to an implied *vedova* (widow) who should, in her soul, feel and respond as the paragraph indicates. The ambivalence may reflect either a subtle rhetorical

to say: whether she is aware of the presence of a mortal sin she has not repented and confessed; whether she is weary of this world; whether she has a great desire for her homeland; whether she delights in sacred Scripture and in the things of God; whether she willingly hears the word of God; whether she enjoys reciting her prayers; whether she often feels herself moved by some internal inspiration; and whether she has such other suggestions of grace, which are nearly infinite and are known only by those saintly souls who practise divine contemplation, through which they feel in many ways something like the assurance that they are in the grace of God. If, therefore, a soul does not have signs such as these, she must stand at the foot of the cross and cry for her sins every day until she feel the internal inspiration and consolation of the Holy Spirit, which is a sure indication that grace has redeemed and forgiven her sins. And this soul must confess often and implore the just with great humility to pray for her. If, however, she feels in herself the signs of grace, she must not boast in her spirit because, of all the virtues, only perseverance will be crowned with victory. On the contrary, she must be greatly afraid and always remember her past, considering God's love towards her, for He has taken her away from the world, and out of the mud, and He has remade her in his grace: because this is a greater gift than if He had made her queen of the world, for all the treasures of the world cannot offer the smallest fraction of a degree of the glory that grace bestows. Therefore, she must be careful not to be ungrateful, and on the other hand she must consider how great the snares of the world are, and how many the devil discovers every day: from which snares, as Saint Anthony said,[10] only true humility can spare us. Therefore, the Sage says in his book *Ecclesiasticus*: 'If you do not keep yourself constantly in the fear of the Lord, your house will soon be ruined.' [Ecclesiasticus 27:4(3)] Therefore, every day the

---

manoeuvre on the part of the author, or yet another example of sloppy work and lack of revision on the part of the fifteenth-century translator.

[10]St Anthony the Hermit (250–356). Born in Egypt, when he was orphaned at about age 20, Anthony placed his sister in the care of a community of holy women, sold all his possessions, and retreated into an ascetic life near his home under the guidance of an aged hermit. He subsequently moved into the desert and lived on his own, but his fame as a holy man kept attracting attention and disciples, while his own concerns for the faith brought him repeatedly back into the world to fight against current heresies.

soul must gather itself under God's commandments and never stop, but on the contrary it must always begin anew, and every hour it must repeat, together with the singer of the Holy Spirit: I do not think I have ever done good, and so I have decided to start doing good now, and I do not take credit myself for this, but *it is a change of the right hand of the Most High*, Who will fill me with his mercy and will turn me from evil to good. [Ps 76:11(77:10)]

To prove that what I have said is taught to us by our widow Saint Anna, I will now expound it through a moral interpretation.

First of all, you hear that her name is this word 'Anna,' to indicate that all widows must bear this name not so much in the literal sense of the word, but in its meaning, for Anna means 'grace.' A widow, therefore, must be purified in her heart by the grace of God.

It is then written that she was the daughter of Phanuel, and so must every widow be, for Phanuel means 'the face of God,' and our bliss will be to see the face of God, which all means that you are in the grace that comes from this bliss: which grace proceeds from the face of God and is similar to it. And so, whoever is begotten in grace, has his life from the face of God, for grace is the life of the soul, and, consequently, he is the child of the face of God, and so he waits for his father's inheritance, which is the eternal bliss that comes from seeing and knowing God, for our Saviour says, speaking to his Father: 'This is eternal life: to know you as the only and eternal God, and Him whom you have sent, Jesus Christ.' [Jh 17:3] We also include the Holy Spirit, for He is the love of the Father and the Son, as if to say: eternal life is to know only one God, who is three persons, Father, Son, and Holy Spirit.

And it follows that this Phanuel was from the tribe of Asher, for his name means 'blessed.' For, just as the grace that comes from the face of God is ordained to bring the soul to the vision of that face and that most high godhead, similarly our vision of God, which is our bliss, is ordained to the glory and honour of God, 'who alone is truly blessed' — as the Apostle says to Timothy — 'and a powerful king of kings and lord of lords, who alone is truly and perfectly immortal and lives in an inaccessible light, which man has never seen, nor will ever see in this present life, nor in the next will he know it perfectly;' [1 Tim 6:15–16] for God sees in himself an infinity of things that the blessed cannot see, even though they see in his essence marvellous things without number. And so all the blessèd are from the tribe of Asher, for they are all blessed by the face of the blessèd God. Thus it is necessary that a widow be regenerated through grace by the face of God, so that she may come to look upon the face of the blessèd God.

And notice that first the tribe of Asher was mentioned and then Phanuel, and first Phanuel and then Anna: this was to indicate what we said above, that a widow must first seek the glory of God; second, her salvation; third, the purity of her heart through grace and divine love. These three things, then, must always be in the thoughts of every Christian, and especially in the thoughts of those widows who have decided to serve God with all their heart.

Therefore, to recapitulate, it is necessary that a widow be like this if she wants to live a saintly life: to be named Anna, daughter of Phanuel from the tribe of Asher. And so, at the beginning, when she wants to enter into this state, she must diligently confess all the sins she has ever committed, and remove from herself all occasions for sin, and then she must say in her mind: 'My Lord, I intend to serve you and to live a good life, first for your praise and glory; then, for the salvation of my soul: therefore, I will force myself to show my heart to you, so clean that you will deign to fill it with grace and charity, so that I may achieve the glory of the blessèd, who praise you with joy for ever and ever.'

Therefore, after our widow has been thus constituted, we will explain in the second part how she should live.

Book Two
On the life of the true widow

Wanting to deal with widowhood, we have placed Saint Anna, daughter of Phanuel, in front of your eyes as a mirror in which to contemplate what the life of every widow must be, and we have shown, drawing from the first part of the Gospel, what her intention, her mind, her purpose must be, so that she may be fit to serve God, so now we must come to the second part, where we will demonstrate, with God's help, through your prayers, how she must live.

The holy Gospel, therefore, continues by saying that Anna, serving God in fasts and prayers, never left the temple day or night. From these words we see first Saint Anna's solitude, for it says that she never left the temple day or night; second, her abstinence; and third, her devotion through constant prayers, for it says 'serving God in constant fasts and prayer.' Observing these three things, as they must be observed, each widow will serve her creator worthily.

So that I may share in your prayers and in your merits, I will strive to show you how these three things are observed.

Chapter 1
On the solitude of a true widow

When I think how Saint Anna did not leave the temple day or night, I seem to see a turtle-dove deprived of her mate, going about alone, languishing and lamenting, delighting more in her lament than in all other external consolations, and especially since she did not so much grieve about being widowed of her earthly, bodily husband, as much as she grieved in her spirit about being widowed of her spiritual husband, the true God, whom she always wanted to see. Do not, however, understand by this that she never left the temple, but rather that she carried out very much, day and night, her visits to the temple, never failing in those hours that were due and appropriate for her state. In fact, sometimes we say of a devout person who prays often, 'This person does nothing else but pray,' even though this person does other things, for it is customary to speak in this manner when we want to express great eagerness and constant effort on the part of a person.

A widow, therefore, must be like a turtle-dove, which is a chaste animal who, when she loses her mate, never again mates with another, but goes about the rest of her life lamenting alone. Thus the type of widow we are discussing, as we mentioned above, after she has lost her husband, must resolve firmly not to pair herself again with another man, but to serve God with all her heart, considering herself a widow both corporally and spiritually: corporally, because she has lost her carnal husband, spiritually, because she is still separated from Christ her spiritual husband. Then, since she cannot regain her carnal husband who is dead, she must try not to lose as well her soul's husband, but to find Him in the other life, for, finding Him, she may perhaps also find her carnal husband, if by chance he is in the place of salvation. Being, therefore, widowed in this world, she must turn her mind not to live in worldly mirth and comforts, but rather to live always in tears and wailing.

According to praiseworthy custom, widows dress in black and go about very much veiled for the entire length of their widowhood, which dress is one of frequent tears and not of laughter. And so a widow, considering that in having lost her husband she has already lost the consolation of the world, for amusements are no longer allowed for her, and that she is still outside her heavenly homeland, widowed of her true spouse Jesus Christ, with the danger of perhaps never finding Him should she pursue sin, she must gather within herself and separate herself completely from worldly conversations and, as the Apostle says, 'not conform in any way to this age, but seek to renew herself internally' day after day. [Rom 12:2]

And first, she must detach herself completely from conversation and from the company of extraneous men who are not related to her, or who have nothing at all to do with her, especially of young men, because from such conversations one always acquires some stain of sin or disgrace. And if they should presumptuously meddle with her, a widow must use such gravity and harshness in her voice, and display such a countenance that she will indicate to them that they have no hope whatever of gaining access to her; for these people, when they realize from a certain smile, or a tender eye, or from some sweet little words, that the mind of a woman can be easily turned to their purpose, with a thousand ways and skills, under the guise of doing good, trained by the devil, little by little they draw near her, and many times they attain their purpose, which they would not have done if, from the beginning, the woman had revealed herself completely alien to such a thing.[11]

A widow must also, whenever she can, distance herself from conversation and familiarity with all her relatives, and especially from those on her husband's side, from brothers-in-law, cousins, and even from brothers, and especially from young ones, so that she does not have close familiarity with any of them, for lust is all the more stirred up against reason the more its expression is forbidden. Thus, if it is not beaten back, it licentiously approaches even what is most illicit and most bestial. Because of this, there have been many, and even today there are not a few who, because of such familiarity, did not consider, nor do now consider the respect that is due to a relative, nor the legal prohibitions, but have instead immersed themselves like donkeys and mules in the filth of their own blood, even in very close degree. And so, one must speak with relatives, kinsmen, and brothers only as much as is necessary, and about matters dealing with the household, or about spiritual matters, or other necessities, and one must speak rather less than too much.

---

[11]For the question of 'young men' lusting after and chasing after widows, see Eisenbichler, 'At Marriage End,' forthcoming.

And if a widow is so old that she is free from this danger, I still forbid her such familiarity, either because this is a bad example for young women, or because it distracts her mind from her contemplations and prayers, of which I will speak later, and also because too much familiarity breeds contempt, and then she is not held in reverence, and so her example is of no use.

A widow must also flee conversations with extraneous women who are not her relatives and have nothing to do with her, and especially young and vain women, for, as Solomon says, 'the friend of crazy people becomes like them.' [Prov 13:20] Seeing how they dress vainly, and hearing their light words, and considering their worldly conversation, she will be pierced to the heart, and her desires will grow, and her good thoughts will fly away, and she will be so caught up that she will find it difficult to repent. Therefore, she must completely abandon such companions, even if she developed them before her widowhood.

She must also guard herself against too much familiarity with her female relatives or with those women who are in the house, because they will lead her mind astray, and also because it will be necessary for her to chat as well with those strangers, male and female, who come to visit these relatives and to keep them company. Many dissolute men use this method whereby, when they cannot speak as they would like with their female friend, they strike a friendship with some relative of hers and, through the relative, they are then brought inside to converse with her. Thus she must flee all companions and live as solitary as she can, so that our enemy will find no place through which to enter.[12]

A widow must also flee from conversation with those men who call themselves spiritual, but are, however, secular, for often the spirit turns into flesh. Men who are truly spiritual flee from women, and women who are truly spiritual flee from men. Every widow must do the same, for conversation with, and the company of such men is much more dangerous than those we discussed above, for temptation, the more it is hidden and subtle and cloaked by the spirit, the more dangerous it is. Therefore, with such men, she must speak little and only of godly matters, and in no way should there be conversation or familiarity. And one should not speak with such people unless it is in the presence of other persons, briefly and

---

[12]That is, the devil.

rarely, for, as Saint John says: 'The entire world is evil,' [1 Jh 5:19] and especially in our times.

She should also not develop too much familiarity with spiritual women if they are not first fully approved, for one finds many women these days who wear the mantle of piety, but have the devil in their hearts, and evil on their tongues, and bile in their minds, and so it is enough to greet them and pass by.[13] Nor do I want you widows, because of this, to judge these spiritual women badly when the matter is uncertain, but rather to leave the judgement of each of them to God, and instead always think the best rather than the worst. Nonetheless, guard your soul from each of them, for fear that she might not perhaps be one of those perverse messengers for men who, under the cloak of humility carry the venom of pride and of every lustful desire.[14] You must not, therefore, be familiar with any woman reputed to be devout; love them with moderation unless you have first tested them over a long time. Be careful, for the Apostle says: 'These are evil days.' [Eph 5:16]

You must also not be familiar with any friar or secular priest, even if he is your relative, but you must honour them all equally with reverence. And if you should realize that they come to visit you often, be suspicious, for good friars and priests, who must always speak with God and handle the sacraments, flee from women whenever they can and they stay alone so as to be suited to his mysteries.[15] And you must especially flee those who are of an easy-going nature and are called in everyday speech 'good fellows,' because from these you can gain nothing but infamy and

---

[13]Savonarola is subtly alluding to a passage from Dante's *Divine Comedy* when Virgil and Dante approach the gates of Hell and find the uncommitted left to wander for all eternity outside the gates. When Dante asks about them, Virgil answers 'let us not speak of them, just look and move on' ('non ragioniam di lor, ma guarda e passa'); Dante, *Inferno* 3:51.

[14]For an example of such a woman in sixteenth-century Florentine theatre, see the character of Mona Verdiana in Giovan Maria Cecchi's 1549 comedy *L'assiuolo* (translated into English as *The Horned Owl*. Ottawa: Dovehouse, 1981). The Savonarolan movement and many of its ideas continued to have influence in Florence well into the sixteenth century; see Lorenzo Polizzotto's recent study *The Elect Nation. The Savonarolan Movement in Florence 1494–1545*. Oxford: Clarendon Press, 1994.

[15] Savonarola's words echo the orthodox Hebrew regulation against rabbis touching women.

scandal. You must also flee from those other friars and priests who are of a strict life and habit, especially if they are prompt in their visits and delight in giving you pictures of the saints, rosaries, and other such trinkets, for these frequent visits and gifts often change spiritual love into carnal love. Briefly, then, I exhort all widows not to be familiar with either priests or friars of whatever type, for I view such conversations with suspicion. And let no widow rest at ease because she is very old, or because the friar or the priest is very old, for the fire of lust remains in us as long as there is flesh on our body, and the devil, who always endeavours to light it, never dies. Therefore, you must keep your distance from persons in this state,[16] and hold them all in such reverence that you will think yourself unworthy to speak to them.

You must also be careful with your confessor, because many depraved priests, who care not for God's souls but for their own will and pleasure, delight greatly in confessing widows, especially those from whom they can draw some use or with whom they can fulfil some desire of their own. Under the guise of piety they easily lead them to a bad end, for women are such that they are very much inclined to go along with men, for they cannot live without the company of men on account of their imperfect nature.[17] Therefore, when a woman loses her husband, since she is not allowed to converse with lay men, very often under the excuse of the spirit she seeks conversation with priests, and since there are many evil priests, many women are caught with a thousand snares. Seek, therefore, a confessor who leads a holy life and has a good reputation, one who is either very old or of a good age, and, briefly, one who is such that he cannot give you any suspicion of infamy. Do not be familiar with him, so that you do not lose your reverence for him: he must not visit you at home, nor call for you often, nor be afraid that you should leave, nor smile cheerfully at you, but he

---

[16]That is, the religious state.

[17]There was a long philosophical, theological and scientific tradition that saw women as 'imperfect' males. From the Christian theological perspective, the tradition was grounded on the Genesis account of the creation of Eve, while from the 'scientific' perspective it was based on Aristotle's comments on the nature of women in his *On the Generations of Animals*. For an excellent discussion of this, see Ian Maclean, *The Renaissance Notion of Woman. A Study in the Fortunes of Scholasticism and Medical Science in European Intellectual Life* (Cambridge: Cambridge University Press, 1980).

should be such that he must always be forced [to carry out his duties with you]. He must not invite you or have you invited, as some do nowadays who go about looking for women and frequent them everywhere, promising them a blessed life and saintliness and other spiritual things, which, truly, if they had them, they would flee women as one flees from snakes and they would not draw near them if they were not obliged to do so out of charity. Such priests, however, do not have such charity, unless falsely so, for it is not an aspect of perfect charity to work for the salvation of others and not to take care of one's own. Let them go read the lives of the holy Fathers of the past, and brood over Holy Scripture, and they will find that all holy men have fled women; and, if they looked after women, they were obliged to do so by their superiors or by such charity that they thought they could not do otherwise without offending God.

Thus, devout widows, I urge you to be careful to choose a saintly confessor and never to speak with him of anything else but confession and matters pertaining to confession, that is, of matters of conscience, and this you should do briefly and rarely. And even though it is good to confess often, it is not however good to converse too much in churches with priests for it gives cause for scandal in the spirit of those standing nearby, and it is a waste of time, and sometimes one commits other sins. Therefore, after you have chosen your confessor, stay with him and do not be like many other unstable women with a frivolous brain, who wander about all the churches and seek to speak with as many renowned men of the cloth as can be found in the city; and as many preachers as come to preach, they want to visit them all, saying that they do this out of devotion. This devotion of theirs dissipates the purity of their mind; this devotion of theirs is a great lightness of their brain. These are those widows of whom the apostle Paul spoke to his disciple Timothy saying that, being 'lazy, they learn to go about all day to other people's houses and they are not only lazy, but also verbose, loquacious, and curious, and they speak of things they ought not.' [1 Tim 5:13] Thus grave widows remain alone and keep themselves from any type of conversation, knowing that Jesus is not found except in solitude, as God says through the mouth of the prophet Hosea: 'I will lead the soul in solitude and will speak to its heart.' [Hos 2:14] Remain, therefore, in solitude as our Saint Anna did; by this I mean as much as it is possible for each of you, for, the more you will draw yourselves away from conversation with people,[18] the more you will have greater conversation with God and with the angels and the saints of Paradise.

However, since regardless of how much a person can withdraw from human conversation, he can never separate himself from conversation with the flesh, which is always repugnant to the spirit, therefore, after having discussed solitude it seems to me necessary to continue by discussing how we ought to deal with our flesh and how to converse with it, so that it may aid the spirit and not be repugnant to it. We will do this in the following chapter.

Chapter 2
On a true widow's fasting

Since, as the apostle Paul says, 'the flesh is repugnant to the spirit and the spirit to the flesh,' [Gal 5:17] and, nonetheless, it is necessary to feed this flesh of ours —as he says in another place, that 'no one ever hates his flesh, but on the contrary nourishes it and favours it' —; [Eph 5:29] it is necessary that each of you who wants to live righteously in this world be so discreet in her fasts as not to exceed by mortifying her body too much, and also not to be so negligent that she allows the thorns of the flesh to grow and suffocate the spirit. It is very useful for our widows to know this balance and discretion, for theirs is always to fast and pray, as the holy Gospel says about our Saint Anna, who 'served in the temple with fasts and prayers all day and all night.' [Lk 2, 37]

In truth, it is very difficult to advise in this matter, for one cannot offer any fixed rules on account of the diversity of people's constitution and the diversity of lands and provinces and habits and times and many events that occur from hour to hour. Nonetheless, one can give some general rules in accordance with the teachings of the saints which, if you should observe them, though you will not be able to attain in this manner the true means to virtue, at least you will draw near to it, keeping in mind that whoever who does not in some way sin in his intentions is quite perfect.

It seems to me, therefore, that our widows should fast in this manner. First, with respect to the fasts decreed by the Church, those women who are healthy and do not have a legitimate excuse must observe devoutly all the fasts ordained by the Church. And because

---

[18]The original reads *la conversazione degli uomini*; I interpret this to refer to people in general rather than to men in particular.

the Samaritan, that is, our Saviour Jesus Christ, said to the inn-keeper: 'Whatever you overspend, I will repay you when I come back,' [Lk 10:35] it seems to me that, aside from the fasts decreed by the Church, you must also observe some other fasting days. At least those who are healthy should fast once a week, and this on Fridays, out of respect for the passion of our Saviour, for, if we will suffer with Him, we will be glorified with Him. And this seems to me to suffice when the weather is hot; and this is generally the practice in religious orders. And even if some time, for some special devotion or because there is a vigil, some woman would like to add another day, I do not condemn her, as long as there always is the salt of discretion.

Second, one should note that there is another fast that should be observed by every person of whatever position and condition in life, and this is to live with temperance and to take food as necessary, in quantities according to the needs of nature. One cannot give any rules about this because of the infinite variety of persons; but everyone learns this by himself through the anointing of the Holy Spirit, who teaches his beloved who humbly have recourse to Him with most devout prayers. I inform you, however, that, even though too much and too little are depraved extremes, nonetheless, since it is difficult for all people to find the mean, whoever should not reach that middle mark, as long as he does not exceed too much from it but is near it, does not deviate very much from virtue nor sins very much. Also, it is a lesser evil if, having to deviate towards one of the extremes, one should deviate towards the little rather than towards the much, as long as one does not exceed greatly, for nature is satisfied with few and simple things. Thus I urge our widows to sobriety and to frugal daily living, because this, though it is appropriate for all conditions of people, nonetheless, is especially appropriate for widowhood, for a widow is in the condition of continent persons, and this requires a continent lifestyle. Thus she must fast daily in this manner and abstain in eating and drinking.

Third, a widow must fast also from all superfluous bodily pleasures, because her position and her dress indicate mortification and sadness. Because of this, Saint Paul says: 'That widow who lives in pleasure is dead' [1 Tim 5:6] with respect to God and to his grace. Thus she must restrain her eyes everywhere so that they do not see vain things, especially in church or in public places, otherwise she will be a source of scandal to herself and to her neighbours. I should warn you that one can well recognize a woman's modesty and the seriousness of her life from her eyes, and for this reason the Sage says in his *Ecclesiasticus*: 'The fornication of a woman is recognized in the elevation and the exaltation of her eyes.' [Ecclesiasticus 26:12(27:9)] Thus a widow must always, in every place and especially in the presence of men, lower her eyes and keep them lowered to the earth and with great modesty and gravity raise them as the place and the person with whom she is speaking requires it.

She must also make her ears fast from all pernicious and useless words, which must not be heard or spoken in any way, considering that God's judgement will be so rigorous that at his tribunal we will be called to account for every idle and irrelevant word. One must especially guard oneself from hearing someone speak ill of someone, for the person who hears does not sin less than the person who speaks ill, but many times more. However, since it is difficult to converse with people who have a weak tongue and not hear many badly spoken words, it is necessary, as much as possible, not to converse, especially in our times, when even those persons who seem to be spiritual and seem to lead a good life do not know how to speak of God's things and about the religious life without mixing in their speech other people's failings. It is necessary, therefore, every day to decide firmly not to want ever in any way to speak with other persons about evil things, either specifically or generally, either about public matters or secret matters, except in such cases as charity should oblige us, as when we would do it to correct our neighbour, or if it were necessary to speak with someone who could or knew how to advise our neighbour, or for some other reason with a good purpose. And in order better to rein in our tongue and our sense of hearing one should every hour resolve to speak little and only as is necessary. As in the case of hearing, so it is with speaking:[19] for, as Solomon says: 'There will not be lack of sin in speech.' [Prov 10:19] And Saint James the Apostle says that 'he who does not offend in speech is truly a perfect person.' [Jas 3:2] And certainly experience shows that, when one begins to speak, one word leads to another, and so little by little from good words one proceeds to idle words, from

---

[19]There seems to be some confusion here in the Italian version about hearing and speaking; I retain the confusion and translate directly as the Italian reads.

which one comes to slander and many other things in which one commits grievous sins without even realizing it. Among venial sins there is none, in my judgement, that draws people away from prayer and devotion more than unnecessary speech. As Saint James the Apostle says, 'He who thinks he is religious and devout and does not hold his tongue back should know that his religion and devotion are empty and useless.' [Jas 1:26]

A holy widow must also fast with her sense of smell and be on guard in every way that she not delight in lustful smells, such as in certain oils and ointments, powders and waters, which are used not only in medicine, but also for sensual pleasure, because these things emit an odour of bad conscience and little modesty in those who use them. One should also guard against all other odours women are accustomed to place on their clothes, their kerchiefs, and their veils, saying as an excuse that they do it in order to preserve the cloth, even though they do it for the sake of sensuality, because we know very well that cloth can easily be preserved by other means. These odours, of whatever type, must be forbidden to widows and to all spiritual people, who must rather give off more of an odour of good reputation and holy life everywhere they go, and not a sensual odour that stinks in the nose of the holy angels of Paradise.

She must also fast with her sense of taste from sensual things that are not necessary to nature, and this is a hidden fast and an abstinence that is not seen. Therefore, besides what we have said above about fasting, we will add this, that every day one can fast in the sense of taste by abstaining from all things that are made in order to satisfy gluttony rather than necessity, for many times these things are more harmful than profitable, for example salads, relishes, and fruits and other such things. However, since abstinence that is manifest engenders vainglory, I urge you whenever possible to hide it from your dinner companions. That is to say, when you eat with your family or with other persons you know, you must not completely abstain from these foods, but you must taste a little of each of them, or of most of them, and silently avoid, either completely or partially, all those foods that please you the most, so that your appetite should never be satiated but remain full of desire for the food you are avoiding, and thus, by restraint, you may have merit with God. Know that, even though this abstinence may appear to be little, it is, nonetheless, very great and it is of great merit to abstain from what we are allowed out of love for

God and in memory of the passion of our Saviour Jesus Christ. Even if it should do no other good, at least it has this benefit, that every time we abstain from some little thing at the table, we remember God at that moment, for whose love we are abstaining in that little thing, and this thinking of him is welcomed by His Majesty. And many times during that hour he rewards with his own food the soul that does this, and lets it savour this food more than any other bodily food available, as those who have experienced it know.

A widow must also fast with her sense of touch, and not only guard herself against illicit touches, but also from licit touches both from her own self and from other persons, because the temptation of touching is most passionate and sudden and it envelops our reason. Because of this temptation, many women and many men have fallen only because they touched a hand, because, though it may seem to be a trifling thing to touch a hand, nonetheless, it often acts as a seal does on soft and tender wax touching it, leaving its impression on it. And so the flesh of a woman is like wax which, when touched by a man, retains the impression of his touch and then only with great effort loses it. Thus the blessed Jordan,[20] who followed our patriarch Saint Dominic, reprimanded a friar who had touched the hand of a respectable woman of good morals. The blessed Jordan said: 'Son, the earth is good and water is good, yet when one mixes them together one gets mud.'[21] Therefore, a widow must be very careful with this sense because, having already experienced such pleasure and now finding it is forbidden to her, that fire could flare up more readily in her than in a woman who has not experienced it or to whom it is not forbidden. Therefore, she must stay far away from it and flee any memory of past things.

Because of this, not only must she make her external senses fast, but also her internal senses; for just as she must detach and distance herself from all things delightful to the senses, similarly inside she must not admit any extraneous fantasy, but ensure that all her thoughts be on God, if at all possible. And when she has unclean

---

[20]The Blessed Jordan of Pisa (1260–1311) studied in Pisa, Bologna, and Paris; travelled in France, England, and Germany; and eventually settled down to teach in Pisa and in Florence. Appointed to teach in Paris, he died while on the way there. He was particularly famous for his preaching. His feast day is 6 March.

[21]I have been unable to locate the source.

and vain thoughts, she must quickly send them away by having recourse to prayer and to saintly meditation or to some other good exercise, so that her heart be always pure in the sight of God, because Jesus wants a pure mind.

Our saintly widow Anna fasted all these fasts, and thus she attained such purity of heart that she was worthy of having the spirit of prophecy and she was worthy of announcing to the children of Israel the coming of our Saviour Jesus Christ. And since, aside from fasting she also prayed,[22] for the Gospel says that she 'prayed day and night,' after having spoken about fasting we will now speak of prayer.

Chapter 3
On a true widow's prayers

Prayer is so necessary to spiritual life that to want to be saved without it is a useless effort. Because of this our Saviour says that 'one must always pray and never fail to do so.' [Lk 18:1] This is what opens the treasures of God's grace; this is what makes one fervent; this makes the soul intimate with Christ; this enlightens our intellect and inflames our affection for divine and holy things; this gives us a foretaste of the joys of Paradise; this, briefly, is the passion of true Christians that yields all the fruits of the Holy Spirit. All widows must be intent on it, as the Apostle says to his disciple Timothy: 'A true widow who is destitute should hope in God, constant in her supplications and her prayers day and night.' [1 Tim 5:5]

Therefore, if we consider ancient things well, we will find that, because of the great constancy the first Christians had for prayer, they came to such perfect holiness. But nowadays we have fallen off because we have not been constant in our prayers. Note that in our times many widows and other women and men, both lay and religious, do nearly nothing else but recite *Our Fathers* and psalms, and yet they hardly ever pray, because, as the Damascene says, 'prayer is a rising of the mind to God.'[23] Many recite many

---

[22]The Italian original reads *serviva* (she served), but the rest of the sentence and the following chapter do not substantiate the use of this verb, so I have corrected it to 'she prayed.'

[23]St John of Damascus (c.645–c.750), one of the most significant theological thinkers of his time, though not necessarily an original one; as B. Kotter puts it in his entry on the saint in *The New Catholic Encyclopedia* (7:1049), 'he tried

good prayers with their mouth, but their heart is not with God and thus they do not pray. This happens to those people who do not have a mind pure enough for a true love of God, and so they never reap a profit one day or the next.

Even though one could say many things about prayer, nonetheless, in order not to be tedious, I will limit myself to what I believe is more necessary at this time, leaving aside doctrinal matters and dealing instead with the practice of prayer.

Prayer, first of all, requires a mind that is tranquil and raised to God. Therefore, those who want to dedicate themselves to this practice and in a short time acquire God's friendship and peace of heart, must remove as much as possible from themselves all those things that disturb the mind and first of all sin, confessing themselves often and guarding themselves against falling even into venial sin. They must also guard themselves from speaking too much, for this strongly impedes prayer, and certainly it impedes it more than one might think, pointing out to you that the father of prayer is silence and its mother is solitude,[24] for in conversation one cannot pray. However, when the soul that desires God is alone and in silence, it is nearly forced to gather unto itself and rise above itself and pray, as the prophet Jeremiah says about the holy man in his Lamentations: 'He will sit, — he says — alone and he will keep quiet, because he will raise himself above himself.' [Lam 3:28] Thus, when one is about to pray, one must first gather together one's thoughts and feelings, and drive away any other fantasy, and make God present, seeking him nowhere else but inside one's heart, for God is in all things and he is in our hearts and especially in the hearts of those who love him, as Saint John the Evangelist says: 'God is love, and he who abides in love abides in God and God in him.' [1 Jh 4:16] Then, having raised one's mind to God and joined it with him, one must thank him for all the benefits one has received, briefly recalling them, that is, the gifts of creation and redemption, of baptism and all the other infinite specific gifts, and especially for all his good inspirations, and all the other good deeds that God has wrought in that individual: because all the good deeds

---

to adapt himself to the whole patristic learning without indulging in originality.' In 1890 Pope Leo XIII declared him a Doctor of the Church.

[24]The awkward grammatical structure of this subsidiary clause is such in the original, and therefore I have retained it.

we do are by his grace, and it is He that has done them and not us, or, rather, He does them all, and we do nothing else but evil and we are always rebellious to his light. So, after this thanksgiving, one must ask forgiveness for all one's sins, gathering them up *all together* and *succinctly*; and succinctly in one's mind, and pray that He might deign, by his infinite goodness and by the passion of our Saviour, to erase them. One must also pray that He might deign to grant the supplicant his perfect love. This prayer should be repeated many times with one's heart rather than with one's tongue, and, saying it, one should think about the passion of our good Lord Jesus and about the sweetness of his breast, doing for one's part all one can to become inflamed with divine love, which alone is necessary and sufficient for us: for he who has this love perfectly, has perfect spiritual life and need not ask for anything else. Lastly, one must ask for perseverance in one's love and, if because of some other need, one still wishes to ask for something in particular that is honest and allowed, this is not bad, on the contrary it is good, as long as one should first do what I have written.

And since, aside from all its other good and perfect benefits, prayer is ordained in order to light the heart of people with divine fervour, it is necessary that we pray often because we have many things that are opposed to this fervour and often we wane cold, and thus we must often return to the fire. Because of this it is better to recite short prayers with fervour and often, rather than long ones rarely. One Our Father recited with devotion and attention is worth more than a thousand Our Fathers recited without paying attention, because one recited with attention generates fervour and spirit, but a thousand recited without devotion generate bother and tedium. For this reason I urge you to recite short prayers often, and especially in order to pass time. That is to say, if you are with other people working or conversing, you must often in your heart cast your mind's eyes to God and briefly say: 'Lord Jesus, help me and have mercy upon me,' and similar other words, as the Holy Spirit moves you. Do this also at the table, or when you go somewhere, or when you can separate yourself easily from people's company and go in some room or private place, as if you were doing something else, and here you must briefly pray. If you do this as a practice, it will benefit you more than the great number of psalms and prayers other people recite because, even though it is a good thing to recite a lot of prayers and psalms, nonetheless, it is better to give oneself to contemplation and mental prayer, which inflames the heart with divine love. And if you say 'When I give myself to mental prayer and contemplation, I cannot recite my rosary and the other prayers I have been given,' I answer you that, unless you are not obligated by a vow or by some other commandment to recite those prayers, if you cannot recite them you should let them be, because the prayers you have said through contemplation are much better than your other prayers, because these are made for those.[25] And blessed be you if you could not pray except mentally, for this is the prayer of those who are perfect and it is an angelic thing.

And although I have proposed this form of prayer, I do not wish to say that it should be followed always, but I have done this in order to exhort those women who are not perfect towards true prayer and contemplation. For this reason the apostle Paul says to the Romans: 'We do not know how to pray, but the Holy Spirit helps us in our infirmity and makes us ask for what pertains to our salvation with undescribable tears.' [Rom 8:26] Thus, if you often give yourselves over to mental prayer, the Holy Spirit will teach you all the sweet ways of love and you will be consoled by Him, and your life will be all angelic on earth as was the life of Saint Anna who 'served God in prayers and fasts day and night.'

We could say many other things about prayer, but since one learns better from practice than from theory, I do not think I should say anything else except that you should practise it, day and night, and you will experience what I have said. Then, because we have completed the second part of our little volume, I will briefly begin the third part.

Book Three
On how true widows should teach their neighbours

At the beginning of our treatise I proposed to examine three things about widows: first, how widows should be; second, how they should live; third, how they should teach. Therefore, since we have absolved ourselves of two of these, we are left, with God's help, to absolve ourselves of the third. And since our intention was to propose Saint Anna to widows as a mirror of saintliness, and having

---

[25]That is, oral prayers such as the rosary are intended to assist in mental prayers, or contemplation.

already shown the manner of her life, we are left with showing how she taught others. The holy Gospel continues in this manner: 'And this woman, when Christ was presented at the temple, came forth praising the Lord and speaking of Him to all who were waiting for the redemption of Israel.' [Lk 2:36–38] With these words widows are taught to be careful to teach first by their example, for it says that Anna praised the Lord when he was presented at the temple, thus showing her affection for Christ; second, by their exhortation, for it says that Anna spoke about Him by preaching about Him to other people; third, she must not teach everybody, but those who are disposed to receive his words,[26] and for this it says that Anna spoke about Him to all those who were waiting for the redemption of Israel. Once we have examined these three aspects we will have finished our presentation.

Chapter 1
On teaching by good examples

Examples move better than words, and therefore those who do not do what they preach bear no fruit, because, since they do not do it themselves, those who are taught by them believe that they are not telling the truth, but swindling them, and many are scandalized by this and say 'Doctor, heal yourself first, and then come to heal us.' Certainly, to teach something without doing it oneself is nothing more than to hand to God one's own sentence and say 'Lord, judge me by my words.' And so, let him who does not do so not be so quick to reprove his brother or his sister. One must, therefore, first do and teach not with one's words but with one's example.

As far as a widow is concerned, aside from what we have said above, it seems to me that, if she wants to be the cause of other people's salvation because of her good works and examples, she must first of all guard herself against being a bad example in exterior matters, such as in her dress, that she not tend to gather in groups or withhold the salary of those who work for her, or be tightfisted in giving alms as she should according to her status and wealth. She instead must show herself completely detached from this world. She must also not seek the glory of this world either

---

[26]The Italian phrase, *le sue parole* could refer both to Anna's words or the Lord's words.

for herself or for her children or for her relatives, but show everybody that only the glory of Christ is fixed in her heart.

Her dress, as well, should not be too sumptuous, nor too tidy, but also not too humble and cheap, because one and the other extreme gives rise to vainglory within oneself, and in other persons it elicits disdain or sets a bad example. Let it, instead, be of medium worth and ornamented according to her status. If she still must lean towards an extreme, she must rather lean to the least rather than the most. And, above all, both at home and outside she must be completely decent in her clothes, for I tell you that a widow can never be too decent in her dress.

She must also hold her tongue, as we said above, and she must not be too prone to conversation, for if she talks too much she will then not have so much authority.

Above all and in all places she must guard herself against wrath, for when someone is angry he is like a beast, and says many things and makes many gestures that are a great cause for scandal in those who hear him and it makes servants lose respect and become disdainful, and this leads not to reproof, but rather to great scandal.

In all her works she must also show great humility of heart, for the reproof and teaching that come from a humble spirit are accepted, but those that come from a haughty spirit are scorned.

In all her conversations she must also show herself to be sweet and mild and similar to other women, when this can be done without sin, because those women who show themselves to be too austere and different from other women do not bear fruit in other people, because those women who are not perfect believe that these women do it out of pride and a desire to appear saintly. Thus the apostle Paul said to the Corinthians about himself: 'I have conformed myself to all people, to the Jews, to the Gentiles, to the infirm, in order to win them all'; [1 Cor 9:19–22] and this he meant with respect to those things he could do without sin. Therefore, in all your conversations, show that you have a passionate care for those persons with whom you are speaking and that you always wish to please them, not taking anything from them, but rather giving them your things as they need them. And on your tongue you should always have words about God, all sweet and sugary,[27] for such words draw people to divine love, and for this reason the Gospel says that

---

[27] *inzuccherate*; the term is clearly used with positive connotations.

Saint Anna praised the Lord when she suddenly appeared in the temple. Therefore, since Christ is always present in the temple of our hearts, we must always utter words of praise and love.

If you follow this, and what we said above, you will be able to reach the second level of teaching, that is, to teach with words of exhortation. We will speak about this in the following chapter.

Chapter 2
On teaching with the tongue

Even though the Apostle forbids women from preaching in public [1 Cor 15:34–35], nonetheless, they are not forbidden from exhorting someone privately when there is need to do so. On the contrary, it is meritorious for them to do so. It is true that women should not be quick to teach, for their duty is more to remain silent and to learn with humility. And rightly it does not pertain to them to teach anyone but their inferiors, such as small sons and daughters, or their grandchildren and servants.[28] However, a woman must not try to teach others to whom she is not superior, unless she has been asked to do so, and nearly forced to do it, even though she be learned and wise, so that it does not seem to others that she speaks out of vainglory or in order to be considered, among other women, virtuous, well-bred, and of saintly and good manners. And since it is not possible to teach others what one does not know, it is necessary for a widow first to be instructed in all those things she wants to teach others and especially in two things. First, in the ways of God, through preaching, private lessons, exhortations and their own experience, so that on the road of spiritual life she may know by heart the articles of faith, the ten commandments, good counsels. These things she will have learned from preachers and from great men, from her reading of books in the vernacular or in Latin, if she has studied Latin, or from her own experience in living a wholesome life; and this is much better, for the knowledge that comes from experience is expressed with better and greater effectiveness than the knowledge that comes out of someone else's mouth, and especially when one learns it from divine enlightment during holy prayer and when the words come forth

---

[28]The word *nipoti* refers both to grandchildren and to nieces and nephews; I have opted for the first, as the more appropriate translation for the term in this case.

from a divine love. Let her beware, however, of giving great faith to visions, because the devil is subtle and has deceived many women.[29] And so, if these visions come into your mind, reveal everything to your confessor if he is a discreet man, learned and of good character, otherwise go out and find one that is such that he can counsel you well. Do not tell other people about your visions if he does not advise you to do so, for this could do great damage to your soul.

The second thing in which a widow must be instructed is in the governance of the house and in good and genteel manners, which pertain to everyone according to one's status, and she must instruct and teach her entire household in these.

However, it does not pertain to every widow to teach such matters, because not each one is an expert and instructed in the things I have mentioned above. Therefore, for young widows it is more appropriate to learn rather than to want to teach. Notice here for a moment that I do not mean young in age as much as young in manners and customs, because, as the book of Wisdom says: 'Old age is not computed by the number of years,' [Wis 4:8] but by good judgement. For this reason some widows are old in years and young in judgement, and it does not pertain to these women to teach, but first to learn and to become old in judgement; and other widows are young in years and old in judgement. And although youth diminishes somewhat the authority one has, nonetheless, the maturity of such a widow is such that she can carry out the office of teaching. Nonetheless, that widow who is old both in judgement and in years will gather greater fruits.

If, therefore, a widow is instructed in these two matters, holding fast to what we have said above, she will be able to reap great benefit even for the souls of others and announce Christ to many people, as did Saint Anna. However, since one must not preach to

---

[29]Savonarola may well be voicing a concern against female mysticism that would soon become widespread in Counter-Reformation Catholicism (in spite of eminent women mystics such as St Teresa of Avila and, in Florence itself, St Maria Maddalena de' Pazzi). It is particularly noteworthy that in the early 1500s his own order would look with great mistrust at women who, embracing Savonarolan ideals, also laid claim to mystical experiences. For an excellent article on this last phenomenon, see Lorenzo Polizzotto, 'When Saints Fall Out: Women and the Savonarolan Reform in Early Sixteenth-Century Florence' *Renaissance Quarterly* 46:3 (1993): 486–525.

everybody, but must be selective, in the following chapter we will briefly speak about who it is a saintly widow must teach.

Chapter 3
On discretion in ministering one's teaching

Some people are superior to us, some are equal, and other are inferior. In my opinion, neither a widow nor any other person should teach one's superiors except in two ways: one is through the preaching that is one's good example, which can move more than words; the other is when the inferior person should see that his superior is wandering off the path of salvation, because in this case the inferior becomes superior. And so, when you see your father or mother or another superior of yours walking along the path of evil, if you think you can lead him to the path of righteousness, you are obligated to do so, but you must do it humbly and skilfully. If you do not have enough strength to do so, seek the advice of your confessor or of some other discreet person about what you can do for the salvation of his soul, and do not in any way let that soul be damned if you can save it. And if it should be a desperate matter, pray for him that God should perhaps deign to move his heart.

We can teach our equals not only with our prayer and example and with humble corrections when they should err, but also with exhortations and some reproofs, not by using authority or superiority over them, but by showing charity. You must not, however, search out all your neighbours and all the women in town, nor find out and examine other people's lives in order to correct them and direct them towards eternal life, because this would be tantamount to abandoning oneself for the sake of others. We have so much to do for our own soul that we do not need to go looking into our neighbour's life. However, when you happen upon a person who needs to be corrected and taught out of charity, with good discretion and great prudence you must take care of his soul, as the Sage says in *Ecclesiasticus*: 'God has commanded that each person should take care of his neighbour.' [Ecclesiasticus 18:12(13)] And this prudence is taught by the anointing of the Holy Spirit, which is obtained especially by prayer.

Inferiors must be taught not only in the manner we have mentioned for superiors and equals, but also by showing some superiority, always, however, keeping holy humility in our hearts. And when they cannot be corrected with sweetness, you must correct them with harshness. It is true that one must have great discretion: for one must teach little ones in one way, youths in another, adults in yet another; similarly, one must correct the proud in one way, the humble in another, the wrathful in one way, the meek in another, the melancholic in one way, the joyous in another, gluttons in one way, the moderate in another, the envious in one way, the charitable in another. But it would be a never-ending labour to write specifically about these corrections.

Truly, there is one general rule you must observe every time you give instruction and correction, and that is to guard yourself against doing it for vainglory or for pride or for wrath. You must do it, instead, only out of charity and out of a desire to save your neighbour's soul. And this charity and this desire will teach you how you must proceed in every person's case in order to save that soul, for the anointing of the Holy Spirit will teach you these things better than books would. And when you cannot reap any benefit whatsoever in your superiors, or equals, or inferiors because of their malice, there is nothing else you can do but pray for them and leave them be; except for inferiors, for they must be forced with threats and blows, so that they do not harm other people. Thus Saint Anna did not announce Christ to everyone, because not everyone was ready, but only to those who were waiting for the redemption of Israel. If you follow this saintly widow as we have written, you will have with her the glory of Paradise in the pleasures of the eternal spouse Christ Jesus, who lives and reigns with the Father and the Holy Spirit for ever and ever. Amen.

Exposition on the Prayer to the Virgin [after April 1496]

Ave, Maria, gratia plena; Dominus tecum: benedicta tu in mulieribus, et benedictus fructus ventris tui Iesu.

Sancta Maria, mater Dei, ora pro nobis peccatoribus nunc et in hora mortis. Amen.[1]

This most devout and angelic salutation, which the most holy Church offers every day to the most glorious mother of the beloved groom Christ Jesus through the lips of its devout sons and daughters, was composed by the Holy Spirit, partly through the lips of the angel Gabriel, partly through the lips of Saint Elizabeth, mother of Saint John the Baptist, and partly through the lips of the Holy Church.

When the angel Gabriel was sent from heaven to earth to bring the news of the incarnation of the Son of God, he greeted the Virgin of virgins in this manner: *Hail, full of grace; the Lord is with you; blessed are you among women.*

Then, when the Virgin went to visit Saint Elizabeth and had greeted her, Saint Elizabeth, feeling the Holy Spirit within her, among the other words she said in praise of such a Virgin and Mother, in a loud voice she said: *And blessed be the fruit of your womb.*

The Holy Church chose to add the other part; and so this most sweet prayer was completed. And so that devout young virgins

---

[1]'Hail Mary, full of grace; the Lord is with you; blessed are you among women, and blessed is the fruit of your womb, Jesus.

Holy Mary, mother of God, pray for us sinners now and in the hour of our death. Amen.'

Savonarola begins his exposition by reciting the 'Hail Mary' in Latin and then in the rest of the exposition he repeats and refers back to the Latin words of the prayer. I have therefore retained the Latin of the prayer.

might say it more devoutly, I wish to explain it in the vernacular, using a low and simple style, as much as I think they might understand. I pray all of them, to offer it sometime on my behalf to the Mother of my Lord and Saviour Jesus Christ, who is one God with the Father and the Holy Spirit, blessed *for ever and ever. Amen.*

Ave. This is a greeting word and might be translated into the vernacular as 'God save you' or 'May you be saved,' as if to say—I wish you to be saved—: so we greet those whom we love and whom we wish to be well in a way that expresses our wish as if saying: —I pray God to grant you every good and to save you, as I wish—. And so the angel, who loved the Virgin Mary, happy she was well and wishing she might have greater grace from God than she already had, at the moment of his arrival said *Hail*, which means 'May you be saved'; as if to say: —I am happy you are in the grace of God and I wish He would increase your state to greater glory—. In the same way, when we begin to pray to her, we first say *Hail*, that is, 'May you be saved.' Not that we want to say that God should save her, which she might not be, but we show her with this greeting our desire, our love for her, that we are not only happy of her glory, but *also* that we wish her to have so much triumph to last *for ever and ever. Amen.* And so we say *Hail*, as if to say: —Mary, we are happy for your eternal glory and we constantly wish that you maintain it for all eternity, just as we know that without a doubt it will last, and we want all good for you and all crowns for you.

Maria. The archangel Gabriel did not say *Mary*, calling her by her own name, but said *Hail, full of grace*, changing her name, and, instead of Mary, calling her full of grace, because at that time the Virgin was changing from a low state to a very high state. And so the angel called her full of grace, practically changing her name because she had changed her state; as our Saviour did to Saint Peter who, though his name was Simon, because he had changed his state wanted him to be called Peter, as if to say stone, foundation and head of the Church [Mt 16:18]. And in the same way the holy Church customarily changes the name of those who are made pope; and similarly for monks who enter into an order. But the Church has given her her own name, that is Mary, humbling herself to her and confessing that she needs her attention because Mary means 'madonna,' that is, 'enlightened' and 'enlightener', or 'star of the sea',[2] as Saint Jerome says.[3] Thus the Church humbly confesses that she needs her holy help when she says *Hail Mary*, as if she were saying: —May you always be saved, my Lady, light and star and harbour for my tribulations—.

And thus this name is glorious, holy and sweet. Glorious because it means 'Lady', and the Virgin is not only lady and queen of a land, but of all the angelic creatures, both earthly and infernal, for she is the bride of he who is king of the universe, that is of God the Father the almighty, since Jesus Christ is the true son of both of them; and she is the mother of the king of heaven and of earth, Jesus Christ, who is of one being with the Father; and she is the tabernacle of the Holy Spirit, who is one God with the Father and with the Son: because the Father and the Son and the Holy Spirit are one God blessed for ever. And so the Father wants his bride to be honoured by all creatures; and so also the Son his mother; and as its tabernacle, the Holy Spirit.

This name Mary is *also* holy, especially in her, that is, pure; it signifies that pure Virgin from whose most pure blood the Son of God formed his holy corpuscle.[4] So, Mary means 'enlightened and enlightener', because, since she was purified, she enlightened the entire world with celestial light; because she has borne on earth the eternal light, Jesus our Lord, while remaining in the glory of her virginity. Oh happy, oh blessed Virgin, you were worthy of carrying and of bringing into the world the splendour of heaven as a radiant morning star! And thus you truly are holy, that is, confirmed in grace and purified by that light that enlightens all men and women born into this world; and in the same way your name is holy.

It is also sweet, for it means 'star of the sea', and truly the holy Virgin is a star of this sea, that is, of this world full of storms and tribulations, for to her we must raise our eyes when we feel the storm,[5] because she is powerful in her help and most compassion-

---

[2]*Madonna* in fact means 'my lady', but Savonarola is clearly on an ecstatic spiral that creates its own etymologies as it raises. For the sake of a more appropriate translation, I will henceforth render *madonna* as 'Lady' (with a capital L).

[3]St Jerome, *De nomin. hebraic., de Exodo*, PL XXIII, col. 833.

[4]Savonarola is using a precise scientific term for a microscopic group of cells, in this case, an embryo.

[5]Savonarola literally says 'when we feel fortune,' using the term *fortuna* in

ate, and completely inclined to want our salvation. And so this name is sweet: it means that which grants us a thousand sweet consolations, that is, the star of the sea that always comforts us.

Gratia plena. Full of grace. Grace is an enormous treasure, a most precious stone, a light, a splendour, a purest gown for the soul. It joins a rational creature[6] most closely to its most sweet spouse Jesus Christ, for an intimate and pure knowledge and a true, not an imitation love. Anyone who does not have it can consider himself not to have anything in this world; and anyone who has it, let him beware of thieves lest it be stolen from him, for he would lose more treasure than the entire universe is worth. This is that manna that lets us walk easily in the desert of this world. This is that pearl for which we ought to sell and disdain everything else. This is that treasure that enriches every man who is worthy of having it: because grace, when it comes into the soul, brings along every virtue: faith, hope, charity, justice, temperance, fortitude, prudence, humility, patience, obedience, meekness, peace, eternal joy and true knowledge, and every other virtue; and it makes a soul pleasing in the sight of God, and worthy of reverence in the sight of the angels, because, through grace, God dwells in our soul. Now, some are richer in this grace, other less: for God does as earthly lords do, who distribute their money to various officials, to some more and to some less, according to their position and the authority of the offices they hold. Similarly, the Lord of lords distributes his grace according to office: so He grants more to that person whom He has ordained to a higher status; and He gives to each person as much as is necessary to carry out the office He has assigned to him. So we find it written that Saint Stephen was full of grace because he had as much as he needed for the office to which he had been called. But our Saviour was full of grace because He had all grace and as perfectly as one can have it. And, after Him, his most sweet Mother was full of grace: so that there never was, nor will there ever be—except for the soul of Christ—another creature who had or will have as much grace as the glorious Virgin had, and for this grace the true and living God became her true and only-begotten Son: and this was never granted to any creature, but her.

---

the sense of a calamitous event or of a storm.

[6]That is, a human being.

Therefore, he rightly said *gratia plena*, that is 'full of grace.' And this was the gift and the ring God the Father sent her when he married her by way of the angel;[7] and so Gabriel offered it to her right away after the salutation. And we *also* now say *full of grace* because she is in heaven, full of every perfection of grace and glory, in great triumph.

Dominus tecum. The Lord is with you. Most appropriately did the archangel say 'the Lord', for he is lord of everything. Certainly in Ferrara the duke is called 'the lord,' because in Ferrara there is no other lord besides Duke Ercole,[8] and in Milan there is no other besides the duke of Milan;[9] someone in Venice, however, would not call the duke of Milan 'the lord' because he is not lord in Venice, but would say 'the duke' of Milan. And so in Ferrara one does not call the king of France 'the lord,' and if anyone said —The lord has waged war against the duke of Burgundy—one would think, in Ferrara, that one was speaking of duke Ercole and not of the king of France; but if we want to speak of that king, we would not call him 'lord' in Ferrara, but 'the king of France,' because he is not lord of Ferrara. And so, every lord in his own land is called 'the lord'; but in someone else's land, he is at most called 'the lord' of Ferrara, or of Milan, or of another country. And because God is lord of all creatures and his lordship extends everywhere, he must everywhere be called 'the Lord': and so when the angel wanted to say that God was with the Virgin he rightly said: —The Lord—, as if to say: —He that is the only lord is with you, Mary—; because the others who call themselves 'lords' are ministers and officers of God rather than lords, and He is Lord of the universe.

Blessed, therefore, are you, oh holy Virgin, who found grace with the true Lord, who is with you in a unique way that never was nor ever will be the same with any creature, for in other creatures there dwells spiritual grace, but in you dwelt God both spiritually and physically. The Father is with her as a groom is with

---

[7]Savonarola uses a passive construction to suggest that God the Father married Mary *through* the angel; literally, the Italian original would say: 'God the Father sent for her to be married to him through the angel.' In Renaissance Italy the groom gave the bride not only a wedding ring, but also a wedding gift; hence Savonarola's reference to a gift and a ring as tokens of marriage.

[8]Ercole d'Este, duke of Ferrara and Modena (r. 1471–1505).

[9]Lodovico Maria Sforza called il Moro (r. 1494–99), married to Beatrice d'Este (d. 1497), daughter of Duke Ercole I of Ferrara.

his beloved bride, and *also* as a father is with his sweetest daughter. The Son is with her as a son who longs for his mother; and He was with her and in her as a guest in her sweet hospice: He dwelt first in her mind and then in her blessed womb. Oh happy palace, worthy of receiving such a guest and lord! The Holy Spirit is with her as balm in a precious ivory vase, for He filled her with every odour of virtue and of heavenly sweetness. Oh blessed Virgin, you were the city and palace for the entire Trinity: daughter and wife to the Father; mother to the Son, and shrine to the Holy Spirit! Truly the Lord is with you more than He ever was with any other creature: and so it is well said that *Dominus tecum*, the Lord is with you.

Benedicta tu in mulieribus. Blessed are you among women. After it has said: —The Lord is with you—, this benediction continues most fittingly because, since the Lord is with her, the blessing of the Lord follows. But one should note that to bless is nothing else but to speak well;[10] and we bless those of whom we speak well. It is true that the Lord blesses his creature in a different way, and the creature the Lord in a different way, for the blessing of God is nothing else but to do good, as Saint Thomas says.[11] So, when He does something good for a creature, it is called 'to bless the creature,' for in God to speak and to do are one and the same thing, as the prophet David says: *Ipse dixit et facta sunt* [Ps 32(33):9], which means: He spoke and commanded, and it was immediately done. And so his speaking well is his doing well for his creatures; but our blessing God is nothing else but praising Him and thanking Him. Therefore, the three youths who were put in the furnace of burning fire, which by divine power did them more good than harm, thanked God for this and called upon other creatures to thank Him with them, and began their song in this manner: *Benedicite omnia opera Domini Domino etc.* [Dan 3:57/ The Song of the Three 35], which means nothing else but: Thank the Lord, all you works and creatures of the Lord. So, when we bless the Lord, it is as if we thanked Him. In the same way, when we bless his creatures, it is nothing else but praising and thanking God for the grace He has bestowed upon those creatures, or in fact to wish that God bestow upon them some good grace. So, when

---

[10]Savonarola is dissecting the Italian word *benedire* into its two component parts, *bene* (well) and *dire* (to speak).

[11]I have been unable to locate the reference.

a mother says to her son: —I bless you and pray God to bless you—, it is as if she were saying: —I wish that God grant you his grace, and I pray Him to do so—; or, if he has this grace, it is as if she were saying: —I thank God for having bestowed his grace upon you, and I pray Him to preserve you in it and multiply it—. It could also be that our blessing a creature is a way of doing good, as we read that Isaac blessed Jacob, his son, for this gave him his inheritance and made him lord over his brothers. So, to sum up, God's blessing is doing good; and our blessing God is thanking Him for the benefits we have received; and our blessing a creature is thanking God for the grace it has received, or to praise it for that grace, or to wish that it had such grace, or to do something good for it, as Isaac did for Jacob.

Therefore, we say to the glorious Virgin: —Blessed are you among women—, and first blessed by God, who has adorned her with greater gifts and grace than He ever did with another woman or creature; always excepting Christ the man, his sweetest Son, to whom no other creature can be compared, for He is joined in one person with the divine and glorious Word; for, as Saint John says, to Christ Jesus the Holy Spirit was given without any measure [Jh 3:34], and from him, as from the head, the entire universal Church emanated. But, after Him, we justly believe that the most beloved mother is thought to have had greater grace than any other creature ever, be it angelic or human. And so, truly, she was blessed by God; and also blessed by creatures in heaven and on earth, for angels, men and women thank God in her, for He deigned to make one of our sisters his most real mother. And they also praise her every day because she was so worthy that she received the Son of God eternal in her hospice, and by this the entire world was freed from the bounds of hell. And note that he says 'among women' and not among men: for, even though she is blessed above all creatures, nonetheless, since her particular blessing lay in her conceiving and giving birth to the Son of God, which she conceived and bore with no detriment to the glory of her virginity—which was never heard of before, nor granted to any other woman—and since to give birth pertains to women and not to men, so the archangel says: —Blessed are you among women, for you will have this unique privilege among them, that you will be virgin and mother—other women, if they are virgins they are not mothers, and if they are mothers they are not virgins—; but you will have one and the other privilege, for you will be mother and will not lose your virginity—. Therefore, the glorious Virgin is truly blessed among all women.

Et benedictus fructus ventris tui. And blessed is the fruit of your womb. If we think about the holy Son of the glorious Virgin in his human nature, God has blessed him above all creatures, for he has filled him with all the grace one can have from him: and his soul is more splendid and radiant than all the seraphim; and his body, already glorified, is more splendid than the sun and more beautiful than the firmament and the empyrian sky, so much so that even those most noble blessed spirits [in heaven] wish to gaze into his sweet face, as Saint Peter the Apostle says [1 Pet 1:12]. And so he is blessed by God for he has filled him with every grace and made him Lord above all creatures; and He has given Him a name that is above all other names [Phil 2:9]. For Jesus Christ, who is true man, son of one of our women, is true living God, Son of the almighty Father; and in heaven He has a father and no mother, and on earth He has a mother and no father: for the eternal Father begot Him *from eternity* out of his own substance when there still were no creatures; and the Mother generated Him in time, a virgin before, during, and after the birth, without the help of any man. This, then, is that fruit in which are hidden all the treasures of the wisdom of God and all the grace that sustains heaven and earth. This is that blessed fruit that all creatures must thank and bless. This, finally, is that holy fruit to which no other creature in heaven or on earth can be compared in sanctity,[12] who is the universal redeemer of all human generations. And so He is truly blessed by God and must be blessed by all creatures: and every day the heavens with their Church triumphant and the earth with its Church militant bless and praise Him *for ever and ever. Amen.*

Oh blessed fruit, then, and blessed be that holy vase that produced Him, and those holy breasts that nourished Him, and those purest hands that wrapped Him!

Oh blessed Mary, tell me, I pray you, Lady, and do not disdain me, a sinner, who is this fruit of your womb? He who has created the sky with its stars; who commands and is immediately obeyed; who makes hell tremble; who is revered in heaven; who makes the blessed spirits exult; bread of the angels; food of travellers; comfort

---

[12]This may be a subtle jab at the Franciscans, who describe St Francis in reference to Jesus (by virtue of his poverty, his stigmata, etc.).

of the afflicted; hope of the righteous; love of our hearts; teacher of the apostles; prince of martyrs; light of the confessors; spouse of the virgins; highest sweetness of all blessed souls. He is our hope; and there is no other but him. Those who do not hope in you, oh blessed fruit, live in vain, in fact they are dead: for you are our life. Those who do not hope in you, oh sweet Jesus, spend their time and their years in vain, and in the end they will find they have been deceived. You are, therefore, my Lord, the blessed fruit of the holy womb of our Lady, the Virgin Mary, most pure and blessed: you are blessed in your divinity and blessed in your humanity; blessed by God and by all creatures; blessed flower; blessed lily; blessed fruit of that blessed Virgin. And I bless you with your Mother, and glorify you *for ever and ever. Amen.*

Iesus. This name *Jesus* is most strong, venerable and sweet. Most strong because it signifies that most powerful Lord who has cast the prince of darkness from this world: for this reason the infernal demon trembles at the power of this name. This is that name by which the apostles raised the dead; in the name of Jesus they freed the infirm; in the name of Jesus they cast out devils; in the name of Jesus the gave sight to the blind; in the name of Jesus they blessed the unbelievers. This is that name which, when we call upon it, lets us conquer the enemy of human kind and every temptation of the devil.[13] This is that name that soften hardened hearts; that breaks stones; that forgives injuries; that makes the dissolute chaste; that humbles the proud; that makes the avaricious generous; that calms the wrathful, and the envious charitable. This is that name that is above high intellects; that casts down kingdoms; that bends the proud, that humbles princes; and, finally, that binds the entire world into his dominion, and so it is most strong and of infinite power.

It is also venerable because it must be honoured by every creature. Certainly, I have sometime seen reverence done to the name of some earthly lord. What, then, should one do when one names the King of heaven? Those who do not bow at the name *Jesus* must be considered infidel Turks; worse than Turks, even,

---

[13]Savonarola uses the phrase 'human nature' (*umana natura*), but because of its particular connotations in English I have preferred to use the phrase 'human kind,' writing it as two words in order to avoid confusing it with the recent neologism for mankind.

because the Turks hold it in great reverence and perhaps in more reverence than many Christians. Certainly, when we say *Jesus* we ought to bend down to the ground. And so says Saint Paul the Apostle, for Christ Jesus humbled himself even unto death—I say unto death on the Cross—for us [Phil 2:8–9]. God has exalted Him and has given Him a name that is above all other names, so that, in the name of Jesus, every knee should bend; and every creature in heaven, on earth and in hell should revere it, and confess that He who is indicated by this name *Jesus* is, in the glory of God the Father, made lord of the universe [Phil 2:10–11].

This name *Jesus* is also sweet because *Jesus* means something like 'Saviour': and certainly salvation is a sweet thing for someone who feels close to death. We were all dead: because at the very least we had to descend to the prison of Limbo; but the Saviour Jesus has freed us all, as long as we are not remiss. And so, what could be sweeter to our ears than to hear this sweet name? What can be sweeter on our tongue and more sweet to our heart, most tender Jesus? This name is sweet to sinners, for it promises them forgiveness of their sins. It is sweet to the just, for this name gives them hope for mercy from their labours. And so Saint Paul the Apostle had it written in his heart: he sowed it in all his Epistles, so much so that we find this name in nearly every sentence. In the same way we read of Saint Ignatius who, when the cruel tyrant had him beaten and tortured in various ways, never stopped invoking this name Jesus Christ. Then, when his torturers and executioners asked him why he called so much upon this name, he answered: —Because I have it written in my heart—. And after his death they opened up his heart and found *'Jesus Christ'* written in gold letters in the centre of that sacred heart.[14] I have also heard from a reputable person that a young virgin girl, a bride of Christ, was so enamoured of him that, when she heard this name *Jesus* spoken, she would think an arrow was piercing to the bottom of her heart, so that she would lose consciousness from such spiritual sweetness and appear to be dead. So, this name is most sweet and penetrates human hearts.

---

[14]For St Ignatius of Antioch (d. ca. 110) and the legend of his inscribed heart, see Voragine, *The Golden Legend*, pp. 145–49. A few years before in Florence, Sandro Botticelli had represented this legend in the predella to his *Madonna di S. Barbara* (1487), now in the Uffizi Gallery.

Sancta Maria, mater Dei. Holy Mary, mother of God. We spoke above about the name of the Virgin. 'Holy'—as we also said above—means 'pure' or 'confirmed': therefore *Holy Mary*, that is 'pure and immaculate, and confirmed in the vision of God,' of whom holy mother Church sings in her stead: *Et sic in Syon firmata sum* [Ecclesiasticus 24:15(10)], which means: 'And so I am confirmed in Zion.' Zion means observatory and refers to the city of God and the heaven where one admires and contemplates the Holy Trinity. And so we say *Holy Mary*, that means something like: —Oh Mary most pure and confirmed in lofty contemplation of the most high Trinity!—. And then follows 'Mother of God.' Oh incomparable praise! What more can be said in praise of Mary? This word is so great and lofty that, if you think carefully about it, I believe one cannot say anything more glorious to the glorious Queen of the heavens. This praise surpasses all praises. This one includes all her praises: 'Mother of God!' Certainly: Mother and virgin; Mother without husband; intact Mother; whole Mother; pure Mother; immaculate Mother. Whose mother? Mother of God; Mother of her Creator; mother of her Father; Mother of her Redeemer; Mother of her Groom; Mother of the Creator of the universe; Mother of the Father of the angels: so, she is Mother of the angels, as well; Mother of the Father of human kind: so, Mother of human kind; Mother of the Father of all creatures: so, Mother of all creatures.

Oh blessed Mary, oh most merciful mother, turn your compassionate eyes towards your children and make them worthy of seeing your beloved only-begotten Son, Christ Jesus, blessed *for ever and ever. Amen.*

Ora pro nobis peccatoribus. Pray for us sinners. Because we are ashamed to go in front of the throne of the majesty of God for the multitude and frequency of our sins, we therefore have recourse to her as to someone who is most merciful, for she has given birth to the fount of pity, and we say: —Pray for us sinners, because we are not sufficient—. And note that one should not ask such a Virgin something that is contrary to our salvation, for in doing so we would be insulting her, and our wish would not be fulfilled. Nor should anyone ask if he is obstinate in his sins, for he would not be able to be satisfied, and this would rather be a way of tempting her and her Son. However, if you are burdened by your sins, do not be obstinate, but, sorrowful, rush confidently to her feet and say: —*Pray for us sinners*—, that is: —You, Mother of God, to whom the Son cannot deny anything; you, Bride, to whom the

Groom cannot deny anything; you, high Queen, Mother of pity and our Mother, because of which you must have compassion for us; pray not only for me alone, but for all of us sinners here on earth—. And do not doubt that you will be heard.

Nunc. In the present time: that is, in our life. And, truly, Mother of God, you must in your compassion pray for us as long as we are alive at this present time, because we are on this earth as if on an enormous and deep sea, full of rocks, and our little vessel, that is, our human nature, is very fragile: every hour we encounter contrary winds, with rain and storms. On one side, the enemy of humankind; on the other, the wicked world; on the other, flesh. Who can defend himself from so many snares?

And so, holy Mother, pray for us that in the present time God might forgive our sins and give us strength in temptation and in tribulation. Pray, Mary, in the present time, when we need only one thing, which is the love of your beloved Son. Pray, therefore, sweetest mother, your Son for us, that He may pardon us our sins and pierce us to the bottom of our heart with your sweet love, and that He give us perseverance in it until our death.

Et in hora mortis. And in the hour of our death. If ever we need help from the Mother of God, we especially need it at the moment of our death, when whoever wins will never again lose his crown; and whoever loses the war can no longer hope for triumph. On the other hand, at that moment one is in great bodily pain, for death is a most terrible thing, and *also* in spiritual pain because of the remorse of one's conscience; and because of the demon who at that hour insistingly harasses the soul as much as he can.[15]

Oh how bitter is death to sinners! And therefore Scripture says: *Oh mors, quam amara est memoria tua homini pacem habenti in substantiis suis!* [Ecclesiasticus 41:1] which means: Oh death, how bitter is the thought of you to a rich man, who is peacefully enjoying his earthly wealth! Oh blessed are those who reach that moment having kept God's commandments during their life. And so it is necessary that at the hour of our death the Virgin pray her most sweet Son on our behalf; and that she reach out for us with her kind hand; and that she deliver us from so many woes, as we

---

[15]For Savonarola's vivid description of the moment of death, see in this collection his sermon 28 on Ruth and Micah, popularly known as *On the Art of Dying Well.*

read of many of her devotees to whom she deigned, in that hour, to extend her mercy, and to come towards them in person and lead them to holy paradise.

Amen. This word, according to what Saint Jerome says, means 'it is true' so, according to this interpretation, it is rightly placed at the end of the salutation of the Queen of the heavens, as if to confirm what has been said: as if we were to say: —It is true, Mary, that you are full of grace and that the Lord is with you; and that you are blessed among women; and that the fruit of your womb is blessed; and that you are holy and Mother of God—. *Amen* also means 'truly', as if we were saying: —Truly, those praises that I said of you are true—, or as if one said: —God, who is truth, is witness to this—. It also means 'Let it be done' and so, at the end of a prayer we say *Amen*, that is 'Let it be done,' as if we openly said: —I pray you, Lady, that what I ask from you be done, and do not deny me this—.

This, then, is the salutation that is so welcomed by the Queen of the heavens that she deigned to appear to a young virgin who every day offered it many many times to her, and she said to her: —My daughter, I am very much pleased that every day you offer this prayer to me, and especially when I hear you say those words: *Dominus tecum*, for they remind me of the time when I used to carry my most sweet Son in my womb: so I counsel you to persevere in this prayer and to pay greater attention to it when you recite it—. When she reawakened, then, the young girl reduced the number and said it just a few times, but paid greater attention to it: because one *Hail Mary* recited with an attentive mind and devoted love is more welcome than a hundred recited in a hurry and with a wandering mind, because God and his Mother want our hearts. It is true that Saint John in the Apocalypse said he saw a woman dressed in the sun and crowned with twelve stars, and she had the moon under her feet [Rev 12:1]: and some expound this as the Virgin Mary, who was dressed in the sun of justice, Christ Jesus, and full of the Holy Spirit; and crowned with the twelve apostles, in whose midst she remained after Christ's ascension; she had the moon under her feet, that is the inconstant things of this world. So, if anyone would like to have a short rosary so as to recite it more devoutly, let her say four Our Fathers for the sun; let her say twelve Hail Marys for the twelve stars; and let her say the Magnificat, which teaches us to tread on the vanities of this world, for the moon. I have also read that, crossing the desert, a man saw some assassins and, in fear, began to recite the Hail Mary, and immediately the Virgin physically appeared to him and for every Hail Mary he recited she plucked a beautiful flower from his mouth and weaved it into a garland which, when she had finished it, disappeared: when they saw this, the thieves converted to the faith. I therefore pray all young virgins and all other persons who will enjoy this small book that I have written and composed for those who do not understand Latin, and especially for the young virgins of Christ, handmaidens to the Queen of angels, that sometime they might offer this prayer for me, a sinner, to the Mother of our Saviour, as remission for my sins, so that we might all one time meet in our heavenly home and rejoice with the glorious Virgin and enjoy her sweetest Son, who is one God with the Father and the Holy Spirit, blessed *for ever and ever. Amen.*

Index of Names

Publications of the
Centre for Reformation and Renaissance Studies

Renaissance and Reformation Texts in Translation

Godly Magistrates and Church Order: Johannes Brenz and the Establishment of the Lutheran Territorial Church in Germany, 1524-1559. Trans. & Ed. J.M. Estes (2001), pp. 219. ISBN 0-7727-2017-7

Giovanni Della Casa. *Galateo: A Renaissance Treatise on Manners.* Trans. & Ed. K. Eisenbichler and K.R. Bartlett. 3rd ed. (2001), pp. 98. ISBN 0-9697512-2-2

Romeo and Juliet Before Shakespeare: Four Stories of Star-Crossed Love. Trans. & Ed. N. Prunster (2000), pp. 127. ISBN 0-7727-2015-0

Jean Bodin. *On the Demon-Mania of Witches.* Abridged, trans. & ed. R.A. Scott and J.L. Pearl (1995), pp. 219. ISBN 0-9697512-5-7

Whether Secular Government Has the Right to Wield the Sword in Matters of Faith: A Controversy in Nürnberg in 1530. Five Documents trans. & Ed J.M. Estes (1994), pp. 118. ISBN 0-9697512-4-9

Lorenzo Valla. *'The Profession of the Religious' and Selections from 'The Falsely-Believed and Forged Donation of Constantine'.* Trans. & ed. O.Z. Pugliese. 2nd ed. (1994), pp. 114. ISBN 0-9697512-3-0

A. Karlstadt, H. Emser, J. Eck. *A Reformation Debate: Karlstadt, Emser and Eck on Sacred Images.* Trans. & Ed. B. Mangrum and G. Scavizzi. 2nd edition (1991), pp. 112. ISBN 0-9697512-7-3

Nicholas of Cusa. *The Layman on Wisdom and the Mind.* Trans. M.L. Führer (1989) pp. 112. ISBN 0-919473-56-3

Bernardino Ochino. *Seven Dialogues.* Trans. & Ed. R. Belladonna (1988), pp. xlviii, 96. ISBN 0-919473-63-6

Tudor and Stuart Texts

Early Stuart Pastoral: 'The Shepherd's Pipe' by William Browne and others, and *'The Shepherd's Hunting' by George Wither.* Ed. & Intro by J. Doelman (1999), pp. 196. ISBN 0-9697512-9-X

The Trial of Nicholas Throckmorton. A modernized edition. Ed. & Intro by A. Patterson. (1998), pp. 108. ISBN 0-9697512-8-1

James I. *The True Law of Free Monarchies* and *Basilikon Doron.* Ed. & Intro by D. Fischlin and M. Fortier (1996), pp. 181. ISBN 0-9697512-6-5

Essays and Studies

The Renaissance in the Nineteenth Century / Le XIXe siècle renaissant. Ed. Y. Portebois and N. Terpstra (2003), pp.302. ISBN 0-7727-2019-3

The Premodern Teenager: Youth in Society 1150-1650. Ed. K. Eisenbichler (2002), pp. 349. ISBN 0-7727-2018-5

Occasional Publications

Annotated Catalogue of Editions of Erasmus at the Centre for Reformation and Renaissance Studies, Toronto. Comp. J. Glomski and E. Rummel (1994), pp. 153. ISBN 0-9697512-1-4

Register of Sermons Preached at St. Paul's Cross (1534-1642). Comp. M. MacLure. Revised by P. Pauls and J.C. Boswell (1989), pp. 152. ISBN 0-919473-48-2

Language and Literature. Early Printed Books at the CRRS. Comp. W.R. Bowen and K. Eisenbichler (1986), pp. ix, 112. ISBN 0-7727-2009-6

Published Books (1499-1700) on Science, Medicine and Natural History at the CRRS. Comp. W.R. Bowen and K. Eisenbichler (1986), pp. ix, 35. ISBN 0-7727-2005-3

Bibles, Theological Treatises and Other Religious Literature, 1492-1700, at the CRRS. Comp. K. Eisenbichler et al. (1981), pp. 94. ISBN 0-7727-2002-9

Humanist Editions of Statutes and Histories at the CRRS. Comp. K. Eisenbichler et al. (1980), pp. xxi, 63. ISBN 0-7727-2001-0

Humanist Editions of the Classics at the CRRS. Comp. N.L. Anderson et al. (1979), pp. ix, 71. ISBN 0-7727-2020-7

To order books, and for additional information, contact:
CRRS Publications, Victoria University
71 Queen's Park, Toronto ON, M5S 1K7, CANADA
tel: (416) 585-4465 / fax: (416) 585-4430
e-mail: <crrs.publications@utoronto.ca> / web: www.crrs.ca